Republican
Rules For ↓ Radicals

Republican
Rules For ↓ Radicals

Revealing the techniques and tactics used to dupe
millions of Americans and propel a racist, militant,
Marxist into the White House
&
How Conservatives Can Create a Republican
Revolution to stop it.

Alexandrea Merrell

Republican Radical

Library of Congress
A catalogue record for this book has been applied for.

ISBN   0 978-0-9822229-9-7

Printed & Bound by Lightning Source in the United States of America

www.AlexandreaMerrell.com

The Republican Party is Broken.

Once the shield and sword of conservative America, the Republican Party has abandoned our values and beliefs. Virtually impotent against a socialist usurper and his army of anti-American, political thugs, the Republican Party seems confused and sulky. It has become little more than a reactionary force, continually chasing Democrat distractions, failing to contain the most extreme and destructive assaults against traditional American values, and moving further and further away from its conservative core.

After supporting grossly irresponsible financial policies, grabbing more and more power away from the States, and refusing to uphold existing immigration and domestic policy, the GOP seems confused as to why so many Conservative Americans no longer call themselves Republicans. Unfortunately, as conservatives, we don't have the luxury of snubbing the GOP on principle. While the Republican Party fiddles, America is burning, and the ultra-liberals are lighting the fires. We have to retake control of the party, strip away all of the dead wood, and reassert the conservative principles and policies essential to the success of this county.

It is my hope that this book will go some way towards helping to repairing the Republican Party. This fight against socialism and abhorrent liberal doctrine must be won.

Conservatives!
Unite and take back our Republican Party!
This is a call to arms.

-Part Two-
The Conservative Republican Revolution

Dedicated To:

My children,
who inspire me to fight for their future and their homeland

My parents,
who have always been willing to sacrifice for this country

All those who come after us:

If you enjoy a strong and proud America,
our desires have been fulfilled and our struggles
worthwhile.

If you live on your knees in servitude and socialism,
our swords were pried from cold fingers, defending
America.

Republican Radical:
A Definition

A "radical" is defined by Webster's Dictionary as one politically "disposed to make extreme changes in existing views, habits, conditions, or institutions." At no point in my life did I ever think that I would fit the definition of radical. Being a lifelong Republican and conservative, a supporter of State's rights and a strong military, and a firm believer in the American Dream, the idea that I would ever be considered a radical was quite laughable. In my mind, a radical was a socialist, a militant, a terrorist, a hate monger intent on destroying our traditions and values. I believed that radical equaled an anti-American or a traitor. But our world has changed.

We now live in a United States in which industries, finance, and our own dollar is being gobbled up by the government, "for our own good." Our basic rights; the right to assemble, to protest, to free speech, to bear arms, are being challenged and withdrawn, "for our own good." Our children are indoctrinated at school to believe that the US is a bad place, full of racists and xenophobes who bully other countries into compliance. Our military is being weakened and our serving soldiers and veterans, villainized. All the while, our "leader" is running around to foes and terror supporting countries, weakening our security, snubbing our allies, and apologizing for America.

If this is the norm, if this is what passes for existing political ideology and behavior, if this is what America has come to represent, then I am proud to say that I am a radical:

I AM A REPUBLICAN RADICAL

It's not enough to simply identify yourself as a **Republican Radical.** It isn't enough to complain about the horrific changes that Team Obama is attempting to sweep into practice, destroying the American Dream, replacing capitalism with socialism, and ending our cherished traditions and values. We must act.

This book examines the ways in which Obama is usurping the power and rights of the American people using techniques developed by Saul Alinsky, a notorious, militant, terrorist, con artist who hid his activities behind the term "community organizer." It identifies the methods and tactics used to deceive and manipulate the American people. But this book isn't just about dissecting Alinsky or revealing Team Obama's playbook. It is about re-establishing the Republican Party's core beliefs and values, changing the way that the political game is played, and ultimately insuring that the best people (from all parties) are not marginalized by special interest groups, shut out by career politicians, or scared away from politics by the tabloid circus.

I am a Republican Radical

I believe in an America where children are taught the value of a strong work ethic, self reliance, and self respect, not to idealize porn stars, gangsters, and lottery winners.

I believe in an America where families can go to sleep at night confident that their bank or business won't have been taken over by the government while they slumbered.

I believe in an America where those in genuine need receive a hand up, not a hand out and that those on welfare should work if they are able.

I believe in an America where people pass the collection plate, not the crack pipe.

I believe in an America where the elderly are revered and respected, not given instructions to go and die so they won't be a burden to the government.

I believe in an America where children are wanted, educated, and protected, not where they simply represent another government check and the next rung on the welfare generation ladder.

I believe in an America where tax cheats go to prison, not to head up government agencies, taking home six figure salaries.

I believe in an America where justice is truly blind and the poor are not simply a conviction statistic to insure the political future of an ambitious District Attorney.

I believe in an America where those who are here illegally should be ejected from the country. BUT that legal immigration should be encouraged from people who have something to give to the betterment of our society.

I believe in an America where the role of the government is to insure that we are respected by allies and feared by enemies. NOT to insure that we are all best friends.

I believe in a strong military with well trained and equipped soldiers who are respected and rewarded with the highest level of medical care, educational benefits, and housing, not where they are blamed for unpopular political choices or forced to pay for their own medical costs because "well, they knew the risks."

I believe in an America where people understand that freedom isn't free and that there are those who willingly make the ultimate sacrifice so that we don't have to…

I am a Republican Radical…..but I don't think that I am alone.

Introduction

I am not a politician. I am not a conspiracy theory follower or an "it's my candidate or no one" voter. I am a fervent supporter of the democratic process, a firm believer that the two party system works, and that the voice of the people, through their vote, should be sacred. Were Obama simply a politician with whom I have philosophical disagreements, I would have simply grumbled and gritted my teeth, as voters from the losing party have done since voting began.

However, Barack Obama brings to our democracy a cancer. A cancer that eats away at the muscle, bone, and brains of our country from the inside, a disease that spreads by mainstreaming the ultra-radical doctrines, vilifying morals, religion, and society, and eradicating the rights and responsibilities of citizens. And like a cancer, the spread can't be contained; the damage can't be repaired unless the cancer is exposed. This book is about exposing that cancer. It is about revealing the methods employed by a racist, militant, Marxist, his ultra-liberal, anti-American cohorts, and his foreign, moneyed, backers (Team Obama) to spread the disease throughout this country.

This book is not only for the Republican Party who seem to have lost their way, but also for Democrats and independent voters who are waking up to the fact that they have been duped by a charlatan schooled at the feet of Saul Alinsky, a man who is arguably the most notorious American socialist of the past century. It is about not only understanding the "game" but identifying the Obama playbook, the rules of which seem counter to anything previously seen in this country. It is about examining the paths that Alinsky established and Obama followed in order to spread the disease throughout this country. Without action, without understanding the method of Team Obama, without rising up to stop the spread of this cancer, we may well be witnessing the disintegration of the United States, the death of the American Dream.

Some Republicans have been playing a great game. Unfortunately it isn't the same game that Team Obama and the financial power brokers behind him are playing. Today in Washington, that means that we aren't playing the game that matters. We continue to try and play the same old game in the same old way and simply cry foul when Team Obama breaks the "rules" or a RINO jumps ship to appeal for cushy jobs from the Obama administration. As a political party, we appear lost, unfocused, and ill-equipped to take the field in arguably one of the most important games in American history. And we are....

The problem, quite simply, is that over the past two years, we have had no idea what game Obama has been playing and so we have wasted a great deal of time and energy speculating and reacting. Republicans have sat on the sidelines, jaws dropped, unable to move when one race card after another is played, when people that should be in prison are appointed to positions of power, and when the established rules are changed or ignored without warning or consequence. We have been reactive instead of pro-active and frankly, reactionaries don't lead countries out of dark times.

But all is not lost, Obama himself gave us the key to understanding the plays and tactics, winning the game, and saving America. He has bragged about mastering the unbeatable "Alinsky Playbook" for his entire political career. Team Obama didn't make up the game or even establish the rules, their playbook is simply the regurgitation of Saul Alinsky's *Rules For Radicals*. I encourage those who read this book to examine the original "playbook" for themselves, to make their own observations, and draw their own conclusions. But use the library, these socialist and domestic terrorists have usurped enough of our tax dollar without increasing their book royalty revenue. It is my hope that by including Alinsky's actual text and context, those on both sides of the political spectrum will research the words upon which Team Obama has based their bid to overthrow the US government and destroy the American Dream.

I have attempted to make this book as "user friendly" as possible. The first section of the book "Deciphering the Alinsky/Obama Playbook" focuses on Saul Alinsky, his book *Rules For Radicals*, and Barack Obama who spent his entire adult life studying Alinsky, teaching Alinsky methods, or working for an Alinsky network organization. In addition to detailing the shocking background and associations of each man, "Deciphering the Alinsky/Obama Playbook" examines the infamous *Rules For Radicals*, Saul Alinsky's step-by-step guide for ambitious but amoral people designed to teach them how to identify the vulnerable and easily duped and organize them into a militant army. Alinsky's guide provides guidance on manipulation, quashing ethical objections, and methods designed to intimidate, harass, and extort.

Without understanding the steps that Obama took to manipulate voters, usurp the power of the democratic process, turn the media into his own personal Gestapo, and hide his radical associations and anti-American agenda in plain sight, we are powerless to combat the greatest threat in living memory to democracy and to the American Dream. By understanding the "Alinsky School" and identifying Obama's use of those manipulation techniques, we can stop reacting to Team Obama's distractions and subterfuge and start flexing the might of the American muscle against Obama's socialist agenda.

The second part of this book "The Conservative Republican Revolution" addresses what we can effectively and practically do to turn the socialist tide, thwart Team Obama, and send the ultra-liberal, America haters back to whatever hole from whence they crawled. Make no mistake, the Republican Party as it stands now is fractured and damaged. Too much time is spent reacting to liberal proposals and distractions and too little time is spent actually championing workable alternatives. Republicans have allowed their brand to be corrupted by association with both the far right fringe and with RINO politicians who pretend to value Republican ideas and values but continue to spend our money and let us down with their vote. We can not simply point the finger of blame at Democrats who were duped by Obama and expect to regain our strength. We must examine the problems within our own party, cut out the diseased organs and dead skin, and heal ourselves.

Rules For **Republican** *Radicals* provides a possible answer to the pressing question, "how do we save our party and our country?" This step-by-step guide to rebuilding the Republican Party both from the ground up and the top down, addresses the issues that we face. By taking control of our own brand and definition instead of allowing liberals to define us as old, rich, white, racist, right-wing zealots, we can support, strengthen, and promote the core values and beliefs of our party. By embracing and championing our values we can reach out to those conservatives who have become disenchanted with the party, we can cull the politicians who are not fulfilling their promises to us and we can promote a fact that liberals would rather the world not know, that the Republican Party is comprised of Americans from every financial and social demographic, gender, age group, race, and religion. The thing that all Republicans share is a love for this country, a faith in the American Dream, and the will to see her restored to her rightful place as a shining example to the world of freedom, democracy, and liberty.

– *Part One* –

Alinsky, Obama
& the
Manipulation
of America

- Chapter 1 -

Deciphering the Alinsky/Obama Playbook

I am a reader. I enjoy reading books on many diverse topics. My own little library includes titles about history, politics, art, and economics I even have a book about infamous serial killers and one about French cooking. Just because I possess a book about French cooking doesn't make me Julia Childs anymore than having a book about Ted Bundy makes me a serial killer. I do not judge a man by the contents of his library or by his occasional reference to something that he has read. However, if I spent my days quoting Bundy, emulating his actions, and praising his techniques, it wouldn't take long before the police would be knocking on my door every time a woman went missing. And rightly so.

Similarly, if Obama had referenced Saul Alinsky in passing or simply tossed out an appropriate quote to illustrate a point, it could easily be explained as information within the scope of an educated man. Instead, Obama has spent the last three decades researching, writing about, emulating, and quoting Saul Alinsky; one of the most infamous "organizers" in American history. The mastermind behind numerous militant, terrorist organizations and corporate takedown schemes, Alinsky, who has been glorified by ultra-liberals for decades, was little more than a con man and thug for hire who used his skills in manipulation and intimidation to create guerrilla armies out of the poor and disenfranchised. Following Alinsky's techniques and teachings, Obama has become the political equivalent of a copycat killer.

To most Americans, Barack Obama seemed to arrive out of nowhere to become the most unlikely of Presidential candidates. Without political experience and saddled with a problematic name and lineage, Obama seemingly pitted himself against the unstoppable, Clinton political machine. Painted by the press as the "everyman underdog," Obama played the role of the hero in the modern day version of the David and Goliath story, toppling both the Clintons and the GOP. For many, Obama became the champion of those under represented in politics; young, non-white, with no political connections or social advantages. With no real voting record and a largely vaporous past, he was the blank canvas upon which voters could paint their own version of the perfect candidate.

Like Hollywood's latest leading man, Obama seemed to rise from virtual obscurity to the heights of fame and power almost overnight with nothing but charm, a winning smile, and a good script. However, like the latest Hollywood heartthrob, the "overnight sensation" is a creation, a manufactured image carefully crafted to appeal to the target demographics and propped up by millions of dollars in advertising, publicity, and palm greasing. Obama was not chosen as the next great hope for America because of brains, temperance, or talent. He was not plucked out of obscurity and bankrolled by billionaire politicos like George Soros because they felt that he was the best chance of a win against the Republicans. Bush's diminished popularity after two terms virtually assured a Democratic win. Selected, massaged, groomed, scripted, and promoted for one reason only, Obama gave the very powerful, anti-Hillary, ultra-liberals their best chance to beat Hillary Clinton.

The media, which had ranged from apathetic to down right hostile towards Hillary during her husband's Presidency, could hardly muster interest in the candidate past speculating on her wardrobe or querying whether Bill would be a "good boy."

Ignoring the historical significance of the probable first female President of the United States, much of the media focused their attention on insuring a Republican loss rather than a Hillary win. The lack of media support, an under current of anti-Hillary sentiment within the party, and fractured opposition from the Republican camp gave the ultra-liberal powers that be the "perfect storm" to usurp Hillary's position and compel millions to take a chance on an unknown. But just any unknown couldn't eclipse the Clinton star, the perfect candidate had to possess the Democrat holy trinity; media devotion, minority votes, and money raising ability. Enter Barack Obama, stage far, far left.

Throughout the 2008 Presidential campaign, both Barack Obama and his wife Michelle peppered their speeches with quotes from a virtually unknown book, published three and a half decades earlier, entitled *Rules For Radicals*. Under normal circumstances a Presidential candidate who cited the works of an extreme radical socialist, a man who had been banned in various communities for agitation and inciting unrest, who had published multiple "how-to-over-throw-the-government" guides, and was held up as the iconic face of home grown and foreign terrorist organizations, would have a very short political career indeed. However, with much of the liberal media fawning over the historical significance of the first black Presidential candidate from a major party and left wing politicians salivating over the potential election of an inexperienced and seemingly idealistic ultra liberal candidate, the contents of the book, so influential to the Obamas, went largely unanalyzed.

Published in 1971, Saul Alinsky's *Rules For Radicals* pledged to be a step-by-step guide for radicals who wanted to move from theory and rhetoric to actual, societal manipulation and governmental overthrow. Unlike other authors of the same ilk, Alinsky didn't focus on the moral foundations or ideology of revolutionaries, instead, he counseled his followers to disregard ethics, to embrace corruption, and to fool the masses. Dedicating his book to Lucifer, whom he claimed rebelled against society so effectively that he "won his own kingdom," Alinsky's works have influenced terrorist organizations around the globe to return to "grass roots" manipulations to deceive and intimidate. The same words that Obama glorified in his Harvard paper "After Alinsky: Community Organizing in Illinois," have provided a "play book" for ACORN, William Ayer's Weather Underground, despots, dictators, terrorists, and of course, Team Obama.

But why Obama? Barack Obama should be a shining example of how well America works and a real proponent of the American Dream. One hundred and forty-five years after the Civil War, when blacks were legally considered no better than livestock, a little over fifty years after the Civil Rights Movement when blacks couldn't attend the same schools as whites, Barack Obama's success is a direct result of the opportunities available to him as an American. In no other place on this planet could a minority, from single parent family rise through the ranks of expensive private schools, Ivy League universities, and into the political corridors of power and privilege.

Yet instead of being a champion of this country and the American Dream that inspires its citizens to achieve, Obama wants to destroy the very thing that made his success possible. He spends his time apologizing for America to leaders of countries whose very laws and traditions would have prevented him from being anything more than a member of the lowest social order, due to his parentage and ethnicity. It seems incredible. But, in the same way that it seems unbelievable that a person from a good, solid, middle-class, American family could run off to join the Taliban, Obama rejected the very society that nurtured him and instead became a follower in the cult of Saul Alinsky.

- Chapter 2 -

Just Who the Hell is Saul Alinsky?

For many Americans, the concept of "welfare generations" in which families live generation after generation out of the pockets of tax payers without ever lifting a finger to work, is abhorrent, counter to the American Dream, and the cause of much of the disintegration of moral society. While organized welfare has existed in limited degrees in the United States since the 1930's, it was the "Great Society" projects in the 1960's that created welfare as we know it. Those who "can't work" because of drug addiction or because they choose to be baby factories rather than productive members of society, are rewarded with a government check, food, and housing. The costs associated with carrying this incredible burden has virtually bankrupted entire cities and states and robs those who truly need short term assistance or are legitimately unable to work due to age or infirmity.

Perhaps most insidious, welfare generations have evolved into entitlement generations, in which an entire segment of society feels that despite generation after generation of sponging off of tax payers and contributing nothing to society except increased crime, disease, fatherless children, and drug addiction, they are entitled to be made financially equal to (or even financially better off than) those who work hard, sacrifice, and save. The roots of the entitlement generation and "reforms" which created welfare generations can be traced back to Alinsky and his contemporaries.

But Alinsky didn't "just" help create the cycle of welfare and entitlement that exists today, he developed the means and methods for those who want to profit from the system to do so. Essentially, he developed a blueprint for a "quasi-legal" version of the protection racket. Organized crime has long used the concept of paid protection as a way to both control the community and earn substantial income from very little actual work. A local crime boss would send thugs to local businesses and demand that the business owner pay "protection money" to the thugs. If the business owner refused, the thugs explained that they could not prevent themselves from attacking the business owner (or his family) or vandalizing the business. Out of fear of violence and financial devastation, business owners paid up. In addition to the physical intimidation and threats, in Alinsky's model, militant thugs used a relatively new, yet extremely effective extortion and blackmail weapon....the race card.

Today, when you see news clips showing the militant "Black Panthers" intimidating voters at polling stations in the 2008 elections, you can look to Alinsky. When you read about Al Sharpton receiving hundreds of thousands (maybe millions) of dollars annually by approaching corporations and demanding to be paid as a race relations consultant or face being blamed for "institutional racism" in the press and through product boycotts,[1] you see the effectiveness of the Alinsky method. Even today, as this book goes to the printer, Alinsky's race card is being used in the press and in the halls of Congress to "tar and feather" anyone who opposes Obama's plans. Political and media thugs attempt to silence political opposition and marginalize tea party patriots by claiming that they are motivated, not by ideological differences, but by their deep seeded racism. While Alinsky may not have "invented" the race card per se, he perfected its use and trained "community organizers," militants, and terrorists to use it globally.

---

[1] Vincent, Isabelle & Edelman, Susan "Rev Al Soaks Up Boycott Bucks: Biz Giants Pay or Face Race Rallies" New York Post June 15, 2008

Today, you could go on to the internet and find web sites that detail the step-by-step methods required to make a bomb, build a gun silencer, use a date rape drug, dismember a body, steal someone's identity, stalk someone, hack someone's computer, etc. etc. etc. When challenged (when they can be found) the authors of these step-by-step guides all say virtually the same thing, "it is for information only, I can't be held responsible if someone chooses to actually use the information provided in a criminal way." Most thinking people however are horrified at the gross irresponsibility of posting that sort of information online and by the legal protections afforded to the authors. Were Alinsky alive today, chances are he would be singing that same "I have no responsibility" tune. Despite teaching hundreds who went on to teach thousands, Alinsky claimed no ethical responsibility for providing people with the ways to destroy businesses, communities, and entire governments.

In fact, while he personally felt no responsibility for the actions that were carried out under his guidance and in his name, he also counseled his students and followers to leave ethics to their enemies, and not concern themselves with morality or responsibility, only with achieving their ultimate aims. Perhaps it is this "step-by-step guide to destruction" without personal repercussion that is Alinsky's most lingering "contribution" to society.

———————————

Some who evolve into militants initially begin their journey with good intentions and "clean hands." These people are often extremely idealistic, naive, and inexperienced in the world, seeing every situation or problem as good or bad, black or white, right or wrong. Saul Alinsky was not one of these idealists. Alinsky's motivation and obsession was power, his means of achieving power, duplicitous. An honorary member of Al

9

Capone's infamous mob in Chicago, young Saul Alinsky learned quickly ways to "get things done" that would provide him inspiration and practical experience for his career in extortion, intimidation, and "agitation." While studying criminology at the University of Chicago, Alinsky, already a petty criminal in his own right, befriended Frank Nitti, Capone's de facto boss. From Nitti and the Capone mob, Alinsky learned the operation of the so called "protection rackets." Alinsky used this "do what we want or you will suffer violence and financial devastation" technique frequently throughout his career.

Capone also taught Alinsky the value of both the "spin" and the malleability of public perception. In a 1972 Playboy article Alinsky explained, "The Capone gang was actually a public utility; it supplied what the people wanted and demanded. The man in the street wanted girls: Capone gave him girls. He wanted booze during Prohibition: Capone gave him booze. He wanted to bet on a horse: Capone let him bet. It all operated according to the old laws of supply and demand, and if there weren't people who wanted the services provided by the gangsters, the gangsters wouldn't be in business."[2] Under Capone and Alinsky's spin, the murders, extortion, drugs, prostitution, and general danger that the criminal element brought to the community was inconsequential because some people (those who wanted access to illegal things) got what they wanted. This has also been a hallmark of Alinsky's basic tenants. Under Alinsky's tutelage, people don't matter at all, as long as the radical group that he has organized or whom has employed him to "organize" or "agitate" gets their demands met.

From Capone, Alinsky also learned the value of positive public perception and usefulness of "relative morality." Despite

---

[2] Playboy Magazine March 1972 "Saul Alinsky; A Candid Conversation with the Feisty Radical Organizer"

10

personally killing and ordering the murders of dozens of people, Capone was reportedly loved by the community. This was attributed to his generosity, though the fact that he had many newsmen on his payroll probably didn't hurt. When the stock market crashed in 1929, Capone opened soup kitchens and donated clothing to the needy, to much fanfare and publicity. He crafted himself as a modern day "Robin Hood" and while those who lived and worked in the neighborhoods affected by the prostitution, gambling, racketeering, and extortion certainly didn't love him, the press made him a hero. Those in the community who benefited from his generosity didn't care that the food that they ate or the clothes that they wore were at the expense of the business shake downs, violence, drugs, prostitution, and murder. These realities so shaped Alinsky that they evolved into one of his rules concerning ethics, "do what you can with what you have and clothe it with moral garments."[3] Capone clothed his $100 million dollar a year criminal empire with the moral garments of depression era charity.

By his mid-thirties, after nearly a decade in the trenches with one criminal gang or another, all the while working for the state of Illinois as a criminologist, Alinsky took a position with the then radical Committee for Industrial Organization, as did many of his gangland associates. Prior to the creation of the C.I.O., "craft" unions restricted their membership to white, male, skilled laborers. The prevailing opinion was that including unskilled "industrial" workers would weaken the union's position. Skilled labor could not be easily replaced and training new people to take their positions could take months, even years. Unskilled workers and female or minority workers however were easily replaced with the constant influx of immigrants.

---

[3] Alinsky, Saul "Rules For Radicals" pg 36 (Vintage Books New York) ISBN 978-0-679-72113-0

11

John L. Lewis, a union member, saw the potential power in organizing the huge numbers of un-affiliated, mass production workers and created the C.I.O. to harness that power. The C.I.O. was essentially an umbrella organization which included international unions (those supporting a particular nationality), industrial unions (mining, steel, etc.), and mass production unions (rubber, clothing, and other mass produced items). However, the C.I.O. was not adverse to teaming up with Communist Party Unions in order to show force at strikes, rallies, and sit-ins.

The common goal of typical industrial (non-skilled) union member was to improve their working conditions and pay. For the union organizers however, increasing membership (and membership dues) at all cost, seemed the primary goal. Not only did large numbers of card carrying union members at the ready make an organizer rich, the kick backs and side deals with factory management, police, and organized crime made them extremely powerful. At C.I.O., Alinsky was able to put much of what he learned shadowing criminals to effective use. As a union organizer Alinsky helped to "convince" workers that they should join a union represented by the C.I.O. as opposed to one of the rival unions. Bitter and bloody battles between rival unions, strikers, scabs (people who cross picket lines to work during strikes), and the police and National Guard were not uncommon.

After riots, property destruction, and deaths, Congress initiated a series of investigations into the Unions and the organizers. One such investigation focusing on "un-American activities" (the Martin Dies Commission Report, published in 1938) revealed that nearly 300 C.I.O. organizers were members of the Communist Party of the United States of America (which incorporated Marxists, Leninists, socialists, communists, anarchists, and other radical liberal organizations) and publicly demanded their removal from positions of authority, Alinsky decided to move away from organizing for the power of the unions and towards organizing for himself. He coined the term "community organizer" to describe his activities.

Alinsky did not look to his own community when he decided to turn his hand to "personal" organization. He instead went the notorious "Back of the Yards" section of Chicago. Despite his previous, paid position as an organizer for the C.I.O., Alinsky set his sites on culling the very people that he had manipulated, threatened and cajoled into joining the union, to now leave it and join him. Alinsky explained, "What I wanted to try to do was apply the organizing techniques I'd mastered with the C.I.O. to the worst slums and ghettos..."[4] But Alinsky was not interested in improving the standard of living for the people who lived there. His goal was to create an army that would provide him the power and clout to push his own socialist agendas. "This was the field I wanted to make my own -- community organization for community power and for radical goals."[5] In a 1972 Playboy Magazine article, Alinsky revealed his early manipulation techniques.

"Well, the first thing I did, the first thing I always do, is to move into the community as an observer, to talk with people and listen and learn their grievances and their attitudes. Then I look around at what I've got to work with, what levers I can use to pry closed doors open, what institutions or organizations already exist that can be useful. In the case of Back of the Yards, the area was 95 percent Roman Catholic, and I recognized that if I could win the support of the Church, we'd be off and running. Conversely, without the Church, or at least some elements

---

[4] Playboy Magazine March 1972 "Saul Alinsky; A Candid Conversation with the Feisty Radical Organizer"
[5] Playboy Magazine March 1972 "Saul Alinsky; A Candid Conversation with the Feisty Radical Organizer"

13

of it, it was unlikely that we'd be able to make much of a dent in the community.

So in order to involve the Catholic priests in Back of the Yards, I didn't give them any stuff about Christian ethics, I just appealed to their self-interest. I'd say, "Look, you're telling your people to stay out of the Communist-dominated unions and action groups, right?" He'd nod. So I'd go on: "And what do they do? They say, 'Yes, Father,' and walk out of the church and join the C.I.O. Why? Because it's their bread and butter, because the C.I.O. is doing something about their problems while you're sitting here on your tail in the sacristy." That stirred 'em up, which is just what I wanted to do, and then I'd say, "Look, if you go on like that you're gonna alienate your parishioners, turn them from the Church, maybe drive them into the arms of the Reds. Your only hope is to move first, to beat the Communists at their own game, to show the people you're more interested in their living conditions than the contents of your collection plate. And not only will you get them back again by supporting their struggle, but when they win they'll be more prosperous and your donations will go up and the welfare of the Church will be enhanced." Now I'm talking their language and we can sit down and hammer out a deal. That was what happened in Back of the Yards, and within a few months the overwhelming majority of the parish priests were backing us, and we were holding our organizational meetings in their churches. To fuck your enemies, you've first got to seduce your allies."[6]

---

[6] Playboy Magazine March 1972 "Saul Alinsky; A Candid Conversation with

Despite liberal doctrine and Alinsky's own egotistical self-aggrandising, his contribution to the Back of the Yards Neighbourhood Council seems restricted to the initial organization of the group. The organization did little to improve the conditions of the people under Alinsky, who used his position to claim that the largely integrated neighbourhood was in fact hated by "everybody" because of its successful integration. This concept of "everybody" (meaning white, middle-class, America) hating minorities became a recurring theme throughout his life as an agitator. In fact, most of the changes to the neighbourhood came about through a combined effort between local churches and labour unions, with real progress coming in the 1950's and 60's when residents banded together to improve their own community by working together to renovate homes, parks, and community buildings.

Alinsky did however use the publicity that he garnered through the Back of the Yards to manoeuvre himself into greater positions of power. By using his contacts within the Catholic Church in the Back of the Yards, he was able to launch an appeal to Marshal Field III, the grandson and benefactor to the Marshall Field Department Store fortune, who ultimately provided Alinsky with the funding to establish the Industrial Areas Foundation Training Institute. The I.A.F. became Alinsky's indoctrination and training camp, designed to instruct radicals in the ways of agitation and community organizing.

Throughout the next twenty years, Alinsky bounced from one "paid outside agitator" position to another, focusing primarily on black inner-city communities and using the "race card" to extort money from municipalities and corporations alike. His "fame" as a white man able to publicly "stick it to the man" on behalf of blacks and in some cases, latinos, insured that small

the Feisty Radical Organizer"

radical groups around the country were willing to pay his fees and provide manpower for his stunts, all so that they could get their name in the paper. These groups believed that Alinsky would use his publicity to bring some benefit or respect to their organization, which would in turn bring them money and power. The reality is however that few organizations that hired Alinsky received what they believed that they had paid for and the money that Alinsky took was largely funnelled to his own training institute and not the communities that he was paid to organize.

Alinsky's real gift was in locating well positioned "weak links" among the wealthy and powerful. He befriended Eugene Meyer, the former Chairman of the War Finance Corporation, Federal Farm Loan Board and the Federal Reserve, who quickly became a financial benefactor and gateway to Washington and Wall Street. The fact that Meyer and his wife Agnes owned The Washington Post didn't hurt either. The struggling newspaper globed onto self-promoting Alinsky and the romanticized version of his work, making him the hero of a six-part newspaper series extolling his virtues and rescue of Chicago slums.

But Alinsky didn't target wealthy business owners who were "self made" millionaires, he targeted their disenfranchised children. To those who felt overshadowed and ignored by their famous parents, Alinsky offered fame. For those who wanted for nothing and were bored of everything, he offered adventure. And much like some middle-class and wealthy children today emulate gangs and behaviour of the lowest common denominator, the wealthy children Alinsky targeted were able to play revolutionary, all without ever leaving their own backyard.

So disdainful of the people who supported him, Alinsky bragged, "*I feel confident that I could persuade a millionaire on a Friday to subsidize a revolution for Saturday out of which he would make a huge profit on Sunday even though he was certain to be executed on Monday.*"[7]

By the time Alinsky was in his 50's, he left the actual, physical side of agitation largely to his handful of disciples and concentrated on training a new generation of radicals to take his place. I.A.F. now received its primary funding from Gordon Sherman, heir to the Midas Muffler fortune, who "channeled" money from the company to support Alinsky. Upon discovery, franchise holders, dealers, and customers started abandoning Midas Muffler to such a degree that Nate Sherman, the founder of the company, came out of retirement to retake control of the business. However, while the physical aspect of agitation may have been relegated, like a fabled Mafia Don, Alinsky still pulled the strings behind the scenes. In addition to community agitation for cash and corporate and government extortion, an aging Alinsky turned his hand to infiltrating; planting or recruiting undercover "operatives" from within the government who insured that money earmarked by President Lyndon Johnson for his War on Poverty initiatives funded Alinsky's pet projects.

Alinsky's fame brought paying "students" from around the world who wished to learn radical agitation at the feet of the master. The Industrial Areas Foundation promised politicians, clergy, and wanna-be cult or revolutionary leaders the techniques to organize the poor, manipulate them into action, and extort "for the common good." By his own account, most would never achieve any level of success. Though most students had a passing association with Alinsky at best, his personally trained disciples went on to train students in his techniques. It is the culmination of

---

[7] www.catholiccitizens.org

17

some of these training sessions that resulted in his book *Rules For Radicals*. However, there were some students with whom Alinsky took a personal interest. One of whom later went on to become the First Lady of the United States and a powerful politician in her own right. That favoured student was Hillary Rodham Clinton.

Like Obama, Hillary Clinton extolled Alinsky's virtues and sang his praises in University papers and articles and called him a significant influence in her memoirs. Alinsky returned the praise by publicly offering Clinton a position within the I.A.F. as a community organizer. When Clinton turned him down to attend Yale Law School, many liberals felt that she had abandoned "the cause." However a close look at the people who pulled stings to pave her way through her law career and into politics reveals that Alinsky, his financial contributors, and board members of the I.A.F. and its offshoot organizations have been the guiding force behind her success. Instead of abandoning the cause, Clinton has simply carried on Alinsky's work in infiltrating the government to gain ultimate power.

By the time of Alinsky's death in 1972, much of his revolutionary "agitation" was starting to wear thin, even within communities that once courted him. Religious leaders suggested that a Christian could not follow both Alinsky and Jesus. Newspapers decried his latest tactics, such as "Shit-Ins," where his followers would tie up all toilets at O'Hare Airport for hours or "Fart-Ins" in which his followers, after eating copious amounts of beans would disrupt the Rochester Symphonic Orchestra, as juvenile, self serving, and attention seeking. Government organizations were also outraged that he had managed to infiltrate antipoverty programs and divert attention and funds towards his own organizations.

Even the Chicago Tribune, a long time publicity machine for Alinsky panned "Rules For Radicals" upon it's release saying:

> "Rubbing raw the sores of discontent may be jolly good fun for him, but we are unable to regard it as a contribution to social betterment. The country has enough problems of the insoluble sort as things are without working up new ones for no discernible purpose except Alinsky's amusement."

Upon his death, Alinsky slipped out of the headlines and out of mainstream America's collective conscious. However, the disciples, the financial power brokers, and the politicians eager to use Alinsky's methods to insure political victory and personal wealth went quietly back to work, infiltrating churches, corporations, and every level of the government. They established a network of foundations from which they channeled federal funding, educational endowments which helped to mainstream extreme liberal ideology in Universities, and they pulled in ambitious radicals from around the globe to train in Alinsky's methods at the Industrial Areas Foundation. A decade after his death, Alinsky's most famous disciple was already busy laying the groundwork to infiltrate government at its highest level.

- Chapter 3 -

Creating Barack Obama

"Don't let facts interfere with a good story."
Unknown

"Only Malcolm X's autobiography seemed to offer something different. His repeated acts of self-creation spoke to me."
Barack Obama

The official Obama biography suggests that his youthful "identity crisis" is hardly surprising. The product of a white, mid-Western bred, rebellious, teen mother and an absent, Kenyan bigamist. Dragged to third world countries in conflict by his mother and largely ignored by her new Indonesian husband. Sent off to attend the expensive, private Punahou School in Honolulu (where he was a minority) largely on scholarship and with assistance from his white, conservative, Grandparents who loved but didn't understand him. It seems logical that a confused young Obama would reach out to find acceptance from the black community, find hope in "community organizing," and wander unknowingly into associations with Rev Wright, Louis Farrakhan, and Saul Alinsky's Industrial Areas Foundation. This story resonates with Americans. It is the fill-in-the-blank formula for the Great American Novel. It is also a complete fabrication, designed to romanticize Obama as the "everyman" American hero, in a hero starved world. It is also designed to conceal Barack's real and very disturbing upbringing.

In Don Fredrick's fascinating book *The Obama Timeline*,[8] Fredrick suggests a much darker picture of Ann Dunham (Obama's mother) and the Dunham family. While Team Obama paints a picture of the Dunham's as a traditional, hardworking, religious family from rural Kansas, according to Fredrick, Stanley (Ann's father) was a Marxist activist, who was rumored to be involved in acts of espionage and sabotage during WWII. The Dunham's lived a rather vagabond lifestyle after Stanley was released from the Army, settling finally in Mercer Island, Washington, where Ann attended infamous Mercer Island High School. Operated by notorious Communist John Stenhouse, Ann studied under Jim Witcherman and Val Foubert, radical Marxists who counseled students to reject traditional values, family, religion, and embrace radical socialism.

When the family relocated to Hawaii (at the time, a hotbed of activity for the Soviet backed Communist party), Stanley became fully immersed in a world of drugs and socialism, turning the Dunham home into a Marxist meeting place and drug den, with marijuana and cocaine supplied by his old friend, Frank Marshall Davis. Davis, who made his living as a drug dealer and pornographer, was a radical racist and Communist party leader, under investigation by the FBI for "anti-American" (terrorist) activities in Chicago where he had worked as a "community organizer" alongside Thomas Ayers, father of Weather Underground terrorist and Barack Obama colleague and friend, William Ayers.

Fredrick details Ann Dunham's early University of Hawaii experiences, where she met fellow pro-Soviet Marxist, Kenyan, Barack Obama Sr. in a Russian language class. Obama Sr. was attending the University of Hawaii due to the political string pulling of his friend Tom Mboya, the Secretary General of the

---

[8] Fredrick, Don "The Obama Timeline" IUniverse ISBN 978-1440-150-739

22

Kenya Federation of Labor and radical racial separatist, Malcolm X. Funded in part by the Laubach Literacy Institute (with alleged links to the radical Nation of Islam organization and a goal of achieving a "socialist world without national borders") and "community activist" Elizabeth Mooney Kirk, Obama Sr.'s radical socialism proved to be a seductive match (short term) for Ann, who idealized both Malcolm X (whom she had heard speak in Washington) and the destruction of the American capitalist system.

It would be grossly unfair to attribute any of the anti-American activities and beliefs of his grandparents or parents to Obama, who clearly had no control over their activities prior to his birth or during his childhood. However, while Obama's place of birth, nationality, and even parentage have provided much fuel for the anti-Obama speculation, one thing is certain, Obama was not the product of a simple African student and a rebellious, mid-western teenager who was raised by traditional, farm stock. His connection to socialism, anti-American values, radical racism, home grown terrorists, and the destruction of capitalism is lifelong and ingrained from birth. What should also be noted is that the very same radical organizations and players who financially supported and nurtured his grandparents and both parents were also instrumental in Obama's education, financial support, and political life.

There is considerable conjecture and speculation concerning Obama's early childhood in Indonesia and the radical associations of his mother and step-father. However, Obama himself details in his own book *Dreams From My Father*, the influences that shaped his teen and young adult life. By the time Obama was back in Hawaii and attending Punahou High School, a racially and socially diverse school where whites were actually the minority (counter to the stories that he was marginalized because he was one of the few blacks in a predominately white school); he spent most of his free time with Frank Davis consuming drugs, alcohol, and socialism. Davis hated whites and frequently discussed the destruction of white society at Communist and community meetings. The strange friendship between Stanley Dunham (Obama's grandfather) and radical racist Davis centered around drugs and the Communist party. Stanley Dunham, impressed with the scope of Davis' activities and knowledge about socialism, democracy and the evils of the US, suggested that Davis take Obama under wing to provide a powerful, black roll model for the young man. Impressionable "Barry" as he was called, was tutored by Davis in socialism, the evils of capitalism and white establishment.

In addition to the lectures provided by Davis, Obama spent his time reading the works of famous (and infamous) black authors. However, it was Malcolm X, who had been an inspiration to his mother and a financial benefactor to his father, who impressed Obama the most. In *Dreams From My Father*, Obama explained that Malcolm X taught "history proves the white man is the devil" and that Islam, which he is credited with spreading throughout black America was the "true religion of black mankind." The influence of growing up in a Marxist home and early indoctrination into radical socialism and racism lead Obama to attend a small, extremely Liberal Arts College in California, Occidental College.

College freshman "Barry" (as he was called at the time) spent much of his first year taking drugs and partying with his Pakistani roommate Imad Husain, Pakistani Muslim Mohammed Hasan Chandoo and Wahid Hamid.[9] His trip to Pakistan, during

[9] Rohter, Larry "Obama Says Real Life Experience Trumps Rivals Foreign Policy Credits" New York Times April 10, 2008

the holiday break between his freshman and sophomore years has been the source of great speculation and leads to further questions about his birth place, birth records, and citizenship. What is certain however is that after his Pakistani trip he became much more involved with militants and anti-American organizations, both on and off-campus.

By his sophomore year, Barry had returned to his birth name, "Barack" and began practice "race card" politics on campus. While some students and professors remember Obama fondly, others recount his claims of prejudice anytime he received a low grade, refusing to acknowledge that his own alcohol and drug use could be the culprit.[10] He began to seek out the more radical professors, activist students, and to participate vocally in the cause de jour, antiapartheid.

Obama's first known public speaking engagement was at the behest of the SED (Students for Economic Democracy) who sought to force the College to sever financial ties with companies who supported white-ruled South Africa. SED was one of the student branches of the notorious Campaign for Economic Democracy, a radical, pro-Marxist group led Tom Hayden (ex husband of Jane Fonda). Hayden was also active in the Students for a Democratic Society (SDS) from which domestic terrorist organization Weather Underground culled its members. The Weather Underground was lead by William Ayers, the son of Thomas Ayers, one of Frank Davis' closest friends.[11] Barack's involvement helped him gain the much desired credibility with radical black students. When many decided to stage a protest and leave the school because of its lack of diversity, Barack left too, transferring to Columbia University in New York.

---

[10] Wolfe, Richard "When Barry Became Barack" Newsweek March 31 2008
[11] Fredrick, Don "The Obama Timeline" IUniverse ISBN 978-1440-150-739

One of the most perplexing aspects of Obama's background is that while he claims Columbia as his alma mater, a New York Times article states "Obama has declined repeated requests to talk about his New York years, release his Columbia transcripts, or identify even a single fellow student, co-worker, roommate, or friends for those years."[12] Other students also claim to have never seen or heard of Barack Obama, despite being in attendance in the same political science program at the time he would have attended. Speculating as to why not a single person remembers Obama and why he is the first candidate in history to take action to prevent his transcripts from being released, continues to fly in the face of his proposed "transparency." In a New York Sun article, Geoffrey Kabaservice, a political historian suggested that, "Mr. Obama has acknowledged benefiting from affirmative action in the past, and details about his academic performance might open him up to critics eager to accuse him, probably unfairly, of receiving a free ride."[13] However, it is not logical that his reluctance to share his transcripts is simply down to affirmative action assistance or even poor grades. A man who admitted to openly using drugs through much of his high school and college years and acknowledges less than stellar grades during that time would have no fear of that same information being revealed. What we do know about Obama's time at Columbia is limited to what the University has been legally allowed to release. A spokesman for the university, Brian Connolly, confirmed that "Mr. Obama spent two years at Columbia College and graduated in 1983 with a major in political science. He did not receive honors," Mr. Connolly said, "though specific information on his grades is sealed. A program from the 1983 graduation ceremony lists him as a graduate."[14]

---

[12] Scott, Janny "Obamas Account of New York Years Often Differs From What Others Say" New York Times Oct. 30, 2007
[13] Goldberg, Ross Obama's Years At Columbia Are A Mystery Sept. 2, 2008 New York Sun
[14] Goldberg, Ross Obama's Years At Columbia Are A Mystery Sept. 2, 2008

While students seem not to remember Barack Obama at Columbia, he was active in the local "socialist scene" attending socialist conferences held by a Columbia University English Professor named Edward Said. Said, a pro-Palestinian, anti-Israel political activist was the focus of an article published in 1989 in *Commentary Magazine,* by fellow English Professor Edward Alexander. In the article entitled "Professor of Terror" Alexander documents Said radical teachings concerning Palestine and terrorism, his support of the death of "collaborators" (those Palestinians who associated in any way with the Jews), as well as his membership in the Palestine National Council, the "mouthpiece" organization for the PLO.[15] Obama was not the only person recently in the headlines to find a mentor in Edward Said. William Ayers also attended the same intimate socialist meetings and the two men continued to count Said as a friend and colleague until his death in 2003.[16]

Genocidal sympathizer Edward Said was not Obama's only controversial mentor during the Columbia years. Raised by pro-Soviet Marxists, Obama was drawn to Zbigniew Brzezinski, "a CIA expert on the Soviet Union, who teaches International Relations and is the head of the Institute for Communist Affairs at Columbia. (Obama is one of only eight students chosen to study Sovietology under Brzezinski.) Obama is heavily influenced by Brzezinski—who, as National Security Advisor for President Jimmy Carter, was instrumental in encouraging America's betrayal of the Shah of Iran (which then led to the Islamist revolution in 1979, the takeover of Iran by Ayatollah Khomeini, the 444-day American hostage debacle, and the eventual rise of the Islamofascist regime's nuclear weapon-seeking Mahmoud Ahmadinejad). Brzezinski also served as director of the Council

New York Sun
[15] Alexander, Edward Professor of Terror Commentary Magazine August 1989
[16] Fredrick, Don "The Obama Timeline" IUniverse ISBN 978-1-440-150-739

on Foreign Relations. In his book, *Between Two Ages*, Brzezinski wrote, "National sovereignty is no longer a viable concept," and "Marxism represents a further vital, and creative stage in the maturing of man's universal visions."[17]

College, for many young men and women, is a time for experimentation, rebelling against family or community values, and even flirting with controversial or dangerous experiences and beliefs. It would be disingenuous to suggest that a person's attendance at a few radical professors' lectures would equate a lifelong leftist philosophy. However, Obama didn't rebel against his upbringing at Occidental or Columbia, he embraced it. Perhaps more importantly however, identifying those people with whom Obama surrounded himself throughout his life is an essential key to understanding the motives, methods, and morals of the man. *In Dreams From My Father* Obama wrote, "I chose my friends carefully. The more politically active black students. The foreign students. The Chicanos. The Marxist professors and structural feminists."

While it would be conceivably possible to rise unaffected above the din of radicals, racists, militants, anti-American socialists, and even domestic terrorists with whom Obama consorted, one has to wonder why an intelligent person would surround himself with such people in the first place. Obama claims that many of these people were either passing acquaintances or were virtually unknown to him and that their radical views were hidden. It is a completely fantastical notion however that Obama, whose surrogate father Davis counted Thomas Ayers as one of his closest friends, who lived a few blocks from William Ayers in New York, AND who attended the same intimate, radical, socialist meetings as William Ayers would only discover his existence when the two happened to share an

---

[17] Fredrick, Don "The Obama Timeline" IUniverse ISBN 978-1440-150-739

28

"education project" in 1995 in Chicago. Ayers was a virtual "rock star" in the leftist world thanks to his domestic terror activities, self-aggrandizing rhetoric, and fugitive status. Suggesting that Obama was oblivious to his existence is akin to being a lifelong member of a 1950's Music Fan Club and never having heard of Elvis, despite your parents working for his record label, and your home being across the street from Graceland.

After leaving Columbia with a degree in political science, Obama went to work for a small business newsletter publishing firm that specialized in helping businesses with foreign operations or aspirations understand the international marketplace. Obama's recollection of his time at Business International Organization and that of other employees differ significantly. Despite Obama's assertions, there was no suit, no secretary, no international consulting, just a bunch of young people in jeans, rewriting newsletters in cubicles. In a New York Times interview, former co-worker Dan Armstrong explains, "All of Barack's embellishment serves a larger narrative purpose: to retell the story of the Christ's temptation. The young, idealistic, would-be community organizer gets a nice suit, joins a consulting house, starts hanging out with investment bankers, and barely escapes moving into the big mansion with the white folks."[18]

This picture of the "spiritually awakening of a black man trapped in the evil white man's world" is a frequent theme for Obama. He recounts in his book *Dreams From My Father* "When the weather was good, my roommate and I might sit out on the fire escape to smoke cigarettes and study the dusk washing blue over the city, or watch white people from the better

---

[18] Scott, Janny New York Times October 30 2007 "Obama's Account of New York Years Often Differs From What Others Say"

neighborhoods nearby walk their dogs down our block to let the animals shit on our curbs."

Clearly Obama counts on the vast majority of Americans not being familiar with the area. New Yorkers can tell you however that while a lovely area now, in the early 1980's, East 94th Street and 1st Avenue was NOT a place where the rich would walk their dogs. A high crime area, 8 city blocks (roughly ½ mile) from the unofficial "safe zone" most Manhattanites of the day didn't venture above East 86th Street. So why the fabrication? Is this to suggest that the wealthy whites walked from the comparative safety of their neighborhood into the heart of an area of town that (at the time) was dangerous, all so that their dogs could defecate on Obama's doorstep? The persecutory tone of his "spiritual awakening to the inequities of race and class" is an affectation, an attempt to create a metaphor for rich whites "shitting" on the poor.

The complete improbability that the rich were migrating in mass to poor areas to walk their dogs is a very telling commentary on Obama's basic beliefs. First, he negates the existence of poor and working class whites in the neighborhood. Could they not have owned dogs? Or are ALL whites painted with the same brush as being rich and vindictive? Second, it shows that Obama, who has had the benefit of private schools since childhood and an Ivy League education, tries desperately to tie himself to experiences that he imagines will resonate with blacks. Perhaps most importantly, coupled with the radical, racist associations that have both been thrust upon him in childhood and that he pursued in adulthood, the continued reference to experiences in which he is the protagonist against an uncaring or evil white society surely shows that there is a difference between a man who can reach across the isles to shake the white man's hand if it gets him what he wants and a person who truly believes in the equality of man.

If nothing else, examining Obama's early background should provide a very valuable lesson to us all. Americans love the underdog story. We love the idea that a regular guy, without advantage, can rise to the top of the pile and become the hero in his own lifetime. And, "The Barack Obama Story," as told by Barack Obama, is the classic American underdog story. We are presented with a young man, the product of a wayward teenaged girl and a simple African exchange student who fell in love and had a child. We are told that he was bullied for his bi-racial background and may have met with a few radicals in his youth, but only because he was seeking some understanding of his black heritage. In the tale, through his own true grit, he was able to rise above his disadvantage and now, through hard work and determination, Barack Obama has risen to the heights of power. Classic American Novel stuff. Because this story seems so romantic and believable, it is easy to digest and we have accepted it as the truth. But, we need only scratch the surface to see that this was a carefully crafted lie designed to seduce us, created to lull us to blissful sleep, allowing Team Obama to do as they will with the economy, the military, and our tax dollar. Millions closed their eyes when they heard the Barack Obama fairytale. But it is time to WAKE UP, open everyone's eyes, and take back our country.

- Chapter 4 -

What is a Community Organizer?

"The organizer is in a true sense reaching for the highest level for which man can reach – to create, to be a "great creator," to play God."   Saul Alinsky

What does the word "community" mean to you? Do you think of your neighborhood? The local theatre or restaurants? What about sports teams or parks? Do you think of your children's schools or your church? Maybe when you think of the word "community" you think of the people that live around you. The family whose over-the-top Christmas lights could practically be seen from space. Or the guy who is always mowing his grass at 7am on a Saturday morning. Of course the components that make up a community vary from place to place. When I lived in a small Midwestern town, my community was dominated by high school football, weekends at the lake, and my house proud neighbors who spent their free time tending their lawns and personalizing their little homes with handmade crafts. When I moved to the city, my community revolved around my University, weekends exploring museums and theatre, and the eclectic people who lived in my apartment building. But, no matter where I have lived (and I have lived all over this great country), the term community always meant the positive connections that I had to the people and places around me.

So perhaps it isn't surprising that when I first heard the term "community organizer" I assumed that it was something wholesome and positive. For me, it brings to mind little old ladies holding bake sales to raise funds for planting flowers or families coming together to clean abandoned lots to turn into baseball diamonds. Over the past few years, Team Obama has relied on average Americans imagining that positive, even nostalgic concept of community and assuming that his activities as a community organizer meant something positive, wholesome, and pro-American. Unfortunately, behind the Norman Rockwell-eque visuals that spring to mind, the reality is that the term has little to do with making a community a better place and everything to do with manipulating vulnerable people into acts of harassment, intimidation, and even crime. To Saul Alinsky and his adherent Obama, the term "community organizer" is just a euphemism for power grab.

Clearly not every aspect of any community is positive. All communities have negative aspects and some are worse than others. Poverty, crime, drug addiction, poor educational facilities and unemployment can devastate a community. It is in these situations where the real fraud of the "community organizer" can be seen. Instead of organizing those in impoverished areas to band together to fight crime, clean up their neighborhoods, renovate their parks and buildings, raise money to improve education or employment opportunities, Alinsky and those who trained in his methods, including Obama, used those whom they organized to develop personal revenue streams and propel themselves into positions of ever increasing power. Were benefiting the community the true goal, the inner cities, from where the "community organizer" culls their personal armies from the disenfranchised and desperate, would be a very different place.

––––––––––––––

By the 1940's Alinsky's self promotion and extortion tactics were working so effectively, that he was in constant demand. He traveled around the country as a "paid agitator," who would enter a community at the behest of an established organization or small group seeking organization, whip up trouble and publicity with a series of stunts (or the threat of stunts). Then he would appeal to other disenfranchised people or angry organizations and consolidate them into one "army." Alinsky would train the local organization leaders in the art of mobilization, rhetoric, publicity stunts, intelligence gathering, blackmail, and mass manipulation and then leave town with his pay and blackmailed politicians or businesses in his pocket. Of course, without the master manipulator at the helm, the communities that he "organized" soon reverted to their previous states of impotence.

Alinsky preferred the short battle that resulted in headlines prior to his arrival and often resulted in a "win" based on his target's fear of what might happen. These battles required minimal amounts of his personal time. However, some corporations or government agencies took longer to blackmail or intimidate. Unable to be at more than one place at a time, Alinsky sought to train a team of assistant agitators who would keep things stirred up after he breezed in and out of town making headlines and collecting fees. The Industrial Areas Foundation was established by Alinsky to train assistant "community organizers," who would take direction and work under his name.

Those assistant "community organizers" were often implanted as the new head of either an existing organization or a newly created organization, that Alinsky thought would be beneficial in the future. He developed a network of race and/or geographically based organizations that he called upon when he needed either a show of manpower or the appearance of a nationwide movement. Most significantly however, much like the Capone mob that trained him, Alinsky's organizations all paid "dues" up the chain to Alinsky and the Industrial Areas Foundation. This is extremely significant in that it enabled Alinsky to divert charitable and government funds earmarked for a specific program, seemingly unrelated to Alinsky into his pockets.

By the 1960's, the Alinsky method of intimidation, harassment, and corporate and government extortion had proved so successful that militants from around the world were signing up for a 15 month long training course in "agitation." Alinsky details with no shortage of glee that often rival "gangs" would sign up for the course. "We didn't, of course, care why they'd joined us – we just knew we'd be better off if they did."[19] This sums up Saul Alinsky. He was a mercenary for hire, unconcerned with the legality, moral or ethical obligations or responsibilities, or even insuring a positive outcome for his clients. He was interested in headlines and paychecks and didn't care who gave him either. Alinsky's goal was not the betterment of a community. He didn't organize people to improve their own lot.

In the same way that we can appreciate the complexities and the chutzpa of Bernie Madoff and his multi-billion dollar ponzi scheme while at the same time deploring the crime, one must marvel at the organizational brilliance of Saul Alinsky. The sheer size and complexity of the Alinsky extortion network can be seen today in ACORN, an Alinsky based organization. Church groups, charities, state government, and the federal government are waking up to the fact that money donated or earmarked for one particular special interest organization or project is being diverted through a series of shell companies and front charities and landing in ACORN's pockets. Whether you are donating money to help starving children or to save the panda, chances are, a portion of your money is headed to ACORN to fund anti-American activities here and abroad. Alinsky's network today includes hundreds of organizations and charities, including every concealable religious or charitable specialty and all are taking

---

[19] Alinsky, Saul "Rules For Radicals" pg 76

money from private citizens, small businesses, corporations, churches, and government agencies under the guise of benefiting a particular cause. Alinsky developed one of the greatest and longest lasting pyramid scams in history and his organizations continue to take in millions, if not billions of dollars every year.

It is significant to note that Barack Obama was trained at the Industrial Areas Foundation prior to teaching there himself. He spent years training militants in Alinsky's methods of mass manipulation, blackmail, extortion, harassment, intimidation, and media control. He also worked for two other organizations in the Alinsky network; Developing Communities Project and the Project Vote arm of ACORN.

———————

"From the moment the organizer enters a community he lives, dreams, eats, breaths, sleeps only one thing and that is to build the mass power base of what he calls the army." Alinsky

Much has been made in the press about Obama's work as a "community organizer." Alinsky himself used the term to provide a positive sounding phrase for members of the sympathetic press to describe his activities. However, Alinsky referred to his own activities as "agitation" rather than organization, describing his goal to "rub raw the resentments of the people of the community; fan the latent hostilities of many of the people to the point of overt expression."[20] His goal was simply to stir up anger and dissatisfaction until people were angry enough to join his organization under the guise of being able to do something about their issues. Alinsky's book, *Rules For Radicals*, is a guide book which describes the methods and tactics that an

———————

[20] Alinsky, Saul "Rules For Radicals" pg 116

agitator must use in order to create a wealth and power generating "army."

Once he achieved a level of notoriety, Alinsky's community agitation was often at the request of a small militant group. Being invited into a community made the job of organizing an army, collecting fees, and creating a commotion to intimidate and extort much easier. However, when he was just starting out, he faced the difficulty of getting a disenfranchised group of the population to accept him, listen to him, and join him. This was especially true as he generally "organized" blacks who were wary of a white, Jew who claimed that he could help them....for a fee. Alinsky realized that the newly trained "community organizers" would have the same issues of acceptance and respect.

"In the beginning the incoming organizer must establish his identity or, putting it another way, get his license to operate. He must have a reason for being there – a reason acceptable to the people."[21]

"His success as an organizer depends on his success in convincing key people – and many others- first, that he is on their side, and second, that he has ideas, and knows how to fight to change things..."[22]

"The organizer's job is to inseminate an invitation for himself, to agitate, introduce ideas, get people pregnant with hope and a desire for change and to identify [the organizer] as the person most qualified for this purpose"[23]

---

[21] Alinsky, Saul "Rules For Radicals" pg 98
[22] Alinsky, Saul "Rules For Radicals" pg 99
[23] Alinsky, Saul "Rules For Radicals" pg 103

Before an organizer can gain any real power, he must be able to infiltrate the organization which he has selected or he must create his own organization from the members of the community. He must be a chameleon, able to put aside his own personality, experiences, beliefs, or feelings in order to become someone who would be accepted by the group he wishes to infiltrate. "He learns the local legends, anecdotes, values, idioms. He listens to small talk. He refrains from rhetoric foreign to the local culture [which will serve] only to identify the speaker as "one of those nuts" and to turn off any further communication."[24]

When the color, nationality, sexual identity, or religion of a group or community would be a natural barrier to assimilation and acceptance, Alinsky sent recruits who would "fit-in" in order to talk to people and discover upon which organization they blamed their dissatisfaction, then he had a topic or a focus that he could use. "The first and most important thing you can do to win this acceptance is to bait the power structure into publicly attacking you. In Back of the Yards, when I was first establishing my credentials, I deliberately maneuvered to provoke criticism. I made outrageous statements to the press, I attacked every civic and business leader I could think of, and I goaded the establishment to strike back. The Chicago Tribune, one of the most right-wing rags in the country at the time, branded me a subversive menace and... denounced me as a dangerous enemy of law and order and the minute [the average Joe from Back of the Yards] saw those attacks he said, "That guy Alinsky must be all right if he can get those bastards that pissed off; he must have something or they wouldn't be so worried." So I used what I call psychological jujitsu on the establishment, and it provided me with my credentials, my birth certificate, in all the communities I ever organized."[25]

---

[24] Alinsky, Saul "Rules For Radicals" pg 70
[25] Playboy Magazine March 1972 "Saul Alinsky; A Candid Conversation with the Feisty Radical Organizer"

By goading an organization or politician or company spokesman into attacking him publicly, he was almost assured of acceptance into whatever community he desired, simply because of the axiom, "the enemy of my enemy is my friend." People assumed that if the corporation that they hated and blamed for their problems also hated Alinsky, he must be a good guy and he must have some power. By pretending to be the enemy of one group, he was able to pretend to be the friend of another. It is this duplicity, this two-faced, shameless manipulation of people that made his infiltration so successful.

Once accepted, the "organizer" must make himself the leader or at least, the advisor to the leaders already in place. This is achieved largely by creating and/or naming a specific issue or problem and offering a concrete solution to that problem. "One of the great problems in the beginning of an organization is, often, that the people do not know what they want."[26] Alinsky focused most of his attention on the poor and uneducated, both because they were easier to manipulate and because they had limited frame of reference outside of their own poor community. This insured that he was able to convince the community that they wanted something that was within his achievable scope and would benefit him. When asked how a community organizer would be able to manipulate a group to demand a certain result that would be beneficial to the organizer, Alinsky explained; "He will not ever tell the community what to do; instead he will use loaded questions…..he will want to suggest, maneuver, and persuade the community toward that action."[27]

Power is in the numbers, both in terms of financial dollars and manpower. In order to turn a small organization into a larger more powerful one, Alinsky counseled agitators to cast their nets

---

[26] Alinsky, Saul "Rules For Radicals" pg104
[27] Alinsky, Saul "Rules For Radicals" pg 91

wide and convince people with many different issues that their problems could also be sorted by joining forces. He also warned against achieving any major success too early. If a group felt that their needs had been met early, the organizer would have no more power, just as in a traditional army, if recruits sign up to defend their country against an invasion or against a foreign threat, they often leave the service once the war is over or the threat is neutralized. Alinsky counseled, "Until [the organizer] has developed that mass power base, he confronts no major issues."[28]

However, an organizer has to be seen to be achieving something before he starts seducing other groups to join the organization. This is often achieved by small, public victories. Alinsky explained that every victory or achievement had to be calculated against the potential rewards of more members (and more money) saying, "Every move revolves around one central point: how many recruits will this bring into the organization, whether by means of local organizations, churches, service groups, labor unions, corner gangs, or as individuals. The only issue is how will this increase the strength of the organization."[29] It is important to note that Alinsky didn't care from where these new members came, including enticing gangs and criminals to join. These elements could be a powerful force when illegal activities, threats, and blackmail became options to achieve success.

Guaranteeing small victories, which would inspire courage in the organization and guarantee new members, requires the careful selection and manipulation of a problem. Early losses would almost insure the impotence of the organization and ultimately people would lose interest and dissipate. So a fight that the organization is certain to win has to be created.

---

[28] Alinsky, Saul "Rules For Radicals" pg 113
[29] Alinsky, Saul "Rules For Radicals" pg 113

An example occurred in the early days of Back of the Yards, the first community that I attempted to organize. This neighborhood was utterly demoralized. The people had no confidence in themselves or in their neighbors or in their cause. So we staged a cinch fight. One of the major problems in Back of the Yards in those days was infant mortality. Some years earlier, the neighborhood had had the services of the Infant Welfare Society medical clinics. But about ten or fifteen years before I came to the neighborhood the Infant Welfare Society had been expelled because tales were spread that its personnel was disseminating birth-control information. The churches therefore drove out these "agents of sin." But soon the people were desperately in need of infant medical services. They had forgotten that they themselves had expelled the Infant Welfare Society from the Back of the Yards community.

After checking it out, I found that all we had to do to get the Infant Welfare Society medical services back into the neighborhood was ask for it. However, I kept this information to myself. We called an emergency meeting, recommended we go in committee to the society's offices and demand medical services. Our strategy was to prevent the officials from saying anything; to start banging on the desk and demanding that we get the services, never permitting them to interrupt us or make any statement. The only time we would let them talk was after we got through. With this careful indoctrination, we stormed into the Infant Welfare Society downtown, identified ourselves, and began a tirade consisting of militant demands, refusing to permit them to say anything. All the time, the poor woman was desperately trying to say "Why of course you can have it. We'll start immediately." But she never has a chance to say anything and finally we ended up in a storm of "And we will not take 'No' for an answer!" At which point she said, "Well, I've been trying to tell you...." And I cut in, demanding, "Is it yes or no?" She said, "Well of course it's yes." I said, "That's all we wanted to know." And we stormed out of the place. All the way back to Back of the Yards you could hear the committee saying "Well, that's the way to get things done; you just tell them off and don't give them a chance to say anything. If we could get this with just the few people that we have in the organization now, just imagine what we can get when we have a big organization.[30]

Alinsky provided the above excerpt in his book *Rules For Radicals* to show the importance of "cinch fights" or un-losable battles in order to grow the power and influence of the community organizer. What is much more telling however is that Alinsky creates an enemy where one does not exist. There is no thought for the people whom he villainizes, the effects on the reputation of an organization that he admits provides essential services to many, or to the potential danger to the workers, patients, babies, and members of the general public when stirring up people's hatred and staging a mass demonstration. Alinsky brags about not only manipulating those whom he has deemed the enemy, but also manipulating those whom he is supposed to be leading. For him, this "win" was simply a means to an end, it insured that his power grew and that more people would want to join the organization.

---

[30] Alinsky, Saul "Rules For Radicals" pg 114

His story is also very revealing about the fallacy of "community organizing" as a force for positive change. By teaching the committee of the organization that they could do a little research and improve their own community, Alinsky had the opportunity to give the power of change to the people. This would have had long lasting effects on the entire community, not just on the group that he organized. If people were aware that they could improve their own lives with the help of private organizations or government programs, simply by asking for help, think what a change could take place in a poor community. But that knowledge wouldn't benefit Alinsky or in fact any "organizer" simply because actually improving the lives of people in those communities is not the goal. The goal is only the power and financial benefit of the organizer.

Alinsky's story also brings into focus the tactics and ethics of the "community organizer." Alinsky's actual stated "rules" concerning tactics and ethics follow in subsequent chapters. But it is easy to see the basic concept. ANY tactic or method that brings power and a revenue stream is acceptable and ethics are simply concepts that get in the way of power and success. "It is not a world of angels but of angles,"[31] counsels Alinsky. Of course, the money and power grab of the "community organizer" flies in direct conflict with his stated goals of the organization. In his own example, the tactic of stirring up the community into such a state as to compel them to storm a building and demand a service is based on the lie that action is the only option and that the receptionist or staff at that office are the enemy. The complete lack of ethics is clear. Alinsky manipulated the organization that he was supposed to be helping.

Not only did he put the "enemy" organization in harms way, he also put the community in danger. What if the Infant

---

[31] Alinsky, Saul "Rules For Radicals" pg 13

Welfare Society, upon having this mob storm the building, decided that it might be too dangerous for their staff to operate in that community? Then, thanks to Alinsky's stunt, the infant mortality rate in the community would continue at a dangerous level. What about the potential danger to the members of the community who participated in the mob? If the police were called and they were arrested, would Alinsky be willing to bail these people out of jail? Pay their legal costs? Support their families if they lost their jobs? Of course not. But even if those dire events transpired, Alinsky would have simply used them to further his cause by going to the press and announcing that the infant mortality rate would continue unabated because of the Infant Welfare Society's refusal to help and that arrests were as a result of the oppression of the poor by those in power.

Once the "army" accepts that the "community organizer" can achieve success against the problem or issue that he devised, Alinsky next counseled his students that the members would need someone to blame for their problems. An organizer must create anger and hatred. This would give the organization and the people in the community a person or a company upon which to focus all of their anger. It is too vague a task to blame "the government" or one industry, people needed to be able to focus on a small unit or a single person as the cause of their problems. Alinsky called this act of creating a focus of hate; "polarization." It doesn't matter if the person is actually to blame or not. If his/her position or perceived position within a company or an agency makes them a potential cause of the problem, that is sufficient.

Alinsky relays the importance of carefully selecting the "fall guy." A man who is above reproach or is too distant from the problem makes a poor target simply because it makes it difficult for people to believe that he/she could actually be responsible for a particular wrong. This was one of the problems facing people when they came forward to expose members of the church in child sexual abuse cases. It was difficult for the congregation and even members of the general public to believe that a person who had done so much good in the community and in the church could also be responsible for doing something so heinous. By the same token, blaming someone who clearly has no control over a situation creates public sympathy and makes the organizer appear to be a bully. Of course, organizers understand that by targeting someone who is already unpopular with other groups, he may be able to gain more members to his own army.

The organizer must then portray the target as a person who has, with malicious intent, set upon the members of the group, to his own personal advantage. A perfect example of this polarization can be found today on Wall Street. Despite Barney Frank, Henry Paulson, and Ben Bernanke's culpability in the Wall Street crash, initially forcing the banking industry to subsidize loans for people who were poor, not credit worthy, and in many cases, not even legal citizens, and then washing their hands of the situation, Dick Fuld, the head of Lehman Brothers is the person villainized in magazine and newspaper articles. As the head of Lehman Brothers it is easy for him to be branded as the "face of corporate greed." The fact that he had no control over the government, and the subsequent inability for those who had no business taking out loans in the first place, to pay, is irrelevant. He has been made the target. And with few people understanding the complex banking, Wall Street, and government connections, and interdependencies, it is easier to just join the group blaming Fuld and other CEOs than to examine the real culprit. Since those culprits are part of the group screaming for Wall Street's blood, it is unlikely that they will stand up and admit their role in the global collapse. Meanwhile, Fuld is rich, white, and well spoken, traits not well suited to being cast as a victim in today's culture.

The organizer must be able to make the members believe that the target is 100% bad. That he or she is pure evil and that they (the members of the group) are 100% good. This has been the battle cry of crusades and holy wars from the beginning of time. God is on our side and by beating the enemy, we are beating the devil. In order to inspire people to lend their time, money, and manpower, the organizer must be able to whip the members into a frenzy of moral indignation and almost religious fervor against the target. It isn't enough to simply blame the target, the members must be made to hate the target and blame everything that is wrong with their life on him.

It is however impossible to maintain that heightened state of arousal and hatred. People have notoriously short attention spans. They will quickly bore if the organization doesn't produce results quickly and consistently. Alinsky counseled organizers to seek many small issues as a way to maintain interest and increase the organization membership. "It is impossible to maintain constant action on a single issue. A single issue is a fatal strait jacket that will stifle the life of an organization. Furthermore, a single issue drastically limits your appeal, where multiple issues would draw in many potential members essential to the building of a broad, mass-based organization."[32] Since creating a wealth and power producing army is the goal, an organizer must find multiple revenue streams and recruitment opportunities.

Small victories on multiple fronts are easier to achieve when the organizer understand the negotiation process. The organizer essentially uses the threats available to him, in order to press the company or government agency to negotiate. He knows that he probably isn't going to have all demands met, but understands that, "if you start with nothing, demand 100%, then compromise for 30%, you're 30% ahead."[33] The members of the organization feel that they have received some benefit and the

[32] Alinsky, Saul "Rules For Radicals" pg 120
[33] Alinsky, Saul "Rules For Radicals" pg 59

company or agency which has been attacked feels that they have been able to negotiate away from the "worst case scenario."

Of course the "enemy" left standing can become a valuable asset in the future. Much like the relationship between man and tapeworm, the tapeworm feeds off of the man, but doesn't kill until he is no longer valuable as a host. The parasite that is the militant organization, headed by the "community organizer" will continue to return to feed on the hobbled corporation or government agency, returning for the occasional small victory, until it can no longer provide sustenance. Naturally, the sustenance gleaned from the "host" doesn't have to filter down to the members of the organization. Al Sharpton is the perfect example of the parasitic "community organizer" who feeds off of corporations by using threats of publicly denouncing his target corporation as being racist. Companies find that it is easier to simply pay Sharpton a "consulting fee" rather than risk branding.

With so many issues and so many people to entice to join the "army" an organizer must be wary of "going native" or actually identifying with the group he is organizing. Alinsky warned; "The organizer must become schizoid, politically, in order not to slip into becoming a true believer. What I am saying is that the organizer must be able to split himself into two parts – one part in the arena of action where he polarizes the issue 100 to nothing, and helps to lead his forces into conflict, while the other part knows that when the time comes for negotiations that it really is only a 10 per cent difference – yet both parts have to live comfortably with each other."[34] In other words, an organizer has to be able to convince his army that he believes in the causes that he has devised and will fight to the death to win, but will in fact be happy with any little victory that will benefit his cause. A 100%

---

[34] Alinsky, Saul "Rules For Radicals" pg 78

victory negates the groups need to continue to fight and the organizer's power and revenue stream dies.

This brings us to the end game. No matter the cause, people lose interest. They either feel that their needs have been somewhat met and so return to their lives satisfied with what they have achieved or they are further disillusioned and recognize that their actions were futile. Either way, once the initial zeal has worn off, an organization either moves into a pattern of establishment or it dies. For Alinsky, the life or death of an organization depended upon its potential future usefulness.

By his own account, Alinsky's agitation on behalf of militant organizations and the poor and disenfranchised was largely a failure. Few groups who paid him to enact change for the better actually received the benefits that Alinsky promised. However, to suggest that Alinsky was a failure is to miss the fact that helping those groups was not his goal. It was a means to an end. He was in fact an incredible success. Supported by money gleaned from millionaire miscreants, fees paid by desperate people, and books, public speaking events, and the Industrial Areas Foundation, Alinsky lead a life of fame and fortune.

He was also successful in his two most passionate goals, first to inspire militants to rise up and attack establishment in his name and second, to develop a network of organizations who would support those efforts. Since Alinsky's teachings have become required reading in political science classes in liberal Universities around the globe and have inspired no lesser persons than President Barack Obama and Secretary of State Hillary Clinton to attack and undermine the traditions and interests of the United States of America, clearly he met that goal.

As people are starting to investigate the incestuous relationship between the organizations that trained and supported

Obama through college all the way to the Presidency, as well as the government funded pyramid scam that is ACORN, it is clear that Alinsky succeed in that goal as well. The only goal that has so far eluded Alinsky is the "organization" and socialization of the middle class, though his most famous student is certainly giving it his best shot.

Before we examine Obama the "community organizer," I want to make a final point about the real tragedy that these charlatans have inflicted (and continue to inflict) upon the desperate communities which they prey. For the past nearly one hundred and fifty years, "community organizers" like Saul Alinsky, Al Sharpton, Jessie Jackson, and Barack Obama, have arrived in a depressed, almost invariably black, inner city community and proceeded to sell some form of the same "snake oil." And like Alinsky who refused to inform the community that they could have medical care for their children simply by asking, these scam artists hide from their communities the truth about the real options and opportunities available to them. After hearing, "you can't do it for yourself and the white, rich, government hates you" enough times, many in the inner cities have come to depend upon the Sharptons and Obamas of the world, as the only people who care and can "save" them.

Contemplate for a moment the sheer number of people involved in the Million Man March. Even if the numbers were significantly less than the million envisioned, there were still tens if not hundreds of thousands of people who came together for one goal. Church organizations held bake sales, car washes, and clothing drives in order to raise money so that their congregation could attend. Local businesses donated items, money, and sponsored buses so that people could travel to Washington. There were even those who walked to Washington, just so they could participate. "Community organizers," looking to capitalize on the ultimate show of manpower, convinced people that joining their groups and attending the march, they would force the government's hand into "fixing" the inner cities.

The fact that "community organizers" could convince so many people that they could make a difference in their community, simply by joining their group, traveling across country and converging on Washington illustrates the very fallacy of Alinsky's community organizer concept. If a "community organizer" has the power to convince people that the problems in their community are all the governments fault and that they should wait, hands outstretched, generation after generation, surely a person who truly had the best interests of the people at heart could organize them to improve their own community.

This is not a new concept, throughout history, when foreigners have moved to the United States or even to a new region within this country, they have worked together, even when they had nothing, even when they had been mortal enemies in their homeland, in order to bring the entire community up. Invariably, within a generation, those new to these shores were able to move out of the inner city slums were they initially landed and into the suburbs and self sufficiency, despite initial poverty and language and cultural barriers. To this day, "community organizers" in the largely black communities site the lingering vestiges of slavery and racism as the cause of the disparity between inner city blacks and white "establishment" all the while, they ask for donations to support the "work" of their cash cows; Operation PUSH, National Rainbow Coalition, National Action Network, and Developing Communities Project.

Of course suggesting that blacks are incapable of assimilating into society and pulling themselves out of the inner city because of racism and the 150 year old residues of slavery completely negates the experience of the Africans, Afghans,

Croats, Serbs, Albanians, Greeks, etc. etc. etc. who having personally lived through the horrors of genocide, and come with little more than the clothes on their back to America. It insults the Jews who survived Hitler's death camps and the indescribable depths of man's inhumanity to man, but have built a new life on these shores. It disregards the experience of Mexicans and South Americans who walk across deserts and swim across rivers, at times under a hail of gunfire, to work menial jobs, saving and scrimping until they can afford to bring their families into the country. Perhaps most telling, the "community organizer's" tales that inner city blacks can't move on and succeed in their own country ignores the fact that despite the horrors of war, Vietnamese and Japanese can come to the homeland of their previous enemy, and can build a life of success for themselves and their families, such a sort time after conflict.

So what is so different about the inner city black American and the Jewish, or Russian, or Eastern European, or Asian, or South/Central American, or African that comes to this country and within a generation has assimilated into society and embraced the American Dream? It isn't opportunity. It isn't ability. It all comes down to programming. In the immigrant community, the religious leaders, small businesses, and families come together to support and inspire each other. The American inner city however is the playground of the "community organizer" who teaches residents that their problems are the fault of the majority, the white, the rich, or the government and that they are powerless to do anything about it....unless they join the organizer's group.

And generation after generation, the largely black inner city buys into this notion that they are being held down, held back, and prevented from success. Some version of Malcolm X's "We didn't land on Plymouth Rock, Plymouth Rock landed on us," becomes the battle cry for inertia and apathy. Year in and year out the community continues to listen to speeches about unfairness and being owed something until they believe that they can do nothing without the leadership of the "organizer." While the community continues to live in poverty and despair, the "organizer" drives around town in his expensive car and lives in an expensive house and doesn't consider the people until he needs a headline to bring in more members or more money.

The real tragedy, the real gut wrenching shame of the entire "community organizer" scam is that like Alinsky hiding valuable information that would better the community, the key to the success of the inner city lies within the community. When small towns have been devastated by natural disasters, they pull together and help each other. They don't cry about the unfairness of the situation or wait for the government to provide money or manpower; they simply get on with rebuilding their community and insuring that their friends and neighbors are clothed, fed, and safe. The "community organizer" spread fallacy that the government is supposed to take care of the citizens, clothe them, feed them, and make them all financially equal is a concept common only to the inner city. No one else believes that that is the role of the government, because it isn't. Generation after generation of inner city residents wait for a handout that isn't coming.

Despite Alinsky's "fame" and his claims that the Back of the Yards community was his first success as a "community organizer" the lives of the people who lived there changed very little until twenty years later when the people in the community finally figured it out. They developed a barter system and soon people were trading piano lessons for haircuts, plumbing for painting, and skilled and unskilled alike found that they had something to contribute to better their community. Churches held bake sales to buy trees and flowers. Schools opened the doors in the evening to teach reading and writing to adults. Neighbors drove out the crime and the drugs and reclaimed their children and their streets. When the community stopped being the home of despair, an eyesore and a haven for crime, businesses started moving in, organizations were willing to invest their money and their time to helping a community that clearly valued their contributions, and the lives of those in the community changed.

Now the Back of the Yards area is considered a national success, a model community, and proof that people can come together and change their own lives. But it didn't happen until the community was able to wake up from the coma induced by Alinsky and other "community organizers." They couldn't take care of themselves until they realized that they had been lied to and deceived into believing that they were powerless without the professional "community organizers" and started working together to organize their own communities. Sadly most inner cities across the country are still asleep, still under the spell of the "community organizer."

The inner cities are inhabited primarily by the welfare recipient and the working poor. If a "community organizer" can inspire people to donate their time and what little money that they have to join his cause and march to Washington, it should be simple to inspire them to make a positive change in their own backyard. With large portions of the population out of work, a "community organizer" should be able to motivate residents into creating the cleanest, safest area in town. When parents (even in single parent households) don't work, they should at minimum be able to care for their children, stay active in their education, and keep their kids off the streets and off of drugs. In communities where people have nothing but time, there should be beautifully tended parks, art in the streets, and a sense of helping each other to create a better community. The working poor have manual labor skills. Those that have skills related to construction, or landscaping, or sanitation should be inspired to use those skills to make their own neighborhood a real home. Those without specialist skills can pick up a paintbrush, clean graffiti, and lend a hand to insulating and repairs.

Unfortunately, this simply doesn't happen in most inner cities. Residents destroy their own community through vandalism and neglect. People allow and then embrace crime, drugs, and alcohol. Children are left largely to fend for themselves and learn nothing but blame and self loathing. Hatred and violence erupt when people get fed up with what they perceive to be gross inequities between their lives and the lives of others. And all the while "community organizers" whisper in their ears, "reparations," "they owe you," "racists," "white devils," and on and on. But why? Why can't a person who can inspire an entire community to scrimp and save, even walk across the country to be part of his personal show of force inspire that same community to do what every other religious and ethnic group who has landed on these shores done, and create their own successful communities? Why wouldn't they want those communities to be drug free, safe, and beautiful? Why? Because there is no money in it for the "community organizer."

- Chapter 5 -

Barack Obama
"Community Organizer"

"...Barack Obama's training in Chicago by the great community organizers is showing its effectiveness. It is an amazingly powerful format, and the method of my late father always works to get the message out and get the supporters on board. When executed meticulously and thoughtfully, it is a powerful strategy for initiating change and making it really happen. Obama learned his lesson well..."   *David Alinksy*

While it is largely circulated that Obama took his first "community organizing" job in the slums of Chicago with the stated goal of bettering the lives of blacks, his first "community organizing" position was with the New York Public Interest Research Group (NYPIRG) based at City College of New York. "The job required winning over students on the political left, who would normally disdain a group inspired by Ralph Nader as insufficiently radical, as well as students on the right and those who were not active at all."[35] However, past PIRG organizers, such as Mark Hemingway, reporter for The National Review, have been vocally critical of the group and its money making and disbursing practices. "Originally envisioned and founded by Ralph Nader, PIRGs are grassroots lobbying groups for progressive legislation. Originally started in Washington D.C., the

---

[35] Scott, Janny New York Times October 30 2007 "Obama's Account of New York Years Often Differs From What Others Say"

groups spread to college campuses and started numerous state chapters around the country in the 1970s."[36]

Hemingway charges that while the stated goal of the PIRG is to lobby for the benefit of the students, the hundreds of thousands of dollars they received as a campus group was being funneled to Naderite, a far-left political lobbyist organization. "PIRG organizing everywhere has a shady reputation, even among those who would otherwise be the ideological compatriots of PIRGs. Left-wing blogs run lengthy, detailed exposes of PIRG scams. And over the years, I've found the most rabid PIRG haters are former employees who are dedicated to exposing PIRG lies. That a young Obama would be involved in it suggests that the young Obama was either very naïve or had very radical politics, or both. When US-PIRG head Gene Karpinski met Obama in 2004 at the Democratic convention, Obama reportedly confessed to Karpinski, "I used to be a PIRG guy. You guys trained me well." The fact that Obama still felt that way 25 years after he was a young and impressionable PIRG organizer is a terrifying statement that speaks directly to Obama's competency and character."[37]

After a year spent attempting to recruit students to join the Naderite lobbying front and short stints as a campaign assistant to a failed Brooklyn assemblyman and as a business newsletter writer, Obama set his sites on Chicago. The story goes that by sheer happenstance, Obama came across an ad in a newspaper in New York, advertising for a "community organizer" in the Southside of Chicago, "…..the capital of the African American community in the country. Every strain of black political thought seemed to converge in Chicago in the 1980s. It was the intellectual center of black nationalism, the base both for Jesse Jackson's

---

[36] Hemingway, Mark National Review "Barack's PIRG Past" Sept. 16, 2008
[37] Hemingway, Mark National Review "Barack's PIRG Past" Sept. 16, 2008

presidential campaigns and for Louis Farrakhan's Nation of Islam."[38] The Obama narrative suggests that a disenfranchised Barack looked to connect to the spirit of the civil rights movement and decided to dedicate his life to becoming a "community organizer" for the betterment of the black community. Interviews with co-workers from his days working at Business International Corporation however paint a different picture. Self-aggrandizing, ambitious, and egotistical, Obama painted a picture of himself as a captain of finance, at the top of the business ladder, hob knobbing with business movers and shakers, dinning at the best restaurants, barking orders to his secretary, all while wearing designer suits. The reality was however that Obama wasn't a business titan, he re-packaged business newsletters from a dingy, shared cubical, along with a dozen other newly graduated college kids. No secretary, no suits, no power.

While much of this period of Obama's life is shrouded in secrecy, several sources have come forward to provide some of the missing pieces. At the request of Frank Davis, Thomas Ayers stepped in to provide Obama with guidance and support. Sending a recruiter to New York to collect him, Obama was given a position in the DCP (Developing Communities Project) whose stated goal was to "organize" the black churches in Chicago. Financed by the Woods Fund, DCP organizer Gerald Kellman, who is rumored to have been personally trained by Saul Alinsky prior to his death in 1972, was given a $25,000.00 grant with the specific instruction that the money was to be used as salary for Barack Obama.[39] Although founded as an equal rights organization in the 1940's, The Woods Fund has become a far-left organization advocating wealth redistribution and the expansion of the welfare state. In addition to Staff Director Jean Rudd, who

---

[38] Lizza, Ryan March 9, 2007 "Barack Obamas Unlikely Political Education" *The Agitator* The New Republic Magazine
[39] Lizza, Ryan March 9, 2007 "Barack Obamas Unlikely Political Education" The Agitator The New Republic Magazine

spearheaded the Foundations "left turn" and authorized the 1985 grant issued specifically to hire Obama, The Woods Fund is operated by a small board whose members included domestic terrorist William Ayers and Barack Obama.[40]

It is of interest to note that Obama returned from Law school to sit on the Board of Directors of the Woods Fund. With Obama on the board, the Fund (worth over $70 million dollars) issued donations to the Northwestern University Law School's Children and Family Justice Center, headed up by Ayer's wife and co-domestic terrorist Benardine Dohrn,   ACORN, and Rev Wright's church, Trinity United Church of Christ (where Obama was a parishioner). Obama and Ayers also funneled money to the AAAN (Arab American Action Network) which was founded by, Rashid Khalidi, press advisor for Yasser Arafat.[41]

———————

The DCP had been largely unsuccessful in organizing in Chicago's South Side, primarily because it's "organizers" were white and Jewish. In an area where Louis Farrakhan preached about the overthrow the white establishment using any means possible and were Rev Jesse Jackson, Rev Wright, and others compelled parishioners to avoid the "white devils," Gerald Kellman, Mike Kruglik, and Gregory Galluzzo were met with open hostility. They needed a black face and Obama needed a job.

"Serving as the black representative for a trio of white organizers wasn't exactly the community organizing fantasy he had in mind,"[42] relayed Kruglik. Obama, who had been brought

---

[40] DiscoverTheNetworks.org - Woods Fund of Chicago
[41] McCarthy, Andrew National Review Online "The LA Times Suppresses Obama's Khalidi BashTape" Oct 27, 2008
[42] Lizza, Ryan March 9, 2007 "Barack Obama's Unlikely Political Education" *The Agitator* The New Republic Magazine

up on the concept of "civil rights socialism" had studied the organizing techniques of Carl Marx and Malcolm X. However, at the DCP, Obama was schooled in the organizational methods of founder Saul Alinsky. "Alinsky's contribution to community organizing was to create a set of rules, a clear-eyed and systemic approach that ordinary citizens can use to gain public power. The first and most fundamental lesson Obama learned was to reassess his understanding of power. Horwitt says that, when Alinsky would ask new students why they wanted to organize, they would invariably respond with selfless bromides about wanting to help others. Alinsky would then scream back at them that there was a one-word answer: "You want to organize for *power*!"[43]

"The other fundamental lesson Obama was taught is Alinsky's maxim that self-interest is the only principle around which to organize people. (Galluzzo's manual goes so far as to advise trainees in block letters: "get rid of do-gooders in your church and your organization.")" Rev. Alvin Love, a Baptist minister from Chicago's South Side and one of the first whom Obama approached as a DCP organizer recalls, "I remember he said this to me: There ought to be some way for us to help you meet your self-interest while at the same time meeting the real interests and the needs of the community."[44]

However, the black face and speeches about self interest weren't enough to convince the black ministers to relinquish control over their parishioners. Many were aware that Obama was stumping for an Alinsky based group and knew that the "community organizers" often diverted parishioner's money and time away from their own coffers and causes. For many, Obama's blackness was not an issue, but the fact that they did not consider

---

[43] Lizza, Ryan March 9, 2007 "Barack Obama's Unlikely Political Education" *The Agitator* The New Republic Magazine
[44] Lizza, Ryan March 9, 2007 "Barack Obama's Unlikely Political Education" *The Agitator* The New Republic Magazine

him an African-American was. This lack of "shared background and shared experiences" dogged Obama throughout his career and his Presidential campaign. Many in the black community felt that he couldn't really identify with the "African-American experience" because despite skin color, he had done little more than read about it.

Obama's lack of religious faith was also an issue for many church leaders. "From [Rev.] Wright and others, Obama learned that part of his problem as an organizer was that he was trying to build a confederation of churches but wasn't showing up in the pews on Sunday. When pastors asked him the inevitable questions about his own spiritual life, Obama would duck them uncomfortably."[45] Raised a Marxist, Obama's only formal religious background came from Muslim lessons at Wahabi school in Indonesia where he attended school from 1967 to 1971. However, he could see that he would not be able to gain access to the congregations that he sought to organize unless he started attending church somewhere. Despite being warned off of Trinity Church by many of the other black ministers, Obama decided that Rev Wright, a former Muslim and a Black Nationalist provided a good fit. Obama was especially impressed with Rev Wright's "Black Value System" which counseled parishioners to avoid societal assimilation and the pursuit of middle class values.

While the DCP had wanted a black face to grant them access to organize the black churches, what they got in Barack Obama was unexpected. Instead of simply regurgitating the Alinsky playbook, Obama excelled in distilling and rephrasing Alinsky's concepts and teaching them to others. He taught workshops on Alinsky techniques, helped other organizers to focus on Alinsky's Rules as they pertained to their own power

---

[45] Lizza, Ryan March 9, 2007 *Barack Obama's Unlikely Political Education* The Agitator The New Republic Magazine

quest, and motivated people to embrace their self interest and ambition. Mike Kruglik, who taught Alinsky methods to Obama at the DCP called him his best student. "He was a natural, the undisputed master of agitation, who could engage a room full of recruiting targets in a rapid-fire Socratic dialogue, nudging them to admit that they were not living up to their own standards. He could be aggressive and confrontational. With probing, sometimes personal questions, he would pinpoint the source of pain in their lives, tearing down their egos just enough before dangling a carrot of hope that they could make things better."[46]

While splitting himself between the worlds of black South Side Chicago "community organizer" and Alinsky method indoctrinator, Obama continued his tutelage under the Ayer's family. Neighborhood sources suggest that Mrs. Thomas Ayers, William's mother, bragged that the family was sponsoring Obama, who had recently graduated from Columbia University. William himself had recently returned to Chicago with his wife Bernadine Dohn, a compatriot in the Weather Underground domestic terrorism attacks. Despite involvement in bombing the New York City Police Department, the United States Capital Building, and the Pentagon, charges against Ayers were dropped due to a technicality; he had returned to school and received a Masters Degree in Early Childhood Education. Back in Chicago, where his wealthy parents and his own infamy held sway with "limousine liberals" and street level militants alike, Ayers was awarded with a series of Board of Directors positions at liberal Foundations and became a professor at the University of Chicago.

It is the networking power of the Ayer's family on behalf of Obama that is most impressive and diabolical. During the four years between Columbia and Harvard, "community organizer"

---

[46] Lizza, Ryan March 9, 2007 *Barack Obama's Unlikely Political Education* The Agitator The New Republic Magazine

Obama was able only to initiate the removal of asbestos in one building and have a job center relocated to the neighborhood. Even those meager "accomplishments" have been mired in accusations that they were actually achieved by other organizers, with Obama sweeping in and taking credit at the last moment. Whatever Obama's actual role in either act happens to be, the fact that he was involved in only two successful public projects in four years shows again that serving the community is not the goal of the "community organizer." Eventually, Obama decided that organizing the poor; already a field well picked over by other "community organizers" and pastors, wasn't going to get him the power which he aspired to possess. After careful counsel with his advisors and financiers, Obama decided to pursue law school.

———————

While the exact steps and timelines are murky, what is crystal clear is that at some point during Obama's Columbia or Chicago years, he became the darling of a whole host of radicals, socialists, domestic terrorists, and militant Muslims, who paved his way financially and politically into Harvard Law and beyond. Despite receiving no honors at Columbia (per Columbia University), Obama was accepted to one of the most prestigious Law Schools in the world, where at the time less than 9% of applicants were accepted.

His attendance seems to have been streamlined thanks to a "recommendation letter" made by Percy Sutton, attorney to Malcolm X and through financial contributions made by Donald Warden who used the name "Khalid al-Mansour" who was acting as financial advisor to Nation of Islam leader Louis Farrakhan and the Saudi Royal family, particularly Prince Alwaleed bin Talal, who famously offered $10 million dollars to help rebuild downtown Manhattan after 9/11, only to have the money rejected by than Mayor Rudy Giuliani after the Prince made a public comment suggesting that U.S. policies had contributed to causing the attacks. Since then, Prince Alwaleed's Kingdom Foundation has given millions of dollars to Muslim charities in the United States, including several whose leaders have been indicted on terrorism-related charges in federal courts. He also has given tens of millions of dollars to Harvard and other major U.S. universities, to establish programs in Islamic studies.[47] Khalid al-Monsour was also mentor to the founders of the Black Panthers, Huey Newton and Bobby Seale.

One can only speculate, but it is no stretch to imagine the response of Harvard admissions if members of the Nation of Islam and Black Panthers showed up with Malcolm X's lawyer to demand entrance for a student. Add the bag full of Saudi Royal family gold and even a student with no scholastic or extra curricular activities (so prized for admittance into the Ivy League schools) and no better than average grades can win a coveted place.

In 1988, Obama entered Harvard Law School with a determination to put his "community organizer" skills to good use. Focused upon reaching the epoch of power, Obama wanted to be made President of the Harvard Law Review. "He didn't get to be president of Harvard Law Review because he was first in his class," said Richard Epstein, a colleague of Obama's at the University of Chicago Law School, where Obama later taught. "He got it because people on the other side believed he would give them a fair shake."[48] Of course this assessment, made by a supporter who didn't actually attend Harvard Law with Obama is certainly skewed. Obama's transcripts are sealed, however those

---

[47] Timmerman, Kenneth R. *Obama Had Close Ties To Top Saudi Advisor From Early Age* Newsmax.com September 3, 2008
[48] Lizza, Ryan March 9, 2007 *Barack Obama's Unlikely Political Education* The Agitator The New Republic Magazine

who did attend with Obama suggest a much different reason for his ascension to the position.

Since the Harvard Law Review was created in 1887, the Presidency had always been a position held by a student of the highest scholastic standing, based on merit and achievement. A mediocre student at best, Obama challenged the merit system and the fact that no black student had been President. Threatening the University with public exposure of its "racist" policies, the conservative board felt it best to acquiesce to Obama's demands that the merit system be abolished. By all accounts, Barack Obama became the first President of the Harvard Law Review to have been given the position based on legal threats instead of achievement. He also has the distinction of reportedly being the only Harvard Law Review President to have never been offered a clerkship with federal Judge or a position with a Blue Chip Law Firm. Knowledge of his tactics for advancement sent shockwaves through Court Houses and high powered law firms around the country who actively recruited meritorious people of all ethnicities, but shunned the "race card" stunt of an undeserving student. Obama has since re-fashioned the legal threat as "convincing a crucial swing bloc of conservatives that their self-interests would be protected by electing him."[49]

Between lessons at Harvard, Obama continued both studying and teaching Alinsky's tactics. This included attending a week long conference in Los Angeles, sponsored by Alinsky's Industrial Areas Foundation. The conference focused on developing power, advancing the Alinsky model into the middle class, and organizing illegal immigrants.

---

[49] Lizza, Ryan March 9, 2007 *Barack Obama's Unlikely Political Education* The Agitator The New Republic Magazine

While it is momentous that a President of the Harvard Law Review would not be offered a stellar position with a Federal Court Judge or with a world class, international legal firm, Obama probably wouldn't have accepted if such a position had been offered. Instead, Obama returned to Chicago in 1991 to start repaying his mentors and financiers, taking positions on the board of both the Woods Fund (which had provided the original funding for his "community organizing" efforts in Chicago) and the Joyce Foundation. Both groups, part of the Alinsky network, funded new "community organization" attempts, liberal indoctrination movements in schools and churches, and of course provided training in Alinsky terror tactics. As a member of the board of the Joyce Foundation, Obama authorized a series of grants for nearly $3 million dollars to anti- Second Amendment projects plus an extra $70,000.00 for himself.[50]

Obama also resumed his connection with Trinity Church and Rev. Wright. No longer interested in even the pretense of organizing the community for their own social advancement, Obama saw the church as a stepping stone into politics. Alinsky had shunned popular politics, villainizing any side and any politician for his own gain. But through Rev. Wright, who had turned a small, poor, inner city church into a multimillion dollar empire, making himself and his family wealthy beyond their dreams, Obama saw the potential power in organizing beyond a single community. "The church helped Obama develop politically. It provided him with new insights about getting people to act, or agitating, that his [community] organizing pals didn't always understand."[51] Organizing the poor, largely black community had been relatively easy, once they accepted him. Blaming the white man or the government for the problems of the people and pledging to take the fight to the establishment was a

[50] Vogel, Kenneth "Obama Linked to Gun Control efforts" Politico Ap. 19, 2008
[51] Lizza, Ryan March 9, 2007 *Barack Obama's Unlikely Political Education* The Agitator The New Republic Magazine

tried and true method of compelling people to join. However, what compelled one group to join his little army, even in the same neighborhood, didn't necessarily work for another. Through Trinity, Obama learned to identify the words and phrases that inspired Wrights parishioners to act and get involved. He learned to appeal to a wider group.

In 1992, Obama put his theory to the test. Obama was hired by the voter registration arm of ACORN and organized a (or depending on whom you believe, inserted himself into an already successful) voter registration drive on Chicago's South Side. The drive helped to propel Carol Moseley Brown into the Senate, making her the first black female to have been elected to the Senate. Obama used the experience to solidify his goal. By 1995, Obama was launching his version of "agitator-politician" to the local media and branding himself as part agitator, part advocate.

One of the most telling events in Obama's early career however was his evisceration of Alice Palmer. Palmer had been an activist in Chicago's South Side since the 1960's and shared many of the same ties, financiers, and friends as Obama. When the popular incumbent decided to vacate her Senate seat for a Congressional bid, Obama was groomed to take her place at the Senate. A surprise loss at the primaries however sent Palmer back to the Senate, where she assumed that her long held seat would be saved. Black politicians and community figures called upon Obama to "wait his turn" and pave the way for Palmer to regain her seat. Obama responded by sending a team of aides to the Chicago Board of Elections. The team went over Palmer's filing paperwork and petitions with a fine toothed comb, discovering that many of the signatures on the filing petition were fake. They then went through the paperwork and petitions of every other political rival for the seat, finding that many of the signatures in their petitions were fake as well. In one fell swoop, Obama was able to launch a legal challenge against not only Palmer, but every other politician vying for the state Senate seat as well, dispatching them all.

Much like his "victory" at Harvard Law, where he won the Presidency of the Law Review but at the cost of the respect of peers and powerhouses alike, Obama had won the state Senate seat, but lost the respect of many leaders in the black community and in the Senate. In an effort to mend fences, Obama returned to the Alinsky network and asked for help in smoothing things over with politicians and community leaders. One of the foundations of the Alinsky method is power analysis and determining who to either attack or entreat in order to meet your goals. This in mind, Obama and other members of the various local Alinsky network foundation boards set their sites on winning over a group of pivotal politicians, chief among them, Emil Jones, a member of the Illinois Senate, considered one of the most powerful men in Illinois politics. Jones had been a staunch defender of Palmer. But like many other politicians and community leaders who owed their positions of power to "community organizers" and Alinsky network organizations, by appealing to self-interest, many (including Jones) grumbled, but welcomed Obama on board. Jones was subsequently elected President of the Illinois Senate. In a recent interview, Emil Jones recalled, "After I was elected president, [Obama] came in to see me one day. He said, 'You were just elected president. You have a lot of power now.' What kind of power do I have?' He said, You have the power to make a United States senator.' That sounds good. Do you have anybody in mind?' He said, Yeah, me.'"[52]

In the interest of fairness, I wish to point out that many in politics, in all parties, are unscrupulous or unprincipled and use whatever means necessary to get the power and all that comes

[52] Lizza, Ryan March 9, 2007 *Barack Obama's Unlikely Political Education* The Agitator The New Republic Magazine

with it. Examining Obama's political background is not an attempt to force him to stand up to a higher standard. However, it is important to recognize two very important facts. First, Obama's associations with domestic terrorists, socialists, militants, racists, and Islamic extremists must be exposed. The very anti-American forces which supported him throughout his life and financed his education and early "community organizing" gigs are the same ones who have propelled and bankrolled him all the way to the White House. Their support is being repaid in almost every plan that Obama puts forward, in socializing housing, medicine, banks, and industry, in increasing our debt by unprecedented and unnecessary numbers, and weakening our military and security.

Second, Obama clearly doesn't care how he gets the power, as long as he gets it. The respect of his peers and the community is completely immaterial. Obama sets his sites on the Harvard Law Review Presidency and instead of working for it, studying, and earning his shot, he threatens, cajoles, and race cards his way into the position. Instead of learning the ropes, working his way up the ladder in politics, he demands that Palmer's seat be given to him and when it isn't, he manipulates the system so that he can take what he wants. Some may see his actions as ambitious or driven. Some may commend Obama on his willingness to see a goal, figure out his opponent's weaknesses, and capitalize. But it should be noted that while being ambitious and even ruthless can be an attribute in success driven American, the ultimate quality of a successful man or woman is loyalty. Obama's loyalties do not lay with America. He has shown this time and time again in his lack of loyalty to the very communities that he "organized." The Jewish communities, gay and lesbian communities, and even the black communities that he seduced into supporting him into the White House are waking up to the fact that the support only flows one way, towards Obama. Now that he has the White House, those groups can do nothing for him and so, they are expendable.

- Chapter 6 -

Emulating the "Shit-in" Master

"You may know a man by the company he keeps."

Proverbs

For a school project, as a kid, I was required to pick someone whom I admired, research their life and write a report about how they influenced my life. As I waited to read my report in front of the class, I listened to other kids read about their influences. Some kids talked about their parents or relatives. Some regaled us with stories of football stars, race car drivers, pop music heartthrobs, and ballerinas. I listened to daring escapades of Amelia Earhart, Pappy Boyington, and Neal Armstrong, the groundbreaking work of Madame Curie, and the selfless work of Mother Theresa.

At various points throughout my University education, I was called on to give a more advanced version of the "who influences you" book report from childhood. For most students, these reports focused on someone influential within their chosen career field. So there was more Igor Sikorsky and less Amelia Earhart, more Frank Whittle and less Tom Petty, and more Leif Ericson and less Leif Garret, but the one thing that the papers all had in common was that the subject provided inspiration to the student and had influenced their desire to enter their chosen career.

When Alinsky's name started to be bantered around, during the campaign, as a person who had influenced Obama, I was a little curious. When both Barack and Michele began quoting

Alinsky, I was intrigued. When I found out that Obama had not only studied Alinsky and his techniques, but had written about the man, taught Alinsky methods in Alinsky's own school, and actually practiced the techniques for years while working for Alinsky network organizations, I was determined to find out what sort of "miraculous" works Alinsky could have achieved that would inspire the man who would be President to follow in his footsteps and sing his praises.

Throughout the campaign, we heard reference to "Alinsky's tactics" and "Alinsky's methods" which gave the impression that Alinsky was akin to some great military tactician. It brought to mind some great General mapping out the battle plan, troop deployment, supply requirements, and even exit strategies in the event that the battle didn't go as he hoped. When I started my research for this book, I wanted to examine other people's reaction to Alinsky's tactics. I assumed that such a masterful tactician would have a great deal written about his actual battles and the methods that he used to win. I scoured books, newspapers, even the internet for reference to the great "battle plans" that made Alinsky's "tactics" so important. I found a lot of references to Alinsky being linked to particular radical groups and landing in jail. I read accounts of businesses large and small, community leaders, and politicians who accused him of blackmail and sabotage. I even read where entire towns banded together to try to keep him out. But, I couldn't find much (outside of his mob attack on an Infant medical Society) about actual "battle plans," detailing how he had achieved success in a particular situation or even how he planned to maneuver his "army" in order to compel his target to meet his demands.

What I did find came from Alinsky himself. While he acknowledged that most of his "community organizing" failed to actually benefit the community, he did write about his most "glorious" battle plans in *Rules For Radicals*. Alinsky, who was a paid "Organizer" for a militant black group who targeted Eastman Kodak in Rochester, New York designed the following "battle plan."

> *"I suggested that we might buy one hundred seats for one of Rochester's symphony concerts. We would select a concert in which the music was relatively quiet. The hundred blacks who would be given the tickets would first be treated to a three-hour pre-concert dinner in the community, in which they would be fed nothing but baked beans, and lots of them; then the people would go to the symphony hall – with obvious consequences"[53]*

In another similar "battle plan," Alinsky targeted O'Hare Airport. After blackmailing City Hall politicians into concessions for the "Woodlawns ghetto organization," Alinsky lost the upper hand when the politicians lost their seats. The incoming group didn't feel compelled to carryout agreements made by predecessors under duress. So Alinsky focused on O'Hare Airport, the world's busiest airport at the time and in particular at tying up all of the toilet facilities, in the entire airport, for the entire day.

> *"...the tactic becomes obvious – we tie up the lavatories. In the restrooms you drop a dime, enter, push the lock on the door – and you can stay there all day. Therefore the occupation of the sit-down toilets presents no problem. It would take relatively few people to walk into these cubicles, armed with books and newspapers, lock the door, and tie up all the facilities. What are the police going to do? Break in and demand evidence of legitimate*

---

[53] Alinsky, Saul Rules For Radicals pg 139

occupancy? Therefore the ladies' restrooms could be occupied completely; the only problem in the men's lavatories would be the stand-up urinals. This too could be taken care of by having groups busy themselves around the airport and then move in on the stand-up urinals to line up four or five deep whenever a flight arrived. An intelligence study was launched to learn how many sit-down toilets for both men and women, as well as stand-up urinals, there were in the entire O'Hare Airport Complex and how many men and women would be necessary for the nation's first "shit-in."

The consequences of this kind of action would be catastrophic in many ways. People would be desperate for a place to relieve themselves. O'Hare would soon become a shambles. The whole scene would be unbelievable...."[54]

Alinsky reveled in these types of juvenile antics. *"The one thing that all oppressed people want to do to their oppressors is shit on them. Here was an approximate way to do this. It connected with their hatred of Whitey."*[55] But what those who chose to follow Alinsky miss is that these types of tactics don't ever achieve the desired result. What do these sorts of tactics prove? Are the blacks who were struggling to gain more access to employment opportunities at Kodak respected more after a "fart-in," or less? Does that sort of behavior further their cause? Are the passengers who are forced to relieve themselves in the corners and hallways of an international airport or those workers who would be compelled to clean such a mess going to be sympathetic to Alinsky's organization? Of course not, but than that wasn't Alinsky's goal, his stated goal was personal power.

---

[54] Alinsky, Saul Rules For Radicals pg 142
[55] Alinsky, Saul Rules For Radicals pg 141

Examining the tactics that Alinsky himself felt were brilliant also reveals his complete disinterest in the consequences to the hundreds and thousands of people that his antics hurt. At Rochester, had his "fart-in" been successful, fewer patrons would be willing to risk paying to attend the next performance for fear that they would waste their time and money on another "stink bomb" experience. Without patrons, the symphony can't pay performers and the orchestra disintegrates. Without a local symphony, people in the community lose an artistic outlet; children aren't exposed to music and aren't inspired to pursue musical studies. The community suffers. Alinsky's selfish stunt robs an entire city of music, affecting generations to come. Of course this doesn't even address the damage that such a stunt inflicts on race relations, which were already tense in Rochester.

The "knock-on" effect in the O'Hare situation would be worse. Thousands of people forced to relive themselves in public would breed disease. People would miss their connecting flights resulting in professional disaster. They would miss meetings that propel the economy. Miss job opportunities that may make the difference between a family being successful and being homeless. Even worse, people would miss the irretrievable moments, weddings, births, deaths, all because Alinsky wanted to blackmail some officials. Shops in O'Hare would lose trade, who wants to buy duty free when your pants are full of pooh? People would plan their next trips insuring that they avoided O'Hare. Alinsky would effectively end thousands of jobs, not only in the airport itself but the support jobs, shipping, construction, fueling, etc. The economy of an entire city is damaged.

So I ask you. What is there in Alinsky that is emulation worthy? What about him would inspire a lifetime of devotion? And what can we say of a politician who chooses to follow the lead of such a man? Barack Obama, the man who modeled his life upon the master of the "shit-in."

- Chapter 7 -

The Organizer & Ethics

"A man without ethics is a wild beast loosed upon this world."
Albert Camus

Perhaps after examining both Alinsky's and Obama's rise to power and prominence, probing their beliefs on ethics seems ironic. And to be fair, it is a short chapter. Alinsky, who lied to those he "organized" in order to insure greater membership, more headlines, and a fatter wallet and then used those improved membership numbers to extort and threaten business leaders, politicians, companies and the government into similarly padding his pockets certainly wasn't a paragon of ethical virtue. Obama has exhibited more faces that Cybil and an open disregard for anyone (no matter how long he has known them and called them friend) who can not benefit his goals. Yet understanding their shared beliefs about ethics is important. It establishes the fact that the old Marquess of Queensberry rules can no longer apply when dealing with Team Obama and perhaps we can all wipe the shocked looks off of our faces when he and his cohorts break the established rules of propriety and politics.

In my experience, when an author writes about current ethics, he or she does so from the standpoint of being a "moralist," someone who prescribes moral behavior and either establishes or interprets rules of appropriate conduct and etiquette. Rarely have I found an author who advises to use the morals and ethics of others as weapons to get whatever the reader covets. This however is the position of Alinsky, who concerned himself very little with the concept of ethics, morality, or right and wrong in the militants that he "organized" and inspired. He considered morals to be the province of theoretical or "arm chair" revolutionaries who talked and debated and fantasized, but never acted.

"The practical revolutionary will understand Goethe's "conscience is the virtue of observers and not of agents of action": in action, one does not always enjoy the luxury of a decision that is consistent both with one's individual conscience and the good of mankind." – Alinsky

"The end is what you want, and the means is how you get it. The man of action views the issue of means and ends in pragmatic and strategic terms. He has no other problem; he thinks only of his actual resources and the possibilities of various choices of action. " - Alinsky

While Alinsky did not concern himself with the morality of militants, he did dedicate an entire chapter of the book *Rules For Radicals* to methods of manipulating the morals of others, ends justifying the means rationalization, and the justification for embracing corruption. Alinsky's rules concerning ethics are listed below.

- "One's concern with ethics of means and ends varies inversely with one's personal interest in the issue.... and distance from the scene of the conflict."

- "Judgment of the ethics of means is dependant upon the political position of those sitting in judgment."

- "In war the end justifies almost any means."

- "Judgment must be made in the context in the times of which the action occurred and not from any other chronological vantage point."

- "Concern with ethics increases with the number if means available and vice versa."

- "The less important the end to be desired, the more one can afford to engage in ethical evaluations of means."

- "Generally, success or failure is a mighty determinant."

- "Morality of the means depends upon whether the means is being employed at a time of imminent defeat or imminent victory."

- "Any effective means is automatically judged by the opposition as being unethical."

- "Do what you can with what you have and clothe it with moral garments."

- "Goals must be phrased in general terms like "Liberty, Equality, Fraternity," "Of the Common Welfare," "Pursuit of Happiness," or "Bread and Peace."

Unlike Alinsky's tactical rules detailing in step-by-step fashion how to manipulate, intimidate, and deceive to gain a position of power, all of Alinsky's rules concerning ethics come down to three basic concepts.

1. History is written by the winners.
2. Ethics is relative.
3. The appearance of ethical behavior is just as good as actually being ethical.

Many of Alinsky's Rules of Ethics concern location (either geographical or political) and distance between the "community organizer" and the "bad smell" or unethical activity. The farther away a "community organizer" can position him/her self from an unethical act, the less it should interfere with goals. Part of the reason that Alinsky trained the locals to follow his instructions, without really understanding the methods or purpose, was to provide him the ability to disavow any knowledge or responsibility in the event that something went wrong.

Obama used this distancing technique particularly well through the internet and through "agents." During the campaign, his team was able to ridicule or attack the opposition on all of traditionally off-limits fronts (race, family, wealth, etc.), without getting his hands dirty. By distancing himself from the comments, he was able to benefit from attacks on Sarah Palin's children, her ability as a mother, her background, and her experience without having to address the deficiencies in his own background or experience. He benefited by appearing "above" the fracas and refusing to comment on controversial attacks that benefited him immensely.

Perhaps even more effectively, Team Obama was able to disseminate misinformation through the same chains. In a 24 hour news climate, where the first to break the news "wins" the audience share and advertising revenue, Team Obama released what seemed like potentially damaging information at such a rate that news teams were unable to keep up with it, reporting without fact checking. The resulting "breaking news stories" reaped benefits for Obama, three fold. First, conservative news outlets were forced to capitulate, frequently, when damaging news items that they had reported turned out to be false. This damaged their credibility and enabled Team Obama to level challenges of racism (again through indirect internet and "agent" channels) against anyone who questioned his credentials or challenged his positions.

Second, gun shy, the same news stations erred on the side of caution when legitimate news worthy stories about Obama's associations and background came to the surface. Unwilling to have "egg on their face" again, news stations either watered down stories about Obama's lack of a birth certificate, transcripts, or experience and links to domestic terrorists, radical socialists, and Islamic fundamentalists or refused to comment at all. Dozens of law suits concerning Obama's legitimacy as a candidate went largely unreported thanks to this fear. So while liberal stations were mercilessly attacking Sarah Palin's young children and John McCain's military service, conservative stations remained largely quiet about Barack and Michele and their myriad of anti-American friends, financiers, and activities.

Perhaps more importantly, Obama was able to use the misinformation stories to hide facts that would end his chances as a Presidential candidate. By including a real fact tucked into an erroneous story, Obama was able to neatly dispose of a real issue without ever having to address it. In one example, information was being gathered that exposed Obama's longstanding friendship with Nation of Islam leader, Louis Farrakhan. Friendship with Farrakhan, a black nationalist who openly declared that blacks will eventually overthrow white establishment using "any means necessary," would certainly make it difficult for Obama to court either Jewish or white voters.

Instead of addressing his relationship with Farrakhan, misinformation about the existence of the so called "Whiety Tapes," was released in mass. In these "Whiety Tapes" Michele Obama was rumored to have made extremely derogatory comments about white people at a Farrakhan sponsored/attended conference. Over the next few days and weeks, the internet and talk radio, as well as some television news channels discussed the "Whitey Tapes" and their potential damage to the Obama campaign. Supposed transcripts of the comments, photos showing Michele and Farrakhan's wife, even claims that the "Whitey Tapes" were a part of a Rev Wright released DVD erupted on the internet. Political commentators theorized on the affects on Obama's campaign. Hillary Democrats and Republicans alike salivated at the impending Obama doom. Through it all, Obama said nothing.

Weeks of anticipation from the right, nervous agitation from the far left, and promises to release the tapes imminently from the secret sources and then…..nothing. No tape, no further contact from the secret sources, no way to follow up and no way to corroborate. News organizations refused to so much as acknowledge that they had ever even heard the term "Whitey Tape" let alone speculated on it's existence and potential fall out and no one was willing to mention Farrakhan and Obama in the same sentence. With one well planned hoax, Obama was able to avoid scrutiny over his close friendship and association with the controversial, militant figure.

The idea that any means is justified in war is probably a fact of simple human nature. The solider may have joined the military to protect his homeland. He may go to the battlefield with the rules of appropriate gentlemanly engagement firmly entrenched. But at the moment when he is faced with his own eminent death, he does what he must to save his own life and that of his comrades. War is ugly and dirty and inhumane, which is why it is easier to romanticize wars from the past, when the real human toll wasn't televised on the evening news.

In the 1960's the government was hesitant to label anything a war for fear of turning off the general public. So "Policing Actions" like Vietnam were under minded, under funded, and went largely unfinished. Today we have the opposite problem. We are faced with constant "wars" on our own shores; the war on domestic terror, the war on drugs, the war on racism, the war on poverty, the war on crime, etc. etc. etc. Everything is labeled a "war," with the rather ironic exception of the situations in Iraq and Afghanistan. Labeling every concerted effort to eradicate a perceived societal problem as a "war" is supposed to make us all feel that the police or appropriate government agency is taking the particular problem seriously.

Alinsky was a fan of turning every issue, no matter how large or small, into a full blown battle. His "hit list" was full of people who he felt personally slighted him or didn't give him proper respect by not simply capitulating to his demands. He delighted in humiliating politicians and business leaders, bullying support staff at the businesses or government agencies that he targeted, and eviscerating anyone that challenged his motivations or methods. To Alinsky, all was fair in war and everything was war.

Obama has continued Alinsky's "walnut and sledgehammer" approach to opposition. Whether he was crushing Alice Palmer early in his political career, declaring that veterans who were not in favor of his ideas were anti-American and potential terrorists, or refusing access to any member of the press who had not sung his praises, like Alinsky, Obama seems particularly "thin skinned" for someone who so spectacularly courted fame and recognition. Obama has launched (or re-launched) multiple "wars" topped off with a dizzying array of "czars" and we should all sleep safely at night, knowing that everything possible is being done to win the battle against whatever.

However, everything is not a war. Just by labeling any social issue or perceived problem as a war simply doesn't make it one. The concept, "in war the end justifies almost any means" is being used as a carte blanch to do or say anything without responsibility or repercussion. This ignores the fact that even in a proper, military war, the entire war is not conducted on an "any means necessary" manner. There are legal requirements, established conventions, and rules of conduct that frame acceptable wartime activities, treatment of captives, and civilians. Alinsky lived by the old adage, "if you are not with me, you are against me" and treated everyone in his life thusly. Obama acts as if any cause that he happens to champion is a war and that the general public, companies, industries, and government organizations fall into either enemy, dispensable infantry, or cannon fodder categories.

The Romans were famous for caging any fallen monarch, chieftain, or General and parading him (or her) through the streets of Rome. Not only did this show the public the power of might Rome, but also completely humiliated the fallen warrior. The Cesar was able to say, "see look at what becomes of those who challenge me!" The Styrofoam colonnade at Obama's acceptance speech was not the only nod to Rome. Obama too parades his vanquished through the streets, hobbling and humiliating them both as a sign of power and as a warning. Perhaps his most famous conquest was that over Hillary Clinton during the Presidential campaign. Not only did he eviscerate her, inspire friends and supporters to stage a mass desertion, and manage to completely ignore the significance of the first female Presidential candidate from a major party, once he had vanquished her, he gave her a high profile position and then immediately removed every vestige of power from the role. Obama neutralized her as a threat, not only during the campaign, but arguably, forever.

One of the dangers facing any challenger is the failure to understand that ferocity with which Team Obama will respond. Even in the arena of "dirty" politics, there are rules and mores defining acceptable behavior. Since Team Obama adheres to the "all is fair in war" concept and considers all opposition a declaration of war, those who find themselves either purposefully or accidentally in Team Obama's sights would do well to remember that they are not concerned with ethics, honor, truth, or even actions benefiting their own supporters. Obama is still a "community organizer" huckster first and foremost and the entire goal the "community organizer" is wealth and power.

"Moral rationalization is indispensable at all times of action whether to justify the selection or use of ends or means." – Alinsky

"All effective actions require the passport of morality." Alinsky

Alinsky counseled that it is necessary to cover one's "naked self-interest" and mask it by using evocative terms such as equality or freedom. This essentially provides the actor with the cover to take just about any action necessary. By claiming that even the most self serving actions are necessary to make the world a better, fairer place, the actor is free attack opposition, usurp power, terminate rights, and trample freedoms.

History is full of dictators and despots who have raped and pillaged their own people under the guise of "moral authority." Whether it was Pol Pot's eco-socialism which forced millions of people to leave the cities to work in collective farms or Hitler's eradication of the Jews, mad men have always claimed that their actions against one group was for the betterment of the country as a whole. While we deplore the actions of those who are removed from us by location or time, we seem blinded by the same tactics used right this second in halls of our own government. Whether it is the bankrupting of industries, forced take-over of businesses, and shoving thousands into unemployment so that a "greener economy" can be built or increasing taxes on working people in order to pay for the food, housing, education, and medical care of those in the country illegally, Team Obama's tactics can be likened to those of every other maniacal leader. Claiming moral authority to cover up immoral actions is nothing new.

By claiming moral authority, Obama has gobbled up entire industries, extended intrusions into the lives of the general public, and taken control of banking and national finance. He has laid the foundation for ending oppositional voices by controlling television, radio, news media, and the internet. Despite appointing tax cheats, criminals, and con artists to positions of power, he is largely unchallenged due to his evocation of moral authority. His ambitions to turn the United States into a socialist country have been relatively un-thwarted. He has used the financial turbulence in the marketplace to act as cover for his systematic dismantling of the marketplace, housing, banking, healthcare, and national security.

At his current pace, Obama is on target to join the ranks of other leaders who have used their position and ambition, coupled with the belief that they somehow knew what was best for every citizen in the country, to remake the United States of America into a completely new entity. Compare any of the dictators who we would consider mad and you will find a similar assent to power and an ambitious attempt to remake their country into their vision of Eden. Barack Obama is following the same path as Pol Pot and his desire to "save us" by forcing us to all live in his version of a socialist Eden with himself as a Guiding Father/Dictator is chilling and to historians, familiar.

While Alinsky believed that appealing to a target's self interest was one of the best ways to secure an alliance or guarantee membership, he was also cognizant of importance of words. Whether the words were used in developing slogans or mantras which would be easy to shout during a rally or were being used in speeches to inspire a community to join his cause, Alinsky counseled his followers to insure that the meaning of the chosen words were pleasing and even inspiring, but were vague and flexible, using Whitman's quote as a warning, "The goal once named cannot be countermanded." Alinsky advised "community organizers" to avoid words and slogans that would box them in or potentially hobble their activities in the event that the situation changed.

Team Obama effectively used the words "Hope" and "Change" throughout his campaign as a slogan for his candidacy. These words were not chosen at random. They were chosen both for their ambiguity and for the emotional response that they elicit. We all have hopes and dreams, we all have aspects of ourselves, our communities, and society as a whole that we would like to change. When the message of hope and change is delivered in a package that is recognizable and acceptable, it is human nature to assume that the messenger shares the same hopes and wants the same changes as the listener. It is in this aspect of basic human nature that lives the deception.

Obama used emulation techniques to "become" a member of whatever organization with whom he spoke. To farmers, he was the grandson of a small town Kansas couple. To the poor, he was the child of a single parent family and a man who dedicated his work to improving the lives of inner city families. To the educated, he was a Harvard man, a lawyer, a scholar. And while being "all things to all people" is almost a tenant of political life,

Obama was able to gain so much support from such a wide range of voters in part because of the disingenuous "Hope" and "Change" mantra. "Hope" and "Change" mean different things to different people. Things that I may want to change, hopes that I have for myself and my family may be vastly different from the changes and hopes of someone else.

Obama successfully avoided committing himself to most issues and allowed millions of Americans (and foreign leaders and citizens) to believe that he was "on their side" and agreed with their concept of hope and the changes that they desired simply by emulating, smiling, and repeating the slogan. It is only now, when Obama has started implementing his plans, do people say, "Hey wait a minute, that is not what we hoped for. That is not the change that I wanted."

- Chapter 8 -

The Tactics
of the Organizer

*"In the world of give and take, tactics is the art of how to take and
how to give. Here our concern is with the tactic of taking; how the
Have Nots can take power away from the Haves." -* Alinsky

Prior to Obama's campaign, most in mainstream and on
Main Street America had never heard of Saul Alinsky. However,
when a mystery man emerges on the national, political scene in
such spectacular fashion and sites Alinsky's teachings as a driving
force through his life, people become curious. While Alinsky's
background and personal motivations are revealing and his
guidance on ethics and deception are shocking, it is the methods
of mass manipulation which have received the most attention.
These methods or tactics, as Alinsky refers to them, are the "rules"
for using a "community organizing" platform to take money,
power, anything of value in order to achieve personal goals.

"Power has always derived from two main sources, money
and people. Lacking money, the Have Nots must build power
from their own flesh and blood. A mass movement expressed
itself with mass tactics. Against the finesse and sophistication of
the status quo, the Have Nots have always had to club their
way."[56] If these sound like the words of a coup leader or a man
attempting to inspire and incite revolution, they are. Alinsky
grounded his teachings in successful military and populous

---

[56] Alinsky, Saul Rules For Radicals pg 127

overthrows throughout history. And in the same way that young officers learn battle strategies, offensive and defensive maneuvers, and troop use and deployment, Alinsky trained his "officers" in strategies to overthrow successful business people, community officials, and politicians. He trained his "officers" in offensive and defensive strategies to either blackmail or humiliate people, businesses, or the government and to extort power and money from them. Finally, he trained his "officers" to use the armies that they create to intimidate or to take action against the businesses, government agencies, and ordinary citizens.

Throughout Alinsky's *Rules For Radicals*, he relays with glee the attacks and planned attacks on small businesses, Corporations, medical service providers, churches, schools, airports, government agencies, and even a Philharmonic Orchestra. Anyone that he perceived could provide him power, fame, or money was a target. Anyone who he felt slighted him or didn't give him the respect that he desired also became a target. By the end of his life, Alinsky seemingly spent as much time on acts of petty vengeance as he did on actually training his followers. However, to be fair, he had spent so many years perfecting the methods and laying groundwork for the networks that he had little to do but act as a figurehead.

I will admit that when I first started research into the Alinsky/Obama relationship for this book, I was chilled to the bone as I read through his "rules." Actually reading mass manipulation techniques are disturbing enough, mainly because they are easy to understand and a person can readily see how they could work. But the aspect that was so disturbing was that in each and every rule, Obama's use of the rule was so blatantly obvious. After reading the Alinsky's book and studying (what we can of) Obama's background, as well as understanding the tremendous significance that Obama himself has placed on Alinsky's teachings, the true and horrifying picture of Barack Obama, the man and his goals, emerges.

"Power is not only what you have, but what the enemy thinks that you have." - Alinsky - Rule 1

It's all about perception. Alinsky explained that those organizations with a large membership can "parade it visibly before the enemy" to intimidate with sheer volume. "If your organization is small in numbers, then do what Gideon did: conceal the members in the dark but raise a din and clamor that will make the listener believe that your organization numbers many more than it does."[57]

The use of "imaginary masses" has well served Obama and other "community organizers" such as Al Sharpton and Jesse Jackson. By using the threat of racial boycotts and bad press if a particular company doesn't comply with demands (generally for "donations" or a paid "consultancy" position), Sharpton in particular has garnered hundreds of thousands, if not millions of dollars by insinuating that he is the voice of all blacks and has control over the "black dollar." The fact that Sharpton is not well respected in much of the black community doesn't matter. The corporations, fearful of being branded as racist organizations, perceive that he has the power and so comply.[58]

The perception of power can also be a great motivator or demoralizer. One of the numerous platforms upon which Obama ran his campaign was that of international respect. Obama claimed that the US had lost respect throughout the world, something that he would be able to restore. To drive this point home, he launched a world tour. US news programs reported

[57] Alinsky, Saul Rules For Radicals pg 126
[58] Vincent, Isabelle & Edelman, Susan "Rev Al Soaks Up Boycott Bucks: Biz Giants Pay or Face Race Rallies" New York Post June 15, 2008

200,000 plus people, in Berlin alone, showed up to hear Obama give a rousing speech. Pictures of huge crowds chanting and waving graced the cover of newspapers and magazines across the country. It truly seemed from the press releases and pictures that the entire world loved Obama. The fact that the crowd was there to see a free rock concert, featuring two of the countries most famous pop acts was irrelevant. Obama took to the stage during the intermission between the two acts, during a time when many had left to sample the free food and beer or use the bathroom. But, the perception that the crowds were there to see Obama was all that mattered. To his followers, it was a further sign that they had backed a winner, loved by the entire world. To his detractors, the sight of thousands of people who seemed to be chanting and cheering for Obama, was a significant morale blow.

While Sharpton's allusion to "Million Man March" numbers at his command and Obama's pop concert photo ops give the visual impression of mass popularity and power, perception is shaped in many ways. Obama used a clever combination of constant statistical releases to demoralize the Clinton camp and scare the Republican opponents. No other political candidate had tapped into the Internet in the same way as Team Obama. While McCain is largely credited with starting the internet campaign contribution revolution in 2000, Obama was the first to really reach out to the public through social networking sites. This enabled him to spread his message faster and farther than any other candidate. It also gave his team virtual carte blanc to issue statistical comparisons that were disingenuous at best and often unconfirmed. A phrase such as "millions of hits" on Obama's web site sounds huge and very formidable. But when put into context, a single YouTube video showing kittens playing or a guy getting hit in the crouch with a football can generate millions of hits in a matter of hours, Obama's "millions of hits" isn't as impressive. However the constant repeating of the phrase gave the perception that the numbers were unique and something to be feared. It also added psychological peer pressure to many who assumed that those "unique" numbers assured an Obama win and they wanted to be on the winning team.

"Never Go Outside the Experience of Your People"
Alinsky - Rule 2
"Whenever Possible Go Outside of the Experience of the Enemy"
Alinsky - Rule 3

Human beings are creatures of habit and structure. Every aspect of a person's life, even those events that seem random or are horrific or tragic (assault, disease, death, etc.), are managed by a series of expected and accepted responses and behaviors. When a person is forced to act in a way that is counter to the expected, they become uncomfortable, fearful, and confused. Alinsky counsels that people who want to manage a group's behavior should look at the activities with which they already feel comfortable and capitalize upon their familiarity with a particular method.

This method has been used quite effectively in protests. When truck drivers wanted to protest the increasing costs of diesel fuel, they drove their big rigs to Washington. The site of hundreds of trucks slowly circling the Capital and honking their horns got the attention of media outlets around the world. Had the truckers instead been counseled to don suits and try and talk about the price issue with politicians or lobbyists, most would have felt uncomfortable and intimidated, their protest poorly attended, and their plight would have generated little media coverage. By staying in their trucks and in their comfort zone, the truck drivers were able to effectively get their message across.

While Alinsky advised organizers to stay within the scope of their member's experiences, he also stressed the importance of forcing "the enemy" out of their own comfort zone. Sighting General Sherman's sweeping attacks throughout the South during the Civil War, Alinsky explained that previously, military movements had specific, organized structures and patterns. Sherman surprised the South when he abandoned the accepted military maneuvers for a guerilla invasion technique. Unable to predict where Sherman's men would strike, and unable to organize an effective, structured military response, the South descended into chaos and ultimately collapsed.

Nobel Prizewinner, Toni Morrison famously called Bill Clinton "our first black President" alluding both to Clinton's own background, his acknowledgement of black voters, and his appointment of blacks to ranking government positions. Hillary Clinton looked to sweep the black vote by association. When Obama initially announced his candidacy, many in the black community suggested that they would stay with the proven track record of the Clintons rather than risk their vote on a largely unknown, Ivy League, elitist.

Unable to attack the Clinton machine head on, Obama turned to community groups with which he was familiar, such as ACORN. Having headed up the DCP, the voter registration arm of ACORN in Chicago, Obama used ACORN to spread the message of his candidacy not initially to those who were already Clinton supporters, but to those who had never registered to vote. ACORN, already familiar in disadvantaged communities as an organization that would assist people to apply for housing and government benefits and voter registration simply added Obama "pushing" to their activities. By using the techniques that ACORN had been successfully employing for over three decades and appealing to a community that trusted and depended upon ACORN, Obama was able to generate huge numbers of voters without having to confront Clinton's base.

Throughout the 2008 campaign, Obama was frequently criticized for his failure to agree to participate in "townhall" style debates. These traditionally unscripted events, which feature citizens asking questions directly to the political candidates are famous for their ability to "make or break" a candidate based on his or her ability to answer questions succinctly. Obama, who was already dodging embarrassing questions about his association with criminals, a racist reverend, and a home grown terrorist organization as well as requests for his birth certificate and University records was understandably less than eager to be put on the spot, on the record, on camera. Coupled with a famous dependency on scripted, teleprompted speeches, Obama was not going to allow himself to be forced out of his comfort zone into a townhall meeting. Unable to confront Obama directly, candidates were forced to ask questions and make claims in their own press releases, giving Obama the time to work with his advisors to craft answers. This refusal to go along with what was considered an essential format also forced the other candidates out of their own comfort zone, but allowed him to stay in his.

"Make the Enemy Live Up To Their Own Book of Rules"

Alinsky – Rule 4

"Ridicule is man's most potent weapon."

Alinsky – Rule 5

"...they can no more obey their own rules than the Christian church can live up to Christianity."　　　Alinsky

What is the difference between President Bill Clinton and his infamous affair with Monica Lewinsky (and others) and the sex scandals of Idaho Senator Larry Craig or New York Governor Eliot Spitzer? Clinton had long acknowledged, even reveled in his reputation as a philandering "bad boy," while Craig, who headed the Senate Ethics Committee and Spitzer, who built his career on prosecuting organized crime (including prostitution) paraded a mantle of moral superiority while engaging in lewd behavior. A philander who cheats is hardly news worthy. However, expose the seedy underbelly of someone who has built their reputation on virtuous behavior and a strict moral code and the resulting chaos of damage control and explosion of ridicule is fodder for the media and an effective weapon for the opposition. The damage is almost always irreversible.

Of course, ridicule or "exposure" need not be fair or honest to be effective. When Team Obama ridiculed the financial success of Senator McCain's wife, attempting to incite an atmosphere of class warfare, the fact that all of the major party candidates were extremely wealthy, including the Obama family was irrelevant. However, perhaps no candidate in history has been more ridiculed and maligned than Sarah Palin. Not only did Team Obama attack her experience, political success, and beliefs (all acceptable in political battles), they attacked her family, her children, her marriage, and her ability to be a mother. While other candidates have been quizzed about their personal lives, no other candidate has been so vilified, dissected, and degraded by the liberal media or an opposing candidate's campaign machine.

Ridicule is almost impossible to deflect or counter. When "the enemy" is caught off guard or embarrassed by revelations or accusations, they lose their poise and their focus. McCain never really recovered from the ridicule that surrounded his wife's personal wealth and property holdings. His failure to quickly list the number of homes that he and his wife owned made him appear either out of touch and uncaring to a society in economic decline or mentally unable to meet the challenges of the Presidency. His hesitance to answer came from the lack of clarity in the loaded question. McCain and his wife held many investment properties and shared vacation properties with other members of the family. However the footage of being caught off guard, open mouthed, and stuttering over a question that most Americans can answer in half a second was used over and over by Team Obama to show McCain as "too old" and out of touch.

In arguably the most distasteful personal attacks in the history of politics, Team Obama's character assassination of Sarah Palin has to mark an all time low in the notoriously dirty game of campaigning. Unable to quell the growing tide of pro-Palin supporters by maligning her experience or positions, Team Obama attacked her children and her family. Palin, a pro-life supporter was accused of "forcing" her teenaged, pregnant daughter into keeping the baby in order to stay in step with publicized anti-abortion stance. Palin's daughter was vilified in the press as a girl of poor moral character because of the pregnancy and accusations about the unborn child's paternity. To add further insult to injury, Palin herself, who had recently had a child afflicted with Down's Syndrome, was accused of being an unfit mother for her mere appearance on the campaign trail. Aside from the shock at being so publicly attacked, Palin was forced to focus her attention away from the campaign and towards protecting her young children and family.

_____

"It should be remembered that you can threaten the enemy and get away with it. You can insult and annoy him, but the one thing that is unforgivable and that is certain to get him to react is to laugh at him. This causes an irrational anger."[59]

---

[59] Alinsky, Saul Rules For Radicals pg 137

"A Good Tactic is One That Your People Enjoy."

Alinsky – Rule 6

"A Tactic That Drags on Too Long Becomes a Drag."

Alinsky – Rule 7

Human beings have notoriously short attention spans. Alinsky recognized that this fact was potentially the biggest threat to any militant organization, as boredom or distraction would collapse a movement from the inside. He advised militants to employ tactics that their members would actually enjoy and that insured some level of success quickly in order to maintain morale.

While Clinton attempted to engage young people by admitting to smoking dope (though not inhaling) and by playing his saxophone on the late night Arsenio Hall Show, Obama successfully integrated college students into his campaign machine by elevating their perceived importance and organizing their participation. It can be argued that this was due in large part to the mass scale liberal indoctrination of college students at the hands of radical University professors (William Ayers, Michael Dyson, Ward Churchill, etc.) or the fairy tale ideology of many young people who lack real world experience. However, this overlooks the fact that Obama engaged young people directly in a way that they understood and could embrace....through electronic media, student specific speeches, and campus events and parties.

When previous political candidates spoke on college campuses, they used the platform to deliver what was little more than another stump speech, hoping for local media coverage. This is due in large part to the notoriously unreliable student vote. While students previously had expressed positions, the numbers that actually registered to vote and cast a ballot was low. However, Obama's speech writers crafted "talks" that directly targeted college students and issues that affected them; tuition fees, scholarships, student loans, and job prospects, as well as military and global warming issues. Perhaps most importantly however, Obama used the platform to invite students to get involved in fun ways that provided almost instant gratification.

Of course their involvement didn't happen by chance. Waiting for students just outside of the lecture halls were Team Obama organized groups designed to capitalize on the lingering feeling of empowerment. Students who fancied themselves film makers were encouraged (and financed) to make pro-Obama (and anti-everyone else) "viral videos" for YouTube, Facebook, and MySpace. Design and marketing students were targeted to participate in Obama campaign art contests. Others participated in "disruption parties" traveling to the speeches and events of opponents with the goal of disrupting and embarrassing candidates. And of course thousands of students got involved with online marketing campaigns that involved a combination of social networking sites and anonymous hate attacks on pro-opposition sites. But the largest groups concentrated on "on-the-spot" voter registration and Obama paraphernalia sales.

All of these activities appeal to those with a short attention span and a need for instant gratification. Whether it is tallying up the number of voters registered at the end of the day or counting the numbers of Obama shirts and pins worn around campus, the young Obama supporter could see the result of their efforts. Add viral videos and social networking sites and a single person could have their opinions, film, or art work viewed by millions of people all thanks to Team Obama. Of course, this can be extremely addictive. By providing tactics and events for student participation, Team Obama carved huge numbers of devoted Obama voters out of a group that had been largely apathetic non-voters in previous election cycles. He made participation fun and easy and reaped the rewards.

"Keep the Pressure On."

Alinsky – Rule 8

With few exceptions, wars are not won with a single shot, they are a compilation of battles, attacks, and woundings that ultimately take their toll and defeat the enemy. Alinsky counseled militants to maintain pressure on the "enemy" by constantly attacking, changing tactics, and drawing the "enemy" to defend or fight on multiple fronts. By physically and emotionally weakening the "enemy" in this way, even small organizations could take on and defeat large opponents.

Team Obama used a very clever combination of launching proxy-attacks against opponents and faux proxy-attacks against himself, to keep constant pressure on Clinton, McCain, and Palin. By using proxy-attacks (attacks that don't come directly from Obama himself) he was able to refute responsibility for the most distasteful personal attacks against his opponents, particularly those against the children and families of McCain and Palin. He was able to benefit from bad press largely generated by pro-Obama journalists and "anonymous" bloggers while giving the appearance of having "clean hands." Proxy-attacks also provided him with a platform to comment on the accusations and attacks from a position of moral superiority.

Perhaps more interestingly however, Obama used faux or fake proxy-attacks against himself to bury real issues. When questions surrounding Obama's missing or falsified birth certificate picked up steam, a series of "attacks" were released by pro-Obama journalists surrounding his philandering father, a poverty stricken half-brother in Kenya, another alleged con artist half-brother in Hong Kong, and his socialist mother. Not only did this overwhelm people with essentially too much information to process, the faux issues all surrounded issues that can't be legitimately laid at Obama's feet. Even those vehemently opposed

100

to Obama's stated positions couldn't blame the man for actions of long dead family members or brothers whom he has never met or had contact. Since most people have family members for whose actions they wouldn't want to be held responsible, pro-Obama journalists were effectively able to wrap the legitimate birth certificate issue with family member non-issues and largely dispose of any real examination of the birth certificate questions by national and international press.

This burying of real issues by covering them with an avalanche of non-issues has been an effective tactic for Team Obama. Not only has it provided him a way to avoid embarrassing and potentially politically deadly legitimate issues, it has created a feeding frenzy for opponents who simply tired themselves out (and looked like reactionary tabloid chasers) by commenting on the barrage of issues that largely came to nothing. This also diverted the focus of opponents off of their own messages and compelled them to focus on often trivial matters, while Obama steamed forward pushing his own agenda.

"The Threat is Usually More Terrifying Than the Thing Itself." Alinsky – Rule 9

Whether the opponent is a single person or a huge organization, fear of the "worst case scenario" can be an extremely effective weapon. By making vague but pointed "threats" the "enemy" is left to imagine their worst fears coming to fruition. This can result in a case of virtual fear based paralysis, where the "enemy" simply stops fighting or can cause an organization to expend a great deal of energy shoring up for what they imagine may happen. The effectiveness of this tactic can't be understated. The threat maker expends limited resources while the target runs themselves ragged preparing for their imagined worst fear, a fear of which the threat maker may have no knowledge or ability to actually inflict. Response to the perceived threat can also create tremendous public backlash if the enemy makes public or overt movements to protect themselves from the imagined danger. This tactic is exhausting and demoralizing for the enemy and is often used as a "final blow" in a protracted battle.

The battle between Obama and Clinton created a unique opportunity for Republicans. Despite being hindered by a President with low popularity numbers and a Republican candidate (McCain) who was arguably a RINO (Republican in Name Only) due to his moderate (even liberal) voting record, the Republicans looked to benefit from a divisive split in the Democrat party. With hundreds of thousands of Clinton supporters refusing to lend their vote to Obama, many going so far as to pledge their votes to the Republican opposition, Obama looked unable to solidify the party machine behind his candidacy.

However, when well timed videos were released showing Obama speaking about a willingness to impose more gun control and even hobble the second amendment, gun enthusiasts and Constitutional sanctity conservatives went into overdrive. Sales of weapons skyrocketed, ammunitions companies had to add shifts in order to meet demand, and the news media showed clips of people who were creating their own personal armories. Fear of a potential Obama win and the possibility that this win would mean a ban on new sales of guns and ammunition created a frenzy.

Around the same time, leaks about "Obama Youth Brigades," Obama backed initiatives to release 1/3rd of the blacks from prison, and connections to the Black Panthers and Louis Farrakhan started hitting the internet and local media outlets. When questioned about the possibility that an "Obama Youth Brigade" comprised of young black men, recently released from prison, and armed would be patrolling the communities, many residents responded by explaining that the very idea of such a development was largely responsible for their own ammunition stock piling and that they would not hesitate to use the weapons to defend themselves, their property, and their community. Of course, by the time that the Pro-Obama journalists were done with their editing, it appeared that thousands of "red necks" were stock piling weapons in the event of an Obama win to facilitate an armed revolution.

Team Obama was then able to use the fear that unless Clinton backers, independent voters, and moderate Republicans voted for him, the result would be an American version of Nazi Germany, in which anyone who was not white and Christian would become the target of armed racists. The fear that an Obama win would result in a loss of the Second Amendment, despite his inability to actually do away with the Second Amendment, resulted in many conservatives over reacting to their worst fears. This, caught on tape provided Obama with the ammunition that he needed to inflict the most damaging wound to Clinton, whose supporters joined Obama in droves. It also compelled moderate Republicans and Independent voters to contemplate their own worst case scenarios and vote against it.

"The major premise for tactics is the development of operations that will maintain a constant pressure upon the opposition." Alinsky – Rule 10

While it is essential to "keep the pressure on" with multiple, changing tactics that keep the enemy on its toes, the tactic that is most effective is one that takes on a "life of its own" continuing to put pressure on the enemy without requiring much additional energy expenditure. Alinsky advised militants to be on the lookout for any developing situation which could be used to damage the enemy. Whether this constant pressure comes from a true revelation or a fabricated link between the enemy and an issue, Alinsky's concern was not honesty or accuracy, but rather effectiveness.

Politicians have long sought the revelation that would cause public outrage and ultimately destroy an opponent. Typically, a politician relied on their muckrakers to expose sex scandals, effectively showering the opponent in bad press, and providing them a platform to "sincerely" question the opposition's honor or ability to focus on the job. A single whisper of a sex scandal, especially if the scandal involved prostitution, homosexuality, or an affair that resulted in a child, could derail a candidate. Not only would the media pick up the story and "investigate" for weeks, they would interview anyone with an opinion about the situation. Gone are the days when a detective would be hired to follow a candidate to find "some dirt." With hidden cameras, email hacking, tracking devices, bugs, social network spying, and newspapers offering lucrative deals to anyone intimately involved with a famous person or public figure, a candidate can't carry on an affair or get up to any other bad behavior and reasonably expect to not be exposed. That being said, many "journalists" don't let truth get in the way of a good story and fabrications aren't unheard of.

Exposing sexual liaisons is not the only way to derail an opponent. Team Obama was successfully able to link opponents to a whole myriad of news items or events that had little to do with the particular candidate or their positions. Despite RINO McCain's liberal voting record, Obama was able to successfully link him to unpopular George Bush. By continuing to claim that McCain was simply a doppelganger of Bush and incorporating sayings like "more of the same" into any discussion of his opponent, news outlets, already covering the growing cry from liberals to charge Bush with war crimes, linked the controversial war in Iraq with McCain. Once the link between McCain and Bush was created, any controversial aspect of Bush's presidency stuck to McCain. Essentially Team Obama's initial tactic of likening McCain to Bush took on a life of its own and developed into a full grown case of guilt by association.

Perhaps the strangest, albeit very successful use of a tactic that attaches to an opponent and continues to inflict injury, is that of a now infamous Saturday Night Live comedy skit parodying Sarah Palin. In the skit, the openly pro-Obama comedian Tina Fey, portrayed Palin as a ditzy, overtly sexy, fame obsessed beauty queen who explains her experience in foreign policy by saying "I can see Russia from my house." Despite Palin never actually saying those words, the satire stuck. Perhaps due to Fey's uncanny portrayal, many believed that the parody was an actual news conference and the clip went viral on the internet. The result was an already largely pro-Obama media using the clip to categorize Palin as being incompetent and stupid. This type of attack is almost impossible to combat.

"If you push a negative hard and deep enough it will break through into its counterside." Alinsky – Rule 11

Alinsky describes an incident in which his militant organization was unceasingly harassing a particular company. In a desperate attempt, the company hired a private detective who broke into Alinsky's home and office to get the company's records from his possession. The company, who had previously been viewed by the public as the unfortunate target of militant thugs, lost their credibility and public sympathy with that one blunder. Alinsky, a frequent target of death threats, publicized that an attempt on his life had been made and that the company had sponsored a break in of his home and office. While he didn't say that the company was responsible for the attempt on his life, he alluded to the fact that the company had so much to hide that they would stoop to burglary and even murder. From that point

105

forward, Alinsky was able to play the part of victim and the company faced with bad press, eventually capitulated. Alinsky's organization's negative position was made positive by the over-reaction of the company.

At least in the short term, this rule is one with which Obama has struggled. During rare moments of unscripted commentary, Obama has frequently attacked an opponent in ways that alienate, even those in his own party and created sympathy for the object of his attack. Whether his comments have been made at an inappropriate time, have seemed insensitive to a voting block, or have added to the perception that he is a dictatorial elitist, an unscripted Obama has often, inadvertently made underdog heroes of opponents. Direct and personal attacks against Hillary Clinton, coupled with statements that indicated that Obama felt that the historical significance of a black President was greater than the historical significance of a female President, resulted in females of all parties swinging direct support to Clinton's campaign. Many who had been apathetic towards Hillary Clinton felt that she was unfairly attacked by both Barack and Michelle prior to the New Hampshire primaries. Arguably, the result was a better than expected showing by Clinton, who carried female voters.

"You can't just listen to Rush Limbaugh and get things done," quipped Obama when berating the GOP leaders about their refusal to blanket stamp his $1 trillion dollar "stimulus" package less than a week after he took office. While Obama was attempting to turn listeners off of the acerbic, conservative radio host, who had been a strong voice against him during his campaign, the idea that a President was dictating to whom people could listen was too much for many. Already the most popular radio talk show host in the country, the backlash against Obama's comments gave Rush a 90 minute, primetime news platform and made the President appear petty and autocratic.

However, arguably the largest backlash against a direct attack came when Obama attacked Alaska Governor Sarah Palin. McCain issued a congratulatory statement (and video) applauding Obama as the first black Presidential nominee for the Democratic Party upon his acceptance of the nomination. However, when Palin was announced as the first Republican female nominee to the role of Vice President, instead of the expected well wishes and civility, Obama attacked her experience, her small town upbringing, and her religious stance before her acceptance speech was even finished. Forced to retract and issue a half hearted apology later in the day, the graceless attack was shocking to many, even within Obama's own party. The backlash of Obama's attacks (which continued, frequently followed by retractions) was to solidify the fractured Republican Party behind the one person who seemed to genuinely unnerve Obama. Palin's popularity can largely be attributed to the fear that she seemed to evoke in the Democratic Party and in particular with Obama.

"The price of a successful attack is a constructive alternative." Alinsky – Rule 12

Alinsky warned militants not to be caught off guard by the sudden capitulation of the enemy. If militants continue to attack a company or a government body demanding an end to whatever practice with which they are unhappy, the entire "war" can end virtually overnight if the enemy suddenly says "ok what would YOU do?" and the militants don't have a cohesive answer. It simply isn't enough to say that someone else is wrong; opponents must be prepared with a popular and feasible alternative plan in order to successfully beat an opponent.

This rule potentially has the highest "backfire" ratio of all of Alinsky's rules. Being forced into a position of not simply attacking but of supplying solutions to a problem places the attacker or accuser into a very vulnerable position. Those who may have been sympathetic to the militants or agreed that the company or government body was doing "the wrong thing" may be equally unimpressed with the solutions offered. This effectively ends support as people will generally choose to back a "bad known" over a "bad unknown."

A good alternative however does not necessarily equal a win. Bureaucracy can be an effective neutralizer. Faced with a public outcry, a company may choose to embrace the offered solutions and publicly begin implementing them, all the while miring the changes down with bureaucracy. The company can then appear to be responsive to the public, while effectively making little more than superficial changes.

Throughout the campaign, Team Obama was very careful to avoid being bitten by this rule. Quick to criticize, Obama used vague words to avoid providing any actual solutions or pin himself to an unpopular policy during the election cycle. Instead of offering his own plans he responded to critics by saying that he wouldn't provide "more of the same" or would be an agent of "change." Both Clinton and the Republicans failed to capitalize on opportunities to press Obama to provide specifics, however Obama's refusal to participate in town hall debates limited his vulnerability.

After the election, when Obama began implementing his policies, many of which were unpopular even with his own party, both Republican and Democrat opposition leaders failed to publicly provide alternative solutions. Obama who had been so vague during the campaign, publicly demanded that Republicans announce their alternatives so that the country could evaluate the ideas. Unprepared, Republicans scrambled. Obama also announced that he would work with Republicans, giving the impression of conciliation, all the while holding secret meetings with his own supporters to quickly pass unpopular initiatives. Without a strong voice, publicly establishing a feasible alternative to Obama's vast socialist based spend-a-thon, Republicans and moderate Democrats appeared whiney and divisive.

"Pick the target, freeze it, personalize it, and polarize it."
Alinsky – Rule 13

The use of a "target" is one of Alinsky's most effective manipulation techniques. Alinsky gained members to his various organizations by taking a general complaint that a particular group had and turning it into someone's fault. The general poverty of a community was blamed on a local factory. The lack of employment was based on City Hall. No link was too tenuous; Alinsky could take any problem and create an enemy. Of course he then swooped in and claimed that if people joined his organization, he would take the battle to the enemy and force them to do something about the perceived problem.

Picking a problem or a target was not based on guesswork or luck. Alinsky's tactics center on power analysis. He counseled students to figure out who had the power and how to take it away. Since it is difficult to take power away from a "friend" or someone with whom your organization may sympathize, an organizer has to create an enemy and that enemy must be named. "The opposition must be singled out as the target and "frozen."[60] Once an issue was established and an enemy created, Alinsky had to find a public face of the enemy, someone who could provide the focal point of hate. Focusing anger on a large group, company, or government agency can be difficult, Alinsky advised "organizers" to find a person upon whom all blame could be attached and to whom all hatred could be channeled. It should be

---

[60] Alinsky, Saul Rules For Radicals pg 130

noted that Alinsky didn't care tremendously if the person targeted was the actual responsible party explaining, "One of the criteria in picking your target is the target's vulnerability."[61]

By stirring up anger and hatred in his organization and then essentially pointing to one person at the targeted company or government agency and saying "it's all his fault," Alinsky was able to control the behaviors of masses of people by manipulating them into hatred for his target. Targeting someone keeps the organization active and in a heightened state of agitation. Where a single person's anger may pass, Alinsky created an environment in which just meeting people on the street would bring new discussions and reignite angers. Each revelation about the target would bring renewed waves of anger and hatred until every aspect of the target's character, family, possessions, and demeanor serve to add further proof that he/she is evil.

Once a target was determined, "It should be borne in mind that the target is always trying to shift responsibility to get out of being the target. [Organizers] must keep this in mind and pin that target down securely. If an organization permits responsibility to be diffused and distributed in a number or areas, attack becomes impossible."[62] Alinsky warned his students not to become sidetracked by other potential targets or by discovering that others are equally if not more to blame than the target, once a target is selected, he/she must be the entire focus and destroying that target is essential in order to meet the "organizer's" goals. So effective is the targeting technique that Alinsky was able to issue effective threats against politicians, business owners, and community leaders simply by insinuating that he intended on making them the target.

---

[61] Alinsky, Saul Rules For radicals pg 133
[62] Alinsky, Saul Rules For Radicals pg 132

Creating a scapegoat has long been an effective strategy in politics and is certainly nothing new. A war that dragged on long after the public's interest waned, perceived irregularities at the ballot box, and a series of financial scandals gave George Bush a vulnerability few liberals could ignore. Targeting Bush became popular sport among Dems who seemed to have forgotten their part in the "war on terror" or the plethora of financial calamities. Liberal media, unencumbered with the pretense of impartiality, attacked Bush on an almost daily basis creating slogans such as "illegal war" that sounded oppressive and evil, despite being totally inaccurate. Bush for his part was at the end of his Presidency and didn't need to battle for his reputation and position. He largely allowed his foes to malign him, while he continued governing the country. By ignoring them, Bush's refusal to accept the mantle of scapegoat made the liberals even more furious

By the time Obama rolled out his campaign circus, blaming Bush had almost become a joke and those that continued the practice were met largely with disinterest. Since Bush was an outgoing politician, continuing to refer to his actions as a President and rehashing perceived failures seemed like beating a dead horse. Obama wanted to be seen as forward thinking, fresh and new. Bush as a target was not going to get the voters to back Obama. He needed a new target, one as "insidious" and "despicable" as the liberal media had made Bush out to be. Enter John McCain.

Attacking McCain on policies and politics was difficult. McCain had one of the most liberal voting records in the Senate and had built a solid reputation of bi-partisanship. Attacking McCain's background was problematic too. He had been a war hero and his capture and captivity had been the subject of several documentaries and books. But, McCain's support of Bush's position in Iraq and the "war on terror" gave Obama the link that he needed to steer the liberal media and much of the left-wing voting public's Bush hostilities squarely onto McCain's back. Once McCain became the target and Obama's supporters accepted him as the target, there was little to stop his annihilation.

Team Obama essentially re-branded McCain as a "Bush lite," a weaker version of a flawed President, who would be a toady to Bush's "imperialistic policies." Every campaign pledge by McCain was countered with Obama's "oh it's just more of the same." So effective was Obama's targeting of McCain that the liberal media started declaring a McCain win would equal a third term for Bush. McCain, once considered above reproach was branded a racist, a financial criminal, even a philanderer. His wife, who had worked with Mother Teresa was branded a Barbie doll, bimbo with a drug problem thanks to a prescription drugs addiction from decades previous.

Perhaps the most damaging label Obama stuck to the McCain campaign bumper was.....RICH. Obama had managed to turn an economic downturn into class warfare with the "rich" blamed as being the cause for the crisis. When McCain was unable to answer how many homes he had, he instantly became the face of the impending financial depression, a position from which he could never recover.

———————

Alinsky's tactics can be distilled into three basic concepts:

- The real action is the enemy's reaction.
- The enemy properly goaded and guided in his reaction will be your major strength.
- Tactics, like organizations, like life, require that you move with the action.[63]

———————

[63] Alinsky, Saul Rules For Radicals pg 136

There is no denying that Alinsky was a masterful tactician. He distilled the complex concepts of society and human nature down until he was able to create a step-by-step guide to mass manipulation and power acquisition. However, with power comes responsibility and a choice; use the talents and skills for good or for evil. Alinsky spent much of his adult life organizing one group after another whose main function was to take something from someone else. Instead of using his talents to organize people into improving their own lives, buildings, communities, etc. he choose to train those people to terrorize, harass, and intimidate. There is little denying that his observations and tactics work, but the price to society is very high.

Alinsky claimed that much of his manipulation was designed to insure a fairer, more democratic society. Since a democratic society is one in which the will of the people is the prevailing force of the government, Alinsky's mass manipulation completely undermines the democratic principles that he claims to be defending. There is a difference between supporting the will of the people if it is manipulated and molded into a concept that insures the wealth and power of the "organizer" and following the will of an informed public. Were Alinsky so eager to follow the will of the people, he would not have needed to deceive and manipulate them through rules designed to hide the truth, create targets, agitate people to a point of irrationality, and manufacture dissent. The very same can be said for Obama. If he truly is the new voice of democracy as he claims, why is so much about the man, past and present shrouded in mystery and secrecy? Why does he court divisiveness? Why does he attempt to marginalize and silence critics? Obama's version of democracy is identical to Alinsky's. That is to say, Obama wants this to be a democratic country, as long as he can be its dictator.

- Chapter 9 -

"Organizing" the Middle Class

"They're still up for grabs - - and we're gonna grab'em."
Alinsky on Middle Class American

At the end of his life, Alinsky admitted that his ultimate goal had eluded him. Above all, he had wanted to be the "community organizer" for the middle class. In the 1972 *Playboy* interview Alinsky discussed the early 1930's "perfect storm" for revolution upon which he had been too late to capitalize.

"You've got to remember, it wasn't only people's money that went down the drain in 1929; it was also their whole traditional system of values. Americans had learned to celebrate their society as an earthly way station to paradise, with all the cherished virtues of hard work and thrift as their tickets to security, success and happiness. Then suddenly, in just a few days, those tickets were cancelled and apparently unredeemable, and the bottom fell out of everything. The American dream became a nightmare overnight for the overwhelming majority of citizens, and the pleasant, open-ended world they knew suddenly began to close in on them as their savings disappeared behind the locked doors of insolvent banks, their jobs vanished in closed factories and their homes and farms were lost to foreclosed mortgages and forcible

eviction. Suddenly the smokestacks were cold and lifeless, the machinery ground to a halt and a chill seemed to hang over the whole country."[64]

While Alinsky lamented missed opportunities in the 1930's, he was excited about what he saw as a coming wave of opportunities for radicals. In the *Playboy* article Alinsky described what he saw as a middle class crying out for radical change.

> *"They're oppressed by taxation and inflation, poisoned by pollution, terrorized by urban crime, frightened by the new youth culture, baffled by the computerized world around them. They've worked all their lives to get their own little house in the suburbs, their color TV, their two cars, and now the good life seems to have turned to ashes in their mouths. Their personal lives are generally unfulfilling, their jobs unsatisfying, they've succumbed to tranquilizers and pep pills, they drown their anxieties in alcohol, they feel trapped in long term endurance marriages or escape into guilt-ridden divorces. They're losing their kids and they're losing their dreams. They're alienated, depersonalized, without any feeling of participation in the political process, and they feel rejected and hopeless. Their utopia of status and security has become a tacky-tacky suburb, their split-levels have sprouted prison bars and their disillusionment is becoming terminal. Their society appears to be crumbling and they see themselves as no more than small failures within the larger failure. All their old values seem to have deserted them, leaving them rudderless in a sea of social chaos.*

---

[64] Playboy Magazine March 1972 "Saul Alinsky; A Candid Conversation with the Feisty Radical Organizer"

Believe me, this is good organizational material. The despair is there; now it's up to us to go in and rub raw the sores of discontent, galvanize them for radical social change."[65]

The true irony of his assessment of the trials and tribulations of the middle class, is that much of problems that oppress us were caused by Alinsky and others like him. Americans were (in the 1970's) and are now oppressed by taxation. Taxes that have been raised again and again in order to support the very programs that he and other ultra liberals blackmailed or threatened the government into creating. Programs that support welfare generations. Programs that pay for the college education of the poor, but insure that the middle classes stay in debt to student loans or can't afford to attend at all. Programs that force mortgage companies and banks to subsidize those who do not have the financial ability to repay the loans, putting us all on the brink of financial ruin when the housing market, placed on an artificially high pedestal, crashes. Programs that pay for the education and medical care of millions of people who are not supposed to be in the US in the first place.

Americans are afraid of urban crime and a youth culture that glorifies violence and degradation. We are confused and horrified that despite doing our best to be good role models, our kids want to be "pimps" or porn stars, so they can be like the people on TV. We do feel like failures when we turn on the television. Not because the "new fangled contraptions" are confusing, but because the shows on television are so counter to the values of middle America that we are fearful that we are either all out of touch or that America is moving so far left, so quickly,

---

[65] Playboy Magazine March 1972 "Saul Alinsky; A Candid Conversation with the Feisty Radical Organizer"

117

that we are on an unstoppable juggernaut to Sodom and Gomorrah.

But how did this happen? What created this "value vacuum" that is stripping America of its ethics, morals, and traditions? Just look to Alinsky and his cult. Generations of people with no work ethic. Abhorrent behaviour excused because "they had a tough childhood." Deviant behaviours glorified by and ultra-liberal entertainment industry guided entirely by the financial benefit of titillation and shock value. Today, on television you can be a "cool" gang member, philanderer, drug addict, rapist, serial killer, or Islamic extremist, but if you are a middle class American, you aren't interesting enough to warrant a mention.

Perhaps most insulting in Alinsky's desire to "organize" the middle class thanks to the very problems that he helped to create, is the idea that somehow Middle America is a bunch of racist. We prided ourselves in being multi-cultural and accepting of people of other ethnicities and cultures and faiths only to discover that while we were patting ourselves on the back for being so advanced, millions were smiling and embracing us, while sharpening their knives. We were shocked at the vitriol of people attending Rev Wright style churches, horrified to find our neighbours sending their children off to terror training camps in the Mid-east so that they could return and blow us up.

We bent over backwards to accommodate the potential sensitivities of others to the point where our children don't say the Pledge of Allegiance in school because the word God might offend someone. Our children can't color Christmas pictures at school for the holidays because someone might not agree with the Judeo-Christian traditions that this country was founded upon. Every part of our society and culture is being stripped away so that those who don't want to assimilate into society don't have to do so, while still reaping all the benefits of belonging.

Middle class America is fed up. We are fed up with paving the way for those who hate us. We are fed up with paying the way for those want to take what we have worked hard to build. We are fed up of being the financier to radical policies and ridiculous programs that only serve to hobble the middle class, offer a free ride to those who refuse to support themselves and contribute to society, and make America more attractive to illegals.

While Alinsky mourned lost opportunities in the 1930's, throughout his life he created the mechanism to help recreate the "perfect storm" of revolution and to capitalize on its ultimate arrival. This was achieved largely on three fronts; "community organizer" training, developing or converting organizations into financial generators for the Industrial Areas Foundation, and re-education programs.

Alinsky appealed to radical organizations, militants of all varieties, and the disenfranchised, but he also actively sold his services to churches, educational institutes, and charities. These groups, desperate for membership, sponsors, or money paid to send their leaders to the Industrial Areas Foundation to train in Alinsky's "community organizing" methods. How many actually stayed on after they discovered that they were being sold something other than the Norman Rockwell version of bettering the community or that the training included a complete lack of ethics and mass manipulation techniques is unknown.

However, what is known is that those who did study under Alinsky and the I.A.F. often became part of an Alinsky network of organizations and organizers who were aligned in method and ideology. Some of these organizations were single branch outfits that functioned as a group for social change within a single community. Others became huge organizations (like ACORN) with multiple branches and thousands of people working in some "community organizing" capacity. All included some form of indoctrination however and pushed the socialist agenda. Many organizations used their training to pressure their local government into creating ever increasing social programs. Others worked within the community teaching a predominantly poor population that they were entitled to lifelong support by the government and assisted them in completing forms to benefit from the various government programs. These types of organizations help to create an American under belly of people who believe that America owes them support and a standard of living equal to the middle class, despite their refusal to do anything to actually earn that benefit.

Other groups in the Alinsky network used their training and their money to fund "agents of change." These groups financially sponsored education facilitators who helped to determine the "direction," curriculum, and hiring practices of schools and Universities. These groups also helped to fund radical educators, guest speakers, and ultra-liberal on-campus organizations designed to indoctrinate the young and naive. Through sponsoring and training these organizations, Alinsky and the I.A.F. were able to effectively "re-program" large sectors of the American population into not only accepting, but embracing ultra-liberal philosophies and socialist expectations. Alinsky's network continues training, funding, and indoctrinating people to this day with tens if not hundreds of thousands of people interacting with an Alinsky network organization.

But how? How do so many people become indoctrinated in socialist fundamentals without the entire country knowing about it? For many, the mere idea that someone would be able to orchestrate a nationwide shift to the left in the course of one lifetime seems unbelievable. Please allow me to illustrate the ease with which this has been accomplished right under our noses.

Larry is a lefty. He is a socialist. He believes that America is an evil and corrupt place. Every Thursday evening, when he attends a socialist meeting in the living room of his friend Saul, he and a handful of other socialists recount stories from the news, stories that illustrate what a bad place American really has become. They talk about revolution. They dream about it. But Larry works at a public library and doesn't have the money or the power to make things happen. Sometimes, kids who have come into the library to gather materials for a school report will ask Larry his opinion on a topic. Larry always suggests that the kids report on "great" men such as Mao, or Castro, or Che Guevara.

Eventually, Larry is promoted to head of the local library. He is in charge of ordering books based on the desires of the neighborhood. He stops ordering religious books or books about traditional American values and increases the number of books that feature America as an evil place, socialism, and left-wing views on social issues. Last year, the previous head of the library sponsored a film series called "Great American Filmmakers" which featured the work of Orson Welles this year Larry is showing all of Michael Moore's films.

Larry's wife Lois is a grade school teacher. She also thinks America is a wicked place and that a socialist system would be better. She doesn't have any money or any power either. But this year, she is supposed to teach the kids about the Civil War. Lois decides that instead of teaching about the economic climate, taxation issues, and the State's rights disagreements that actually

121

led to the Civil War, she is only going to teach the children that Southerners were racists who owned blacks as slaves and that Northerner's went to war to save them. She is going to teach the children that the Southerners were rich, white men who had grand houses and that the women had fancy clothes, while the black slaves were beaten, abused, and their families were split up and sold on. She is going to teach the children about the gentle beauty of the black slave and the soul music that they sang and compare it to the greedy, evil white landowner.

Lois isn't going to mention that the vast majority of whites in the south were also poor and many lived as either indentured servants (slaves) or as share croppers. She isn't going to mention the thousands of Irish slaves that lived in the south. Or that anyone who didn't own land had no rights either. She isn't going to mention that the wealthy in the North had slaves as well. She certainly isn't going to teach the children that the Civil War was only about slavery in so far as the Northern industries didn't feel that they should be taxed in the same fashion as the south, since the south benefited from "free" labor. No mention of slavery on a global scale or that the Africans captured their neighboring tribes and sold them into slavery. No mention that slavery had been around from the beginning of time and that every population had at one time or other been enslaved. As far as Lois is concerned, the only thing that the children need to know was that the rich, white Southerners were evil racist and forced black people into slavery. For many kids, this year was the first time they had ever heard of the Civil War.

When Kelly starts her first year as a school teacher, Lois who has been teaching for several years, is assigned to take Kelly under her wing. When Kelly asks Lois to look over her lesson plan, Lois informs Kelly that she needs to include more information about "non-traditional" families. Kelly who teaches 3rd grade, is shocked that books about homosexual families should be a part of the reading list. But, as a new teacher, she defers to Lois and includes the books.

After a decade of teaching children her version of the Civil War, Vietnam, American Imperialism, and social issues, as the teacher with the most tenure, Lois is asked to act as a temporary principle while they school district searches for a new principle to replace the one who left quickly due to a health emergency. Lois decides that this year, the school will not celebrate Christmas at all, since it is a secular holiday and will instead learn about diversity, celebrating Kwanzaa.

Over ten years, Lois' school has gone from a traditional curriculum to one that teaches extremely liberal doctrine. Teachers that wouldn't dream of slanting subjects so far left are doing so because that is what they are taught to do. With the financial pressures on parents to do more hours and have less family time, most are simply not aware that when they ask "what did you learn at school today Bobby" and he replies "we are studying Vietnam" that he is being taught the Jane Fonda version of the Vietnam era. Without other information, kids are growing up believing the far left lessons are actually undisputable facts and teachers continue to teach each successive year that America is a country of racists and bullies.

These two people, have affected the lives of hundreds, maybe thousands of people, slanting history to fit their arguments, inflicting their socialist agenda, and laying the groundwork for a national shift. Children who grow up believing Larry and Lois' version of America teach those skewed concepts to their own kids and insert those beliefs into their own working environments. The result is Judges who release pedophiles back onto the street, teachers who force children to sing "Praise Obama the Savoir" songs in school, and journalists who report only news that adheres to their opinion. When you recognize that this is happening in every community in the country, it is easy to see how a small group of people can affect the direction of the entire country and how Alinsky has masterminded the destruction of the American middle class.

- Chapter 10 -

Organizer To Dictator

"Experience hath shown, that those entrusted with power have, in time, perverted it into tyranny." Thomas Jefferson

Power and all that comes with it is the goal, how far a person can take that power depends entirely upon their own skills, circumstances, and ambition. "The only answer is to build up local power bases that can merge into a national power movement that will ultimately realize your goals."[66] But there is no denying that once the power has been seized and the goals recognized, the "community organizer" becomes the dictator.

"It's important to look at this issue in a historical perspective. Every major revolutionary movement in history has gone through the same process of corruption, proceeding from virginal purity to seduction to decadence. Look at the Christian church as it evolved from the days of the martyrs to a giant holding company, or the way the Russian Revolution degenerated into a morass of bureaucracy and oppression as the new class of state managers replaced the feudal landowners as the reigning power elite. Look at our American Revolution; there wasn't anybody more dedicated to the right of revolution than Sam Adams, leader of the Sons of Liberty, the radical wing of the revolution. But once we won the fight, you couldn't find a worse dictatorial reactionary than Adams; he insisted that

---

[66] Playboy Magazine March 1972 "Saul Alinsky; A Candid Conversation with the Feisty Radical Organizer"

every single leader of Shays' Rebellion be executed as a warning to the masses. He had the right to revolt, but nobody had the right to revolt against him. Take Gandhi, even; within ten months of India's independence, he acquiesced in the law making passive resistance a felony, and he abandoned his nonviolent principles to support the military occupation of Kashmir. Subsequently, we've seen the same thing happen in Goa and Pakistan. Over and over again, the firebrand revolutionary freedom fighter is the first to destroy the rights and even the lives of the next generation of rebels."[67]

It is clear from Obama's actions since his first day in the Oval Office, that he intends on fulfilling Alinsky's prophesy and squash the very types of First Amendment and social organizing activities that propelled him into power. Obama himself came out early in his Presidency to warn Republicans not to listen to conservative talk show host Rush Limbaugh saying "You can't just listen to Rush Limbaugh and get things done." Members of the media who have not shown their devotion to Team Obama have been denied access to White House functions and Presidential events. Military veterans have been classified as "right-wing extremists" and potential threats to American security. [68] The hundreds of thousands if not millions of people who have taken part in the Tea Party events around the country have been maligned as racists, anti-American, and loons. Bills to reinstate the ironically named "Fairness Doctrine" which would force conservative radio off the air, have been drafted. And as this book was going to press, the Obama administration launched

---

[67] Playboy Magazine March 1972 "Saul Alinsky; A Candid Conversation with the Feisty Radical Organizer"
[68] MacAskill, Ewen "Obama Administration Issues Warnings Over Rightwing Extremists" Guardian News April 15, 2009

attacks against Fox News Network for failure to fall in line with White House doctrines.

Obama ran his Presidential campaign on a platform that included villainizing Bush's post 9/11 abolishment (at least temporarily) of some civil and legal rights under the heading of "homeland security." Once in office however, Obama not only extended the very "homeland security" rights grabs that he rallied against, but also dramatically extended the government's ability to monitor citizens records and activities. Obama's position reversal on civil and legal rights issues shocked his own party as well as the countless liberal groups that had backed him. Perhaps most shocking, a bill is currently being presented that would give Obama an internet "kill switch" essentially disabling all internet connection if he believed that it would be in the interest of national security. As Alinsky predicted, Obama has paved the way to eliminate any organized challenge to his power.

- Chapter 11-

A Call To Arms

"Dissent is the highest form of patriotism"
Unknown

Much of Obama's background has been the subject of conjecture and speculation. Essential past life experiences that we as voters use to evaluate a potential, political representative have been hidden by legal maneuvering. In other instances, half truths and out right lies have been provided as a palatable biography designed to make Obama either a sympathetic "everyman" or to explain away the most radical and insidious associations.

Essentially, a man who is at minimum a deceiver and liar has ascended to the highest position in the land. In the best case scenario, a man whose own behavior would insure that he would not be trusted to borrow the family car, has taken control of the entire auto industry. In the worst case scenario, a radical, racist, socialist has used the skills and techniques learned from birth at the hands of master manipulators, funded by the financiers of both domestic and international terrorists, promoted by the mass media markets whose majority shareholders are among the wealthiest Muslim families in the world to achieve a position perfect to impose the stated goal of many of his associates; a borderless, socialist, Islamic world.

But frankly, no matter which scenario is closer to the truth, the campaign and election of Barack Obama has proven beyond a shadow of a doubt that the political system as it currently stands does not provide the American people with the protection and security required to insure that the land of the free and the home of the brave stays that way.

Saul Alinsky was a con man. He used the failed hopes and dreams of the poorest and most vulnerable in society to create an instrument for his personal fame and wealth. By his own account, after nearly half a century of "agitation" he was largely a failure at creating any positive outcomes for the organizations that paid his fees or for the people that he "organized" on his own accord. His greatest talent, self promotion and financial generation, did little to benefit the poor communities whom he conned into following him in one immature or dangerous escapade after another.

To believe that he was anything more than a vengeful huckster is to ignore his own words and actions. A man who organizes a "shit-in" in order to damage the reputation of O'Hare airport just to prove a point, without the slightest thought for the thousands of passengers who would be inconvenienced or humiliated or his famous "fart-in" where he planned to send one hundred people, after they had been treated to a meal entirely of baked beans, to the Rochester symphony orchestra in order to disrupt the concert, is not interested in anything but revenge and attention.

But Saul Alinsky's buffoonery belies the very dangerous pyramid scheme that he developed and that continues on his in name. A pyramid scheme that Barack Obama has been trained to follow, protect, and expand. Obama's version of socialism, like Alinsky's is not one in which all men are equal, but rather a feudalistic system in which there exists an impoverished socialism for the vast majority of the country and a monarchy in which Obama holds court over czars and patricians who enjoy unrivaled wealth and privilege.

We can see it now. We can see the plan, see the steps that Team Obama has taken to manipulate the masses and hide his intentions in "robes of morality." We can see how he has used ridicule to silence sincere objectors and malign those poised to expose him. We can see that his use of "hope" and "change" were just empty words to Obama, chosen for the vagueness and intangible qualities. Perhaps most importantly, we can see that his goal is not to guide America back to a position of security and strength, but rather to use her dismantling and destruction as a stepping stone to the real goal of a socialized, borderless world. Now that we can see Obama for what he is and understand the tactics and tricks that he and his team have used to usurp the honor and the power of the American people, we can stop him.

This is a call to arms. A call to action. A call to all Americans, no matter what political party with whom you felt affiliated. We must use our voices to compel politicians to return to our service, the job for which they were elected. We must write, shout out, and take to the streets if necessary to put this country back on the path to prosperity and organized progress. We must take back control of the political process. We must plug up the loop holes that allow someone who refuses to produce even basic identification to take control of the most important position in the world. We must insure that politicians, no matter what party they represent, are expelled from positions of power and authority if they breech basic standards of ethics. We must return to the political values of the framers of the Constitution who saw public service a way in which successful people could lend their skills and experiences for the betterment of society, for a short term, before returning to their private lives and not as a way for the bureaucrats, plurocrats, and autocrats to create lifetime positions of wealth and power for themselves and their offspring. We must insure that the political process is fair for all candidates and is about transparency, about fact, and about evidence of positions, beliefs, and values and not a media circus where "news organizations," owned largely by foreign entities push their agendas through slanted journalism and tabloid exposés unworthy of the task of selecting a candidate for the most important position in the world.

Perhaps most importantly, we must understand that for the past several generations, while we have pursued the American Dream, defended freedom, worked hard, played hard, raised our families, and built our lives believing that everyone in America had the same goal, a free, proud, democracy; others were quietly pursuing our destruction. These enemies of America, enemies of our freedoms, enemies of our families have been silently percolating, networking, infiltrating every level of society. They did not wake up yesterday and decide on this course of action, Obama and hundreds, maybe thousands like him have been trained with the single goal of achieving power in order to destroy America. It is so hard for us to grasp this fact. But unless we stand up and do so now our children and our children's children and our children's children's children will live on their knees in the rubble of what was once the greatest democracy in history.

- *Part Two* -

The
Conservative
Republican Revolution

- Chapter 1 -

The New Republican

Sun Tzu, the brilliant Chinese military tactician who wrote *The Art of War*, famously decreed, "Victorious warriors win first and then go to war, while defeated warriors go to war first and then seek to win." Few quotes more succinctly illustrate the current state of affairs. Team Obama and the socialist takeover of this country didn't happen over night, it took decades of careful planning, manipulation, and indoctrination. By the time they were ready to launch their final attack to propel Barack Obama into the ultimate, symbolic, position of power, they had mastered their game plan, paid for loyalties, created almost unlimited funding streams, shored up weaknesses, created misinformation campaigns, pulled out their deck of race cards, and controlled the media. They were virtually assured a win.

In contrast, the Republican Party rushed to war without a plan. After spending a decade deviating from their conservative base, the GOP had little by way of a platform from which to launch an attack. Republican voters were largely disenfranchised by years of irresponsible spending, economic meltdown after historic levels of government interference, and the baffling, continued support of Party traitors like Arlen Specter and Susan Collins. Attempting to be the party of "all things to all people" they lost the trust of their core supporters and the respect of potential voters. The Republican Party never took the offensive position, instead, they rushed around reacting the every Clinton and then Obama move. They never looked commanding or powerful. They never inspired confidence. Without a clear and concise platform or even guiding principles, the Republican Party as a whole, floundered.

The candidates that stepped forward to battle for Republican nomination didn't help inspire confidence either. They seemed as if they were part of a game show/reality TV competition instead of warriors for the Grand Old Party.

- **Fred** -*I don't know anything about politics, but I play a DA on Law and Order*- **Thomson**.

- **Mike** -*Chuck Norris likes me, he really, really likes me*- **Huckabee**.

- **Rudy** -*I am not going to bother with any States except Florida....oh and would you like an autographed copy of the 9/11 picture of me*- **Gulliani**

- **Mitt** -*Yeah I'm a Mormon, but not in that icky Big Love kinda way*- **Romney**

- **John** -*You think I'm old, you should see my Mom*- **McCain**

Liberals, crazies, and half-hearted efforts abound. The Democrats offered their supporters passion and fervor; a return to the Clinton Dynasty with the tough as nails Senator Clinton or the charismatic young upstart Barack Obama. Both historically significant choices. Both inspiring cult like devotion from followers. The Republicans offered us a "lesser of two evils" choice.

Now I am not insinuating that these men are not fine people and do not deserve respect and thanks for service. Anyone willing to put themselves into the media circus in service of their fellow man deserves respect and praise. The problem is that without a clear and concise platform and a well thought out battle plan, candidates who were inappropriate to lead conservative battles or who were not inspiring enough to bring voters to the polls were the only options available.

Team Obama planned ahead and won the battle, but they haven't yet won the war. As conservatives, we should be using this valuable time to return to core values, shore up our defenses, rid ourselves of poor Generals, and map out our plans of attack. We now understand Alinsky methods and how Team Obama has used them to manipulate the public. But we can't simply use random tactical knowledge against Obama and expect to win. As the underdogs in this fight, we have to build and in many cases rebuild a strong support system, upon which the American people can rely.

It isn't simply that people are disenfranchised with the lack of direction seen in the current Republican Party. They are banding together, raising their voices and demanding that the Party return to its conservative roots. Unless it does so, the only option is for a new conservative party to emerge. While that is a possibility, it would be a shame. The Grand Old Party has been around since 1854, it produced Abraham Lincoln, the first Republican President. It developed the first small business support network designed to help move people from migrant, factory, or sharecropper work into their own small businesses and farms and self sufficiency. It produced and defended the civil rights movement and counted Martin Luther King Jr. as a member. This party gave us Ronald Reagan, who ended decades of tyranny with those famous words to Mikhail Gorbachev, "tear down this wall!" resulting in the reunification of Germany and the removal of the Berlin Wall. The Republican Party has so much in which to be proud. But at the core of each of those successes, at the heart of every significant, world changing event lay the conservative platform. As long as the current people in power at the GOP deviate from those core values, they aren't real Republicans at all, they are simply wearing the tee shirt.

On this eve of the first anniversary of Obama's win, I am saddened to report that the Republican Party has not shifted from the impotent, reactionary party of the election. They continue to chase the distraction that Obama and Pelosi toss out at them and whine about how unfair the Dems game plan is for the country. I get my continual string of Michael Steele emails and updates. They all are various regurgitations of the same "gosh did you see what Obama is getting away with now?" It is clear that he is attempting to connect with voters, which is important. And I have no doubt at all that he and others in positions of power and leadership with the Republican Party are trying really hard to regain control. But just yesterday, a quick visit to the GOP website confirmed my deepest fears, they just don't "get it."

The GOP web site was rather shocking. If you covered up the words GOP across the top, you were met with a huge waving banner of deep red, with a scattering of gold stars. I thought I had been redirected to a Chinese propaganda site. For a party that wants to get rid of the socialist agendas in America, designing the Republican Party's internet experience around socialist icons seemed to be a strange choice. This waving comrade red flag also featured a link to "Heroes of the Republican Party." A few observations; 1) If you are trying to establish that you are a modern, conservative party, showing only "heroes" from 150 years ago plus Reagan seems like a bad plan. 2) Over half of these old photos were of blacks. As a party we have been "race carded" to death. I in no way wish to devalue the incredible contributions the blacks have made to the Republican Party. But it is impossible not to see the photo line up as a lame attempt to try and quash the idea that we are the party of rich, old, white, men in order to appeal to minorities. Quite frankly, anyone who would switch affiliations simply because we posted a handful of old tintype photos online is as sad as those who voted for someone just because of his race. I won't even get into the website's complete lack of functionality at this stage. But the point is we should NOT be chasing ethnic demographics at all. We should be returning to our conservative roots and embracing ALL people who have the same values, that includes a lot of black Americans.

There are hundreds, if not thousands of groups, large and small, that have sprung up across America to show displeasure with Obama's socialist agenda and compel the Republican Party to return to conservative values. Some of these groups focus on a single issue; health care, abortion issues, taxation, the list goes on. Some of these groups are effectively mobilizing and getting their message out into the public arena. But few seem to be connecting to each other and many, especially in smaller groups, seem unsure how their actions can affect and effect a change in Washington and in their own community. Yesterdays Republican successes in historically Democrat New Jersey and in Virginia, as well as the incredible success of a conservative politician over the RINO candidate in the 23rd district in New York show that the people of this country largely do not want to follow an ultra-liberal or socialist agenda. They want the Republican Party to re-embrace its conservative core. They...WE...want to be an active part of the Republican Party, just as soon as the Republican Party becomes the Republican Party once again.

We can bring the Republican Party back from the brink of disaster with a return to conservative values.

We CAN win this war.

And here is how....

- Chapter 2 -

The
Conservative Platform

One of the most important aspects of any organization is its platform. A platform is essentially a reason for that organization's existence. It answers basic, fundamental questions. Why are we an organization? For what do we stand? What do we hope to gain by organizing? How do we intend to meet our goals? In the case of political parties, the platform goes a step further by providing a pledge to voters and guidance to member politicians, as to the agreed positions on important issues.

A platform is both a sword and a shield. By providing clear and concise positions on issues, the Party's goal is defined. As a sword, a platform is a weapon designed to cut through the bureaucratic fog. Politicians should be able to look to the Party platform to provide them guidance as they perform their service to their constituents. They should have no doubt as to how they are expected to vote and the nature of the bills that they are expected to put forward. New or unaffiliated voters should be able to look to the platform to determine if their beliefs and values mirror that of the Party. As a shield, the platform protects the Party and politicians from smears and misinformation tactics by the media and opposition forces, simply be eliminating any ambiguity. For voters who are already Party members, a clear platform helps to monitor politicians. When a politician deviates from the expected in terms of voting or bill proposals, there can be no question as to his or her continuing to represent the party. Perhaps most importantly, the party platform helps to insure that the party stays on track, even in difficult times.

Adhering to a conservative, Republican Party platform has brought tremendous advancements to the United States. When the Republican Party has deviated, utter disaster.

The Republican Party – A Brief History

The Republican Party was built on a sold foundation of Judeo-Christian values. "Free Labor, Free Land, Free Men," the original slogan of the Republican Party, perfectly encapsulates the goals and ambitions of those early Republicans. They believed that by promoting small business, the middle and working class would be free to leave the factories and sharecropping behind and become self sufficient. They believed that by offering free land to those who would use it to establish businesses and family farms, a clear path to success could be created. With nearly 2 million legal emigrants entering the United States annually and largely going straight into factory and menial labor jobs, creating a way for people to work out of those low paying positions and into self sufficiency would bring increased prosperity to the country and leave only a very small percentage of people ever at the poverty level at any time.

The Republican Party also espoused the idea that a free market comprised of small businesses would provide rapid economic growth, rendering slavery obsolete and economically unsustainable. By providing a vehicle to self sufficiency to the Irish, Chinese, African, and Caribbean slaves, the Republican Party sought to integrate them smoothly into middle class society. For the first 24 years of existence, the Republican Party adhered to a platform that supported large and small businesses, farming interests, limited issuance of credit, and a pension system for war Veterans. The phenomenal success in the growth and entrepreneurial development of the era can arguably be attributed to the Republican Party policies and platforms.

Then it all went horribly wrong. After two and half decades of following a successful policy of limited government interference, the Republicans who had long supported high tariffs on foreign made products in order to encourage people to "buy American," imposed the McKinley Tariff. Already high, the new tariffs increased prices on foreign products by as much as 50%. Since many foreign made products were used to make American products, the huge cost increased were passed onto the American people. Coupled with their support of the Interstate Commerce Commission and the Sherman Antitrust Act, Republican politicians across the land were unceremoniously dumped by voters. The Republican Party had deviated from its core conservative values as politicians went in pursuit of side deals and kick backs.

But the Party didn't die. Politicians went back to the Republican Party core principles of supporting the middle class, business and entrepreneurship, American products, and self sufficiency. In doing so, they regained the White House and held onto power for over a decade. It was only the Wall Street crash that ended Republican reign. What followed was three decades of destroying businesses and farms, increasing taxes on the middle class in order to support an ever increasing welfare state, and the mass socialization of the United States under Roosevelt, thanks to his New Deal programs. It can not be ignored that the continued Republican defeat during these decades is due in large part to specific politicians who turned away from the party platform and chased any issue that they believed might lead them to power.

By the time the next Republican Superstar came to power, the country had almost collapsed under the weight of decades of social programs. The Cold War, coupled with the rise of Islamic fundamentalist based terrorism insured that the country faced a huge fiscal crisis. Staunchly conservative, Ronald Reagan ran on a platform of states rights, minimal government interference, lowered taxes, and a strong military. He also brushed off his gubernatorial platform crying "send the welfare bums back to work." While Reagan was conservative on most social issues and pressed for both a line item veto and a Constitutional amendment requiring a balanced budget, he left office with an unprecedented level of debt. Reagan increased the gross national debt during his first term by 11.3% and added an additional 9.2% in his second.

While many will argue that the level of debt was required to prevent a complete financial collapse and to support a necessary military build up, the fact remains that his deviation from a conservative fiscal plan laid the groundwork for both a rash of "pick-and-choose" Republican politicians and the pursuit of an increasingly irresponsible fiscal path. George Bush Sr. and George Bush Jr. both followed Reagan's example of selective conservatism, with Sr. increasing debt 13.1% and Jr. increasing the gross national debt by 6.9% in his first term and 11.7% in his second. While much of the increase was due to protracted wars, both also failed to enforce laws already in place to curb illegal immigration, costing the government over $300 billion annually.

Lack of a Platform = "Pick-n-Choose" Republicans & Republicans In Name Only

"Pick-and-choose" Republicans (those who are selectively conservative) and gross financial miss management have evolved into the norm instead of the exception. Politicians, attempting to chase personal political aspirations align themselves with contradictory policies or attempt to ride both sides of the fence. Recently, the national spotlight fell upon New York State Assembly representative Deirdre Scozzafava, who is an excellent example. Residing in a largely Republican district and receiving support from the GOP, Scozzafava supported gay marriage, abortion, and has strong ties to labor unions. During the special election to fill the Republican Congressional seat, Scozzafava, while running on the Republican ticket, was endorsed by top level Democratic leaders, including Chuck Schumer. When it became clear that she couldn't win, she threw her support not behind the conservative candidate, but behind the Democrat. Courted by both the Independence Party and Democrats, Scozzafava may be the poster child to RINO's everywhere, benefiting from nearly $700,000 in Republican money and a Republican seat, but voting for liberal policies.

Unfortunately, Scozzafava is not an isolated incident and party traitor politicians are becoming increasingly common. But why? Why would politicians operate counter to their party or their constituent's wishes? I suggest that there are two different schools at work. On the one hand, some people are motivated by the potential wealth available to high level politicians. If they live in state or region that heavily favors one party, it would make sense to align yourself, at least for a while, with that party. In Scozzafava's case, she grew up and resided in an area that had been largely under Republican control since the 1870's. Her personal beliefs seem to mirror a liberal Democrat platform, but there was clearly little chance of a political career if she entered a party that mirrored her beliefs.

Once she became a State Assemblywoman, her husband (a labor union leader) contacted key Democrats about the possibility of her switching to the Democratic ticket for a run at a Congressional seat. This was apparently not the first time that an offer to switch to the Democrats had been made.[69] But tax troubles and financial shenanigans prevented the Democrats from seeing Scozzafava as a positive addition and they backed other

---

[69] Benjamin, Elizabeth *Democrats Fan The Flames of Scozzafava's Tax Troubles* New York Daily News July 22, 2009

145

candidates instead. Ironically, had the information concerning her desire to switch parties not come out, she was in line to win the Congressional seat as a Republican. At that level, the GOP has been historically hesitant to muscle RINOs out for fear of losing the seat to a Democrat. She would have had the power, financial ability, and political clout to vote as liberally as she wanted, while being virtually assured of GOP support.

While this duplicity is certainly a factor in many politicians becoming party traitors, there are also those who simply don't have a clear understanding of their role. Without a clear platform and guidance, many simply vote their own personal feelings. As these people spend more time in Washington, and less within their own communities, they easily lose touch with their constituents. They are also faced with pressure from lobbyist, special interest groups, and senior politicians and of course there are the financial remunerations and incentives to vote a certain way. With in-practice assurances that there will be no actual ramifications for a politician voting against his party or the voters, politicians feel free to do as they wish.

It should be noted that whether the drift from conservative values happens as a byproduct of personal political ambition to be a "leader" at all costs OR the drift comes from poor direction or understanding of his/her role as a political representative, both are equally damaging to the voters, to the party, and to the country. Both scenarios can also be prevented simply by creating and adhering to a local, state, and national party platform. For those who wish to use the Republican Party's money or seats in order to leapfrog into the heights of power, a clear and concise platform coupled with transparency regarding voting records, fundraising, and lobbyist partners will help to eliminate duplicity as a viable opportunity. A clear party platform also acts as a roadmap for new politicians who may be unsure of their responsibilities or may become overwhelmed at "opportunities" in Washington. If they are provided with a clear, easy to understand "road map" of the values and positions of their constituency and the Party, there should be no confusion.

Without confusion as to the platform of the Party, any willful vote against the values and principles will be seen clearly as a vote against the Party and against the voters. This is useful information for voters at election time. When voters can see where and when and upon which issues a politician has failed to follow the directives of the Party, they can make informed decisions as to whether or not that candidate is an appropriate representative. By creating and maintaining a clear platform and transparent voting record, politicians who may wish to pretend to be Republicans will find that they are not electable in the following political cycle. As conservative Republicans, we must be vigilant in weeding out RINOs from ALL levels of government and end the ability for those just starting in politics to see duplicity as a viable step onto the political ladder.

The Republican Platform

While researching this book, I decided to check out the current national Republican Party platform. Guess what? It isn't listed on the GOP site. There is a "What We Believe" section that gives a nice little sentence encapsulating a belief (Free markets keep people free, Helping those around you is worthwhile, etc.[70]). But nowhere on the site is there the actual national Republican platform. This is a problem.

While the "What We Believe" sentences are "warm and fuzzy" giving me a nice feeling, as a voter, I want to know the ACTUAL positions. I want to know specifics and I want to know how these positions will be addressed and implemented. I don't

---

[70] www.GOP.com Retrieved Nov. 4, 2009

want "warm and fuzzy" from the people that I have selected to be the champion of my values, my family, my community, and my country.

The following is one of the "What We Believe" statements from the GOP web site.

"Our Armed Forces defend and protect our democracy. The Republican Party is committed to preserving our national strength while working to extend peace, freedom, and human rights throughout the world."[71]

Nice. But how specifically? Does the Republican Party support troop withdrawals from Iraq? What is the Republican Party position on selling and leasing our ports to foreign countries, including terror financing countries? What is the Republican Party position on the substandard care at many Veterans Hospitals?

See the problem? Without clear cut statements of policy and principle, without a clear platform, as a voter, I can't be sure what the Republican position is on a specific issue. It is simply too ambiguous. I may believe that when the GOP site says "preserving our national strength" that it means increasing the size of the military, while someone else may read that as investing in more high tech weapons, and still another may understand that statement to mean that the Republican Party supports establishing more bases overseas. This all helps to disenfranchise the base. When we believe that the Party position is one thing, and politicians do another, we feel cheated. It also angers independents and conservative Democrats who have voted with us because of specific issues. As a Republican, I am likely to continue to vote Republican, even after being disappointed. An independent or conservative Democrat however is less likely to give a second chance. Of course ambiguity also ads fuel to the fire

---

[71] www.GOP.com Retrieved Nov. 4, 2009

148

of media and opposition attacks. By failing to define the GOP position, our opposition is free to define us in the most unflattering way.

Part of the reason that politicians are loath to pin themselves down on a specific issue is fear that they will alienate some potential voters. The ambiguity also leaves them some "wiggle room." Without specifics, it becomes more difficult to assign blame or examine voting inconsistencies. While many politicians see this as a way of damage control in the event of failure, the lack of a specific platform also makes it virtually impossible to determine how close we are to success. I am much more supportive of a politician who has a clear platform, votes in support of that platform and fails, than I am of one who uses ambiguous phrasing, shrouds his or her positions in mystery, and then attempts to divert attention and blame away.

A Model Republican Platform

The Arkansas GOP website www.ArkansasGOP.org is an excellent example of a professional and informative political site. The Arkansas Republican Platform is clear, easy to read and understand, and is provided without ambiguity. Each topic is laid out with a general goal concerning that issue, as well as numbered points providing specific positions and assertions.

The Arkansas GOP Platform on Election Reform states in part:[72]

> 7.   We support the current term limits laws as initiated by the people.

---

[72] www.ArkansasGOP.org

8.   Recall legislation should be enacted to give Arkansas voters power to remove elected officials for abuses of power in office.

9.   We support the Electoral College process as it presently exists.

The Arkansas GOP Platform is simple and straight forward. Whether you are already a Republican or a voter interested in finding out the Republican position on certain issues, there can be little ambiguity in the above statements. Does the Arkansas GOP support term limits? Yes it does! It says so right in its official platform. What is the official position on the Electoral College? Well that is pretty clear too. Actually, the Arkansas GOP Platform is pretty clear on all issues and those positions are easy to read and understand and posted right on their web site. This is the way it should be for all Republican web sites, whether it is a local, state, or national party site or a politicians personal site.

Not only does it clearly spell out the official position of the Party on specific issues, it helps us, as voters, keep tabs on the politicians who we elect to represent us. If one of the official positions on Tax Reform and Fiscal Responsibility is; "We support the increase in the exemption on retirement income from the state income tax."[73] but, a Republican politician votes against the exemption, there may be a problem. It could be that the bill was poorly written or that it was onerous in some many other areas that it would have been against other Republican positions to pass it. But no matter what the reason, that politician should be able to quickly explain why he or she voted against the will of the Republican voters. If the politician can't explain why he or she voted against a clearly stated position, this politician may not be an appropriate person to support during the next election cycle.

---

[73] www.ArkansasGOP.org Platform Tax Reform & Fiscal Responsibility Pt 10

A clearly stated position also protects the Party, the politicians, and the voters from smear tactics. While politics may always be a dirty game, at least with a clearly stated platform, a politician or a voter has the ability to point to that segment and defend a position. It is also much easier to point out smear tactics and outright lies. When a member of the liberal media or an unethical opposition opponent falsely claims that the Party or a specific politician supports a position, that person can be quickly discredited since the actual position is available for everyone to review for themselves.

While a clear and specific platform is essential, politicians and GOPs need not fear that committing to a platform means that there can be no deviation. Clearly a pre and post 9/11 platform will have some differences. As long as the changes are thoughtful and are in keeping with the spirit of the platform and with the conservative values and beliefs upon which they are founded, some flexibility, especially in unpredictable times, is essential.

Platform + Solutions

Of course, having a Republican platform doesn't mean that every Republican is going to agree with every issue. This is especially true in regards to social or morality issues. Much of the disagreement however can be set aside if the platform includes not only the edicts...this is what we believe... but also offers solutions as to how to implement positions. Sometimes the solutions would be in the form of clarification and practical alternatives.

One of the conflicts between moderate Republicans and conservatives and between Republicans and Democrats is the same sex marriage issue. In every state in which a same sex marriage bill has been put on the ballot, the bill has been shot down, showing that the concept of "marriage" between same sex couples is not acceptable. Conservatives generally believe in the traditional definition of marriage, as a commitment between a man and woman that is sanctified by God and legitimized by the law. The idea of same sex marriages is against the religious beliefs of most conservatives. Conservatives largely feel that the continual attempt to create same sex marriage laws is a direct assault on religion and morality. They fear that legislation will force churches to perform marriage ceremonies and that legitimizing a "marriage" between same sex partners will lead schools to teach that same sex "marriages" are right and equal to traditional marriages.

However, there can be no denying that there are thousands of same sex couples and no amount of moral indignation is going to change that fact. Same sex couples are often denied access to their partner in the hospital or refused insurance coverage, social security, inheritance, and other benefits. In the same way that a legal guardian of a child is not the same as a biological or even adoptive parent, many feel that creating a legal, contractual, relationship is an acceptable alternative. Creating some form of cohabitation contract could allow same sex couples to share some legal rights and responsibilities, without equating same sex marriages with traditional marriages. By removing the religious connotations, there is no threat to Judeo-Christian beliefs or the sanctity of the church. By creating contractual rights, there is no need to legitimize gay marriages for the sake of legal benefits. There would be no need to discuss same sex partnerships in schools. With contractual relationships available to those adults who wished to pursue them, the continual assault on traditional values from ultra-liberals, concerning same sex marriages could end. As long as it continues, we are in danger of liberals in power passing measures to force same sex "marriages" into our churches and forcing schools to teach children about same sex marriages as an acceptable alternative to traditional marriage.

The Republican Platform and solution statements regarding same sex marriage might include:

"The Republican Party...supports the traditional definition of marriage as a God-ordained, legal and moral commitment between a man and a woman, and we believe that marriage is the foundational unit of a healthy society...."[74]

- We reject the word "marriage" as a description of same sex relationships.
- We reject the mention of same sex relationships in educational settings.
- We support the creation of a cohabitation agreement that would provide two non-related persons with limited rights concerning medical procedures, insurance, benefits, inheritance, and other financial relationships.

While this type of solution doesn't end the religious controversies around homosexuality, it would achieve several goals. First, it would provide same sex couples (and unmarried traditional couples) with a level of legal protection. Second, it would effectively end the same sex marriage debate simply because the legal rights of adults to create contracts with each other, in any capacity, would be reaffirmed. If a same sex couple wishes to celebrate the creation of the contract, so be it.

For conservatives, perhaps most importantly, it would protect the religious and moral sanctity of the term and concept of "marriage." It would prevent groups from seeking to force churches to perform rituals counter to their beliefs, it would end the constant coverage of the same sex marriage issue in the press, and would protect children, especially in primary schools, from being indoctrinated by ultra-liberal concepts of marriage and

---

[74] Arkansas GOP Platform   www.ArkansasGOP.org retrieved Nov7, 2009

family which are counter to conservative beliefs. It isn't the perfect situation for either party, but both sides could walk away with their prime objective met.

A platform and solutions could also be in the form of a "step program" or phase out system. For example, many Americans (myself included) believe that English should be the official language of the United States. We believe that issuing forms and services in other languages does not encourage assimilation into American society and further that it provides ease for illegal aliens to obtain government services to which they should not be entitled, encouraging more illegal immigration. However, simply terminating services would prove detrimental to legal, foreign born, Americans who, because of lax laws in their community for the past several decades, have not learned English.

A platform and solution statements might look like this:

"Republicans believe that English should be the official language of the United States of America. We believe that having a single official language helps people to assimilate in their communities and aids in combating illegal immigration. We don't believe that tax payers should pay for multi-lingual government services."

- Work towards passing a Constitutional Amendment affirming English as the official language of both the State and the United States.
- Nurture a partnership between educational facilities, community centers, libraries, and churches to either add free English literacy programs for legal, foreign language speaking citizens to their current adult education programs or develop a community based program to improve literacy for all adults, including English as a second language for legal citizens.

154

- Nurture a partnership between educational facilities, community centers, libraries, and churches to provide free English literacy programs for children.
- Phase out all non-English forms and services within 6 months of adoption of Amendment.
- Create a media awareness campaign that highlights the ways in which we want to help legal immigrants to assimilate into American society and to fully participate in the American Dream, while celebrating the diversity that maintaining cultural aspects of their native heritage brings to the United States.

Some platform issues require a complete overhaul of the system in order to effectively and ethically work. Simply handing down "in a perfect world" edicts causes more problems. In my opinion, most justice related matters fall into this category. I agree in theory that Judges should have the option to use the death sentence in cases of capital murder. However, hundreds of death row inmates have been exonerated and released thanks to DNA evidence conclusively proving their innocence. In many of these cases, the DA and or police department was aware that there were other viable suspects, but felt that pursuing more than one suspect would weaken their case against the person they focused on first.

Situations like the Duke Lacrosse rape case, where District Attorney Mike Nifong continued to pursue criminal cases against three young men, even after their innocence had been established, simply because it furthered his career and desire for fame, are not unusual. Hans Sherrer of Justice: Denied Magazine sites official FBI and US Department of Justice statistics suggesting that as many as 14% of people convicted of a crime are not guilty. The difficulty for Americans untouched by the criminal justice system is that we were raised to believe that "bad people" go to jail and that if you hadn't done anything wrong, the police wouldn't see you as a suspect. The statistics show otherwise. Many of these people are not simply people who are "usual suspects" who have long criminal records, with increasing frequency those falsely accused and convicted are regular working people, mothers and fathers, who are at the wrong place at the wrong time, bare some resemblance to a suspect in a witness statement, or have been the victim of identity fraud.

The unusual aspect of the Nifong case is that the young men were from wealthy families and could afford to hire the best attorneys. Were they your children or mine, we would be unable to afford the $3 million in legal fees that accrued before the truth came out, Nifong admitted his deceit, and the men were exonerated. Most working class people must rely on the public defender system in which a single lawyer can average over 100 cases at any given time. Compare that to the handful of cases that a private attorney handles and it is easy to see that even with the best of intentions, working class people are not afforded even basic legal protection under the current system.

As long as District Attorneys are rewarded with promotions and salary increases based on conviction rates, we will continue to have more and more working class people arrested, charged, and unable to financially defend themselves, jailed, for the sake of a lawyers career. Until there are significant justice reforms and safe guards to protect people, not only from real criminals, but also from a legal system that penalizes those who can't afford appropriate legal representation, in my opinion, something as final as the death penalty should not be an option.

With this type of issue, a complete system overhaul needs to occur. Laws and sentences are inconsistent. People accused of financial crimes are given more time in prison than those who have committed rape, murder, even sexual abuse of children. Internet related laws have not caught up with technology providing limited legal remedies for those victimized by identity theft, stalking, harassment, child pornography, etc. The prison system is inefficiently operated and dangerous for both inmate and employees. Not to mention the incredible strain that illegal immigrants who commit crimes are putting on the system. DA's are rewarded and promoted base on conviction rates, leading to a doubling of the conviction rate over the past two decades, despite an overall drop in crime. Public defenders are unable to offer adequate defenses. Yet with all that is wrong with the system, it would clearly be impossible to simply scrap the system and start from scratch. This type of situation requires a platform, which states the ideals and goals of the Republican Party as well as both interim solutions and ultimate solutions to the problems.

A platform regarding capital punishment, interim and ultimate solutions may look something like this:

"Republicans believe that judges should have the discretion to issue a sentence of capital punishment in cases of murder, provided that the conviction included conclusive DNA proof verified by an independent, professional organization as established by law."

- An independent, professional organization should be established to process DNA evidence.
- Those currently convicted of murder, who have received capital punishment sentences, without any DNA evidence must have their sentences commuted to life imprisonment.
- Those currently convicted of murder, who have received capital punishment sentences, where DNA was a part of the evidence presented that led to a conviction, must have the DNA evidence evaluated by the independent body prior to having the sentence carried out.

In this scenario, the platform includes the ultimate goal of having conclusive, DNA proof established in all murder cases where the death penalty is an appropriate option. It establishes the need to

157

either create or utilize an existing professional body, separate from the police and prosecution, to evaluate DNA evidence. Finally, it addresses those currently on "death row" and divides the cases into those that do not fit the criteria for a capital sentence and those who need to be evaluated for certainty, prior to the sentence being implemented.

These sample platforms and solutions highlight one of the fundamental problems with the current political climate, a lack of clearly defined goals and plans. Most GOP organizations and politicians do not make their platform clear. Without a clear platform, voters can't make informed decisions or monitor progress towards goals. In addition, while a platform must be clear and concise as to the positions of the Party or politician, edicts are meaningless unless we can provide a workable plan to implement our principles. Voters want to know not only what a politician or a party would like in an ideal world, we want to know how we can all work towards achieving the goals. Finally, many of the social issues that create divisiveness and vitriol could be mitigated by simply devising a working plan alternative.

I applaud the Arkansas GOP for their model web site and for providing a platform that is clear, easy to understand, and concise. I hope that they will build on this and include proposed solutions to create a roadmap of how they propose to implement those plans and involve the general public in making those ideals a reality. All GOP organizations and politicians should familiarize themselves with the Arkansas GOP Platform and use it as a template to create their own, published Platform and solutions.

- Chapter 3-

The Republican Brand

If someone told you that Coca-Cola, with its iconic red and white logo, was a company that produced insulation for houses or hair care products, you would know that that wasn't true. Coca-Cola is a brand that you recognize. Even if you don't drink soft drinks or don't happen to like Coca-Cola products, your familiarity with the brand insures that you know what your getting if you order a bottle. The same can't be said for the Republican brand.

Today's Republican Party bares little resemblance to the conservative party platforms and principles upon which it was founded. Gross financial irresponsibility, the promotion of greater and greater levels of government intervention and intrusion, and the propulsion of increasingly liberal politicians into Republican seats has rendered the party almost impotent. Conservatives are quick to attempt to distance themselves from the current Republican Party, calling themselves Regan Republicans or Conservative Republicans, while greater and greater numbers of moderates and even "Blue-dog" democrats finding themselves more comfortable with an independent label as opposed to being associated with the free-spending GOP.

Voters are confused by RINOs who occupy Republican seats, but walk and talk like liberals. They are confused by the support of policies that are completely counter to the "classic" Republican battle cries. Even politicians themselves seem confused. People who would normally run on an independent ticket because of their "take a little from the right and a little from the left" policies are being financed by the Republican Party, while true conservative politicians are being forced to run on their own dime, often against the "Republican" candidate. No wonder independents and conservative Democrats, as well as a good number of Republicans voted for "hope" and "change" ticket, conservatives hope that the GOP will change back into the party that represents the American Dream, Constitutional supremacy, and conservative values.

Understanding Branding

Product branding is a vital component of any business or organization. The names, symbols, logos, and even packaging are used to create a complete experience. Branding helps consumers to differentiate between the products and services of competing companies. But it's more than just a way to tell the difference between soda pop brands or sneaker makers, effective branding is a defining symbol that expresses the principles and goals of the organization. It conveys a clear message. A brand elicits a response. It helps to establish credibility. A brand can create loyalty and unity, giving people a feeling of confidence and belonging. Perhaps most importantly, an effective brand will help establish the organization as a strong and powerful leader in the industry.

An effective brand is the flag that flies before us into battle, that motivates soldiers to continue the fight even if the tide is against them, it enrobes and nurtures those too weak to hold the sword, it inspires courage in man to achieve his or her greatest potentials, and upon victory, stands as a constant source of pride and security to citizens and allies alike, as well as a warning to our enemies. Unfortunately, conservative Americans have lost their flag. The GOP brand has become confusing and contradictory. It no longer inspires courage. It no longer motivates soldiers to fight against socialist tyrannies. It fails to unite. It has become the reactionary, lap dog chasing the Democrats rubber ball. And without a strong brand, conservative America is becoming fractured and disenfranchised, apathetic or disgusted at the Republican Party, but horrified by the alternative.

To make matters worse, while the Republican Party has failed to create a clear and unifying brand, the Democrats have been hard at work doing the job for us, to our serious detriment. Team Obama and the Democrats have been effectively branding the Republican Party AND conservative Americans as "racists," "morality police," "war mongers," "religious nuts," and of course the party of "rich, old, white, men." The fact that the GOP has completely failed to establish a recognizable brand, meant that these slanders and attacks stuck to voters and politicians like glue.

How Democrats Branded Republicans

A significant aspect of an effective branding campaign revolves around eliciting an emotional response. But that emotional response isn't necessarily positive. The Democrats have done a great job of linking negative emotions and issues with Republicans. In 2004, John McCain was effectively branded as an authentic, American war hero, a brand that the Democrats were unable to shake. However, the "war hero" brand in 2008 wasn't as popular with a country tired of expensive and increasingly unpopular wars in Iraq and Afghanistan. The "war hero" brand was linked to the "war monger" label which the liberal media had attached to George Bush. Capitalizing on the link, Team Obama branded McCain as "More of the same" or a "third Bush term." McCain who had not adapted with the changing circumstances attempted to rely on the old brand.

To make matters worse, John McCain was easily branded as a "rich, old, white, man" because he is a rich, old, white, man. The connotation however was that he was corrupt, out of touch, unconcerned about issues facing the middle class, and a racist.

After the media had spent months blaming Wall Street and highly paid executives for the economic crisis, Team Obama easily swept in and branded McCain a "crook" due to his part, twenty years earlier in the Keating Five scandal. The American public, confused by the financial "mumbo jumbo," were easily lead to conclude that McCain was just another financial crook, responsible for the financial woes of America. McCain's infamous confusion when asked how many houses he owned sealed his fate. Through effective branding, John McCain's war hero brand was replaced with that of an out-of-touch, uncaring, financial crook.

While John McCain's re-branding by Team Obama was successful in large part due to his failure to adapt his own "war hero" brand to changing circumstances, the Democrats have been able to attach dozens of negative brands to the GOP as a whole, thanks to their complete lack of ANY cohesive brand. This provided the liberal media and Team Obama with virtual carte blanc to say whatever they wanted, no matter how fantastical, slanderous, or outrageous, simply because we had nothing to buffer and deflect the accusations. The Republican Party became reactionary, wasting valuable time and resources chasing around slanderous stories, engaging in damage control and trying to defuse politically incorrect accusations. Instead of being seen by voters as the political party of leaders, of defenders, of brilliant administrators who would use their skills to guide the country safely through trying times, the Republican Party was cast in the role of backward thinking, racists, desperately afraid of change, who had only one answer to foreign policy, war.

How Republicans Branded Themselves

While the Democrats did a great job at negatively branding the Republican Party, Republicans did a super job of negatively branding themselves. While an unpopular President and an even more unpopular Congress certainly damaged the Party's reputation, the Republican primary candidates failed to present any forward looking concepts or solutions to campaign focused problems. Instead, they attempted to blame the economic crisis on Democrat initiates all the way back to Bill Clinton. While their assertions may have been accurate, the twists and turns and side deals and nefarious activities and economic mumbo jumbo were too complicated to follow. In the end, all voters could see was that the Republican Party was looking backwards to blame, while Team Obama promised a future of change.

And change was exactly what voters wanted. Nearly a decade of deviating from the main Republican foundations of small government and fiscal responsibility, voters disproportionately turned out for Team Obama. Republicans lost ground in every voter demographic except those over 65 years of age. Simply put, Republicans didn't connect positively with ANYONE except Seniors. While some of this is due simply to the fact that voters felt that the Republican leadership seemed duplicitous, saying one thing (small government and limited intrusion) while doing another (larger government, staggering deficits, and over reaching personal intrusions), Republicans also failed to deliver "sound bite" answers to questions.

Without quick, well thought responses to question concerning Republican strategies on all of the issues, candidates looked bumbling, long winded, slow, and out of touch. On the other side of the table, Team Obama had entire focus groups coming up with just the right "one liners" to make for excellent TV sound bites and give the impression of a quick wit and passionate dedication to sorting out problems. This failure to understand TV culture, where a response needs to fit nicely in a sentence or two was devastating to the Republicans. Already the underdog thanks to the ultra-liberal stranglehold on most major media outlets, Republicans needed every sharp sound bite that they could get.

Perhaps equally problematic, Republicans failed to reach out to the Middle Class in any meaningful way. Already branded as the party of the super rich and powerful, Republicans desperately needed to connect with Middle America. The success of Sarah Palin is a testament to how desperately the middle wanted to connect with conservative values. However, in an effort to make Palin the "everyman" up against the Harvard elitist, Republican spin doctors played up the homey, back woodsy, charm and downplayed her quick wit, incredible speaking talents, and intelligence. The liberal media picked up on the error and ran with it. Inadvertently, Republicans had helped to brand Palin a "dumb hick," not smart enough to manage the economy and international relations. While Middle America was thrilled to have one of their own on the ticket, most Americans don't feel that they personally would be intellectually up to the task of running the country and felt that she probably wasn't either.

Re-branding To Move Forward

Pundits and politicos have called from the "re-branding" of the Republican Party. Noting that over the past twenty years voters have moved away from self identifying as Republicans and have embraced the "independent" label, many seek to reinvigorate the "Reagan Republican" brand. Fearing that the Republican Party leaders have become too institutionalized to make the dramatic shifts necessary to re-engage voters, others are attempting to create a separate, Conservative Party. The current GOP leadership seems to be taking neither position and instead makes half-hearted attempts to reactionary branding, while completely missing the point of why we are at this cross roads.

While each group has different methods and varying degrees of success, the goal is the same. Voters want a thoughtfully progressive, socially and fiscally conservative, Republican Party. The only problem is that those in power don't seem to know how to renovate, reconnect, and re-brand. There is a tendency in life that when things are going poorly, revert to a time when things were going well and start again. This has led many to call for a reprise of the Reagan Republican. While it is important to remember our history, educate people about our history, and of course learn lessons from our history, retreating into our history will not provide result in the Republican Party being seen as forward thinking, problem solvers. In order to effectively re-brand, we have to re-evaluate our Party and our beliefs and build on those constants.

Before Re-branding Begins

Every dime that the GOP spends on advertising and marketing, whether it is the Party web site or a TV commercial, is a waste. I am not suggesting that no one gets the message or that people don't see the ad or commercial and feel inspired. I am simply saying that unless you have established a solid identity and have both a clear message to convey and a directive as to what your audience should do with the message, the best that you can hope for is hit-or-miss success. As a brand, a recognizable and respected symbol that inspires loyalty and devotion, the Republican Party is failing. Half hearted attempts at re-branding have been reactionary at best, focusing on what Team Obama is doing and saying, rather than renovating our own Party and image.

But re-branding the Republican Party can't be effective unless we can understand and convey who we are, what we believe, and how we plan to achieve success. Identifying our core supporters, re-engaging them so that they are confident that we will not deviate from a progressive yet conservative path again, providing safe guards to prevent future deviation, and reaching out to under represented conservatives will be essential to the success of the Republican Party. Without binding the core together, we have nothing to re-brand.

The Republican Brand must convey strength, honor, integrity, loyalty, achievement, personal responsibility, and morality. It must be seen as a forward thinking, conservative and responsible organization. Right now, it isn't seen that way at all. Until we "clean-up-our own-house" and reconnect with our core, conservative supporters, any attempt to effectively brand the Republican Party appropriately will fail.

Supporters and critics alike have legitimately attacked the GOP for failure to adhere to our own stated principles. The Republican Party has always held fiscal responsibility and limited government intervention as core beliefs. Yet, over the past three decades, out of control spending and increased government intrusion have been the norm. Now when Republicans complain about Team Obama's trillion dollar money grab, his allies in the media ask, "Where were you when Bush was increasing debt and intruding into your personal life?"

As a Party, we can't continue to replay, rehash, or respond to events that transpired before today. As they say, hindsight is 20/20 and judging past activities, especially in times of crisis, from a removed time and place is unfair. Instead of apologizing for the times when we deviated from the core values of limited government and fiscal responsibility we must accept that mistakes have been made and reaffirm our commitment to core values.

✪ **The Republican Party must draw a line under the past and return to core values immediately.**

No matter where you look, conservative Republicans are promising a return to core values. However, pledging to return to core values means nothing if people don't know what constitutes a core value. Historically the Republican Party gave four foundations upon which all platforms were built.

1) Limited or Small Government
2) Strong National Defense
3) Personal Responsibility
4) Family Values

The core value then became the heading for subsections detailing actual platforms. Limited Government, for example, encompasses states rights, tax reform, economy, regulation, and fiscal responsibility. The Party's policy on each of those subsections would be broken down as well until each aspect of the platform was established.

Over the past thirty years, Republican leaders have strayed from the conservative core, especially in the limited government arena; increasing taxes, showing limited fiscal responsibility, and implementing a dizzying array of regulations on both business and the personal lives of citizens. It therefore becomes difficult to continue to claim to be the party of small government and fiscal responsibility while passing increasingly oppressive legislation. However, mistakes in the past do not need to render the core values unobtainable. At several points during the past 150 years, Republicans have deviated (resulting in disastrous losses) but were able to return to core values and success.

Core values go hand in hand with platforms and solutions. Rebuilding and re-branding is impossible without assuring that all interested parties, whether they are already supporters, potential voters, other politicians, or the media have a clear and concise understanding our positions, values, and goals.

✪ **Core vales, platforms, and solutions must be clearly stated and well publicized.**

RINOs are ruining the Republican Party. In the GOP's attempt to be all things to all people, they have financed and promoted increasingly liberal people into Republican seats. Fearful that the seat would fall to a Democrat if they attempted to run against the name recognition of the RINO, once in, the GOP continues to support these people despite their continued vote against Republican values. Dozens of "liberals in Republican clothing" such as Dierdre Scozzafava, Olympia Snow, Susan Collins, and Arlen Specter, who after voting liberal for 44 years, all while being supported and funded by the GOP finally jumped ship and joined the Democrats, are destroying the Party.

It is impossible to expect voters to trust the GOP, on any level, if they continue to take campaign contributions and votes and waste them on people who do not represent the will of the constituency or that of the Republican Party. It is ridiculous to support a RINO simply because we may lose the seat to a Democrat, with a RINO in the seat, we already have lost the seat to a Democrat. We must put RINOs on notice that they will no longer be supported for office or with financial contributions unless they return to voting for conservative value issues. RINOs who refuse to return to core values must be removed from office. We must uncover anti-conservative value legislation proposed by RINOs and defeat or repeal it. We must cut off the financial stream to RINOs. Today! This minute!!

✪ **RINOs must choose. They can vote the core values of their constituents and the Party OR they can find their financial and campaign support elsewhere. RINOs must be put on notice that they have no place in the modern Republican Party.**

In order to successfully re-brand, the GOP needs to understand that strength lay with the conservative Republican core supporters. However, these voters are the ones who have been most burned by Republican deviation and are the ones most likely to either refuse to vote or to turn to small conservative parties that are springing up around the country. Sadly, it seems that many Republicans have forgotten who comprises the conservative core. In order to re-engage core conservatives, the GOP needs to identify these essential groups.

- Married couples with children
- People over 35
- Military Personnel
- Rural Communities
- Southern, Mid-Western, & Mountain States
- Christians and Evangelicals
- Business Community
- Middle Class
- Hispanics
- Asians

In order to re-engage them, the GOP will have to reaffirm that they will pursue conservative core values and platforms, stop supporting RINOs, and make visible steps to get the party back on track. Conservatives want to SEE action, not just hear more promises. While on a national level, the GOP should be focusing on halting the spread of Obama's socialist agenda and to offer bills that will bring the conservative values back to the forefront of political debate, local and state level GOP's must look to the core conservatives and address their issues immediately.

✪ **Republicans must identify and re-engage core supporters by affirming (in word AND deed) the conservative core generally, and their concerns specifically.**

One of the most fundamental changes that the GOP can make to instill faith and rebuild trust within the core constituency is to provide completely transparent voting records for all Republican politicians. Voters feel completely helpless when it comes time to vote because we don't have enough information about candidates to make an informed decision. We are therefore left to choose, especially in primaries, based on limited information and PR spins. As Republicans, we want to be passionate about those who we elect to represent us. But we are robbed of that ability to connect and really support because we have no real information.

Of course many politicians are concerned that providing a transparent voting record will shine a light on either their failure to show up for votes or an inconsistent voting record. Still others may worry that simply showing a FOR or AGAINST vote for each bill won't paint the full picture. In some instances, onerous wording or additions tacked on at the end of an otherwise acceptable proposal, render it unsupportable. These issues can be addressed. Again we return to drawing a line under the past. Those who have failed to turn up for votes must understand that they are being paid to support our interests by representing us at every vote. Those who have failed to do so in the past must understand that they are being put on notice that such continued failures will be seen as a breach of their contract with voters. By the same token, the name of the bill and a simple YES or NO vote record is not transparency. A summary of the bill along with a sentence or two as to why the politician either supported it or rejected it, along with a downloadable .pdf file of each bill will be sufficient for voters to make informed decisions. There is additional information about the mechanics of transparency in the "Renovating the GOP" section of this book.

✪　　We demand transparency in the voting records of all Republican politicians.

Once we have put our house in order, we must reach out to voters who share our values, but have been indoctrinated away from our Party. This is NOT the same as attempting to become all things to all people are reach out to those who do not support our values. Doing so only waters down our goals, disengages the core, and returns us to a party of reactionaries instead of innovators.

Clearly our core values and principles are not going to appeal to socialists, ultra-liberals, or any of the other left wing loons who want to destroy America. Good! But there are many groups who share values, but have been the victims of long term indoctrination. Some of theses people can be saved.

- Young people 18-35
- Blue-collar Workers
- African Americans
- Legal Immigrants
- Native Americans
- Catholic Americans
- Jewish Americans

When reviewed individually, each group listed believes in many of the same principles as the conservative Republican. Tradition and years of indoctrination however have created a block that simply continues to vote for the Democrat, without examining their own beliefs and values. On a national level, the GOP must promote the diversity that exists within the Party and initiate education campaigns and deprogramming that target specific groups. On a local and state level, the GOP needs to reach out to these groups, address their specific issues and explain both why the Democrat platform is not working for them and how the Republican platform can.

✪ **We must identify and reach out to conservative groups who have been indoctrinated away from the Party.**

Creating the Republican Brand

The Republican Brand must convey strength, honor, integrity, loyalty, achievement, personal responsibility, and morality. By reaffirming our dedication to core values and our core constituents, we can display strength and loyalty. By putting RINOs on notice, drawing a line under past deviations, and providing clear platforms and voting records, we establish integrity, honor, and morality. By promoting the diversity of the Party and reaching out to new conservatives, we can showcase our commitment to achievement and our core value of personal responsibility. It is upon these issues that our brand is created. However, we can not rest on integrity and honor. We must convey that we are a principled Party of forward thinkers, who can boldly lead our country out of this darkness.

We can't simply create a clever slogan, wave our flags, and hand out party platforms. While those traditional political elements are important, the future of the Republican Party boils down to a single issue. We have to be able to answer the fundamental question, "What will Republicans do for the Middle Class?" Despite Team Obama's assertion that the Middle Class wants to be socialized, the vast majority of Middle and Working Class Americans still believe in the American Dream. They want to be afforded the opportunity to pursue their concept of happiness, success, and personal fulfillment. It isn't about making everyone rich. It is about making sure that the system isn't rigged to insure that they fail.

In this area, Republicans and Democrats differ most significantly. Democrats attempt, with social programs to create a false equality. They have pre-determining that everyone wants to attend college in pursuit of white collar occupations, live in urban areas, and embrace a socialistic concept of government in which the government owns or controls industries. Republicans don't agree. We believe that Americans have a broad definition of success. Some people do consider a college degree and a white collar job success. But what about the millions of Americans who work in manufacturing, agriculture, construction, trades and services? Where are the paths that enable them to create success? Republicans must embrace the ENTIRE Middle Class and not simply respond to the Democrats vision of the Middle Class.

Republicans have a real opportunity to refocus on the people that matter most in this country and connect with them directly. This country rises and falls on the blood, sweat, and tears of Middle America. We must reach out to them with bold plans to help insure that they can build their own vision of success. This will take some re-education. Having been branded the party of the rich, we have to return to basics and explain that we are not the party of the rich, we are the party of wealth creation. There is a huge difference between the two. Wealth creation is about making things that people want to buy, providing services that people want to use, and inventing things that make lives easier and more enjoyable. It is about creating paths for small businesses and farms to be self sufficient, creating financial security for the owners and potential jobs for the community. We must offer practical pathways to non-college degree jobs and for military personnel to reintegrate into working society after their military service is concluded. While it would be a mistake to try and return to a Norman Rockwell vision of America, it is essential that we understand what made those concepts so appealing.

This is the brand. This is the Republican Party that conservatives can support. It isn't about going backwards. It isn't about casting blame for current problems. It isn't about who gets the biggest paycheck. The Republican Party must re-brand itself as THE Party that can bring this country back to an age of prosperity.
THE Party that can resuscitate a dying US economy.
THE Party that can return the sanctity of the Constitution.

The Republican Party
The American Dream Resurrected

- Chapter 4 -

Renovating the GOP
From the Top Down

Affecting change in an organization, especially from the top down, can be very difficult. In an organization that has been around for nearly one hundred and fifty years and is designed to develop strategies and methods to win power and influence, the deeply entrenched behaviors, mores, and codes work against internal change. However, as a Party, we have veered so far off course; a drastic correction is required in order to stay a viable vehicle for conservative American stewardship.

You can sugar coat it any way you wish, but Americans see both major political parties as groups of liars and cheats who use side deals, kick backs, and ear marks to pay for support and votes. Congress has an embarrassingly low approval rating, and most people don't know the names or backgrounds of their national representatives. People simply don't feel that they have the power to change the system and so apathy creeps in. Untended by a vigilant electorate, politicians stray from their core values by financially tempting diversions. Far removed from the issues of their home states, the promises made in campaigns are forgotten. Americans don't trust politicians.

Politicians, on the other hand, feel that their efforts and energies are unappreciated by a fickle electorate who will turn on them based on rumors and innuendos. Faced with proposed legislation the size of *War and Peace*, crammed with references to a hundred other similar sized bills, politicians who came to office, desperately seeking to make a real change on the national stage find themselves impotent. Eventually, some succumb to the pressures of lobbyist, special interests, and big money side deals assuming that they are just the perks of a difficult job.

But, change is not impossible, if all parties see the necessity and are willing to make the (sometimes painful) modifications. In order to make these changes, we need to establish some ground rules.

1. **We must give the benefit of the doubt.** While there are politicians who have used their position only to further their own personal interests and bank balances, there are just as many who genuinely want to help guide this country to greatness. Unfortunately, it is the bad guys that hit the headlines. Painting all politicians with the same brush is unfair.

2. **We must take some responsibility.** Things are changing and people are getting more vigilant, holding their representatives accountable for their actions and their votes. But, for many, many years we sent our reps off to Washington and didn't think of them again until the next election cycle. We failed to monitor our representatives.

3. **We must offer amnesty.** Politicians have followed their own agenda for many years now. Some have done this, aware that they did wrong. But others simply followed the direction of their predecessors. We can't expect politicians to open themselves up for examination if we can't offer them a pass on past errors in judgment. But, that pass ends today. Future ethics violations will not be accepted.

4. **We must draw a line.** Mistakes have been made and in some cases, are still being made. But we can't fix things and move on if we continue to look to the past or find

people upon whom to affix blame. We must be willing to draw a line under the past, admit that mistakes have been made, refuse to get bogged down with cataloging and detailing the mistakes, and put things right from today.

Marketing & Brand Awareness

All marketing starts by answering a single question, "why do we exist?" As a political party, do we exist to thwart Obama? Do we exist to prevent socialist and ultra-liberals from destroying this country? Do we exist to set the country back on its centrist right axis? No. Those are all components of what we need to do in order to achieve the goal, but they are not the overriding goal itself. The Republican Party goal should be to be the conservative, thoughtfully progressive, solutions driven, stewards of America. Until we can agree that this is the goal and focus on that, we will continue to be reactionary, servants to team Obama's whims and an impotent political force. Barack Obama and his wave of socialism will eventually be no more than a speed bump in the history of this country. If we are to survive as a party, we must realize that Obama is a symptom of the problems that we face, a light that shines on the legal loop holes and sleeper cell socialists that lay in wait to destroy this country. To continue to elevate him to any level higher than usurper, traitor, or pretender to the throne is to give Team Obama power that is unearned and undeserved. While it is important to monitor and counter anti-American activities perpetrated by Team Obama, we must focus our attention on the over arching goal.

The Goal of the Republican Party:

To be the conservative, thoughtfully progressive, solution driven, stewards of the United States of America.

177

Once we can get past focusing on Obama, we can focus on marketing the Republican Party as the conservative, thoughtfully progressive, solution driven, stewards of the USA. This must be the message that we send out in every newsletter and press memo. This is the message that we must convey at every conference, speaking event, or interview. Right now the message that we are conveying is largely that of whiney, sore losers. This continues to damage our brand.

Education

After years of misinformation, smears, and our own deviations, the GOP must be a force of education. This CAN NOT wait. The GOP should be funding commercials, viral videos, documentaries, print ads, and all sorts of media designed to educate people about the real Republican Party. This is NOT about attacking Obama. We have to re-educate the general public about our values, our principles, and most importantly, our plans for the resurrection of the American Dream.

The education process is an excellent way to involve state and local GOP as well as the hundreds of groundswell organizations that are already organized and active. These are armies that can spread the word in their states and local communities. They can provide valuable information about what educational efforts are working and where we still need to reach out. Understanding that most effective and appropriate ways to reach different communities and different demographics within those communities is vital. But the GOP at the national level should be spearheading educational efforts across the country.

This is an incredible uphill battle. We have to battle against Team Obama devotional songs in grade schools, Obama Youth Corps, and a network of millions of indoctrinated cult members. We have to counter the major media love affair with Obama. We have to counter decades of being branded as racists, xenophobes, only interested in the rich. This should be the primary focus of the GOP between campaign cycles.

The GOP Web Site

In this age of information, an organization must have an effective web site. The web site is the way that an organization can connect with its members immediately, 24 hours a day. It is a source of information and inspiration. The GOP web site should be the "go to" source for national level, political information for Republicans. It should be. But it isn't. The web site is not well laid out, informative, or inspiring. This must be corrected immediately. Most of failures of the GOP on a national level can be corrected through an effective internet presence. The following details should be a part of that presence.

The GOP Portal

As a matter of functionality, a person should be able to go to the national GOP site and easily navigate their way to the page (or separate linked site) of every national level Republican politician. Not only does this provide ease of information, it also creates a team. Each member of the GOP is a member of the team and since we generally promote people up the ranks, creating name recognition early on is essential.

The national GOP site should also provide links to each state GOP site. This will enable people to easily navigate from national information, news, and activities to that of their particular state and from there, to their local area. Creating a GOP portal helps to build a groundswell movement. It keeps people connected to the "big picture."

National Party Platform

As previously discussed, the national party platform and the proposed solutions to the problems that face the United States must be easy to understand and prominently displayed on the site. There should be no confusion as to our position or the steps that we intend on taking to put the country back on the right track. Failure to provide an easy to understand platform is one of the most significant failures of the site and the GOP as a whole.

Understanding National Politics

While people are getting increasingly, politically savvy, the majority of Americans do not fully understand politics. Ignorance or misinformation is NOT our friend. The GOP site should have at least a page that details the national, political process. In easy to understand terms and diagrams, it should explain the roles of the various representatives, how bills are created and passed, the electoral college, and a general guideline of what issues fall under the remit of the federal government.

Republican History

Focusing a great deal on the past does not inspire confidence that a party can be effective in the future. However, a single page that briefly outlines the history of the party is important. People do want to know upon what values and beliefs the current Party was built upon. Highlighting important players in our history and details the significant, nation shaping events that were inspired by Republicans and Republican platforms is an essential education that is currently, sorely lacking.

The Role of the RNC

While most people recognize that the RNC organizes and operates the Republican National Convention and is involved in fundraising, few people understand the role and makeup of the Republican National Committee. The RNC plays such a substantial role in the politics of this country and in particular in the success or failure of Republican politicians on a national stage, that this lack of understanding must be corrected. A single page explaining the roles of the RNC in campaign fundraising, platform development, and political strategies as well as the makeup of the RNC would be helpful and informative.

Lobbying, Special Interest Groups, & Earmarks

There is a tremendous amount of misinformation surrounding the roles of lobbying groups, special interest groups, and earmarks. However, despite having a limited grasp of the terms, each has come to be synonymous with corruption in the minds of most Americans. Providing easy to understand definitions of these terms, explaining their functions, and how they fit into the political process would help to educate the electorate and prevent negative, knee jerk reactions re-actions for vital aspects of the political process.

Transparency & Accountability

Americans responded to the promise of a transparent government and political process. So let's give it to them! The GOP web site should have links to .pdf files of all bills proposed. Our party members include some of the brightest people in the world. They want to read these bills. They want to discuss the contents and evaluate the merits. Since most politicians complain that they simply don't have the time to read and evaluate the bills before voting, enlist the help of the electorate. Reading groups will develop devoted to particular issues, they will be able to provide valuable, educated, practical insight and summaries of the bills from a constituents perspective, something sorely lacking in Washington.

The site should have a list of the voting records of each politician, and if they are Republican, why they supported or rejected the bill. We understand that bills have all sorts of non-sense attached to them at times, so we recognize that some bills might look good from the name, but would be bad in practice. Tell us! Americans feel largely impotent when it comes to selecting representatives at all levels because they don't have access to information. Providing that information will inspire more people to become politically active and will help keep those elected to serve us on the straight and narrow path.

News

The GOP web site should be the home page of politically active conservatives. But in order for it to be so, the site must include more than just definitions, platforms, and links. News feeds should play an important part of the site. People want to know what their representatives are doing, how they are voting, what they are proposing, and what events are shaping the national scene. However, making the site a "can you believe what Obama is doing this time?" site is NOT effective. Mainstream news covers Obama's socialist maneuverings well enough. Continuing that posture of shock does not inspire faith that the Republican Party is the party of ideas and solutions. We need to concentrate on providing the electorate with information about what we are doing rather than what Team Obama is doing.

Community

In order to create a groundswell, people need to feel connected to something positive and growing. Creating an on-line community is a great way to connect with Republicans who want to be part of that success. A community is a way that people can interact with other like minded people, as well as groups that interest them. It is also a super way for politicians to "meet" their constituents to discuss important issues.

A positive community provides:
- space for different groups to meet on line
- space where people can post photos showcasing their rallies and meetings

- space where people can reach out to other groups to connect for state and national level rallies and meetings
- space where people can post their personal videos, short films, etc. And encourage people to participate. Remember, ACORN wouldn't be falling apart if not for the clever camera work of some amateur film makers. Encourage!

A positive community does NOT include:
- unmonitored, open access, chat rooms. This just encourages hatefulness, stalking, and anger.
- ads or links to non-affiliated commercial operations. The community doesn't want to feel targeted.

Creating a positive community, where people can interact, is an excellent way to inspire people to greater degrees of involvement. The GOP can't wait until six months before an election to reach out. The groundswell has to start now and there must be an outlet for people to connect in a positive way. People want to be involved in the process. They want to feel that their vote is valued and important. They want to feel that they are making informed decisions. Right now, those desires are not being met. The GOP web site should be THE source of information for the Republican Party. It should be inspiring and should show a united front, but above all it should be a source of political information and groundswell connection.

What's NOT Working For the GOP

One of the most challenging, but necessary aspects of leadership is recognizing when something isn't working and taking the appropriate steps to correct the problem. The larger the organization, the more difficult change can be, however, for the Republican Party to succeed, some problems must be addressed.

Republicans In Name Only

Clearly there will be times and locations when getting a great, conservative Republican into a seat will be difficult if not impossible. But, the prevailing wisdom seems to be that ANYONE willing to call themselves a Republican during the campaign is acceptable for support, even if their own stance on issues places them squarely off sides with core Republican values. And further, that once someone has the seat, even if they prove to be incompetent or unacceptable based on the principles and values of the Republican Party, the GOP moves heaven and earth to keep them in that seat. This is not working.

While it is true that the most conservative politician in a very liberal area may not be as conservative as the most conservative person in a conservative area, no matter where a politician is situated, they must share the core values of the Party. If they don't, it is completely inappropriate for the GOP to financially support their candidacy. The idea that it is better to win a seat for the Republicans and then attempt to influence the politician to vote conservatively has been proven time and time again to be ineffective. It leads to the very side deals, special favors, and financial incentives that have destroyed the country's faith in politicians. The Republican voter can see no good reason to fund and support RINOs. If we are unable to win a seat for a conservative in a liberal area, the GOP should be focusing its efforts on re-educating the residents, not funding future enemies. If there is a compelling reason to support a RINO, the GOP needs to do a better job of explaining that reason to the electorate.

Pundit Condemnation

Over the course of the past year, various politicians and members of the GOP leadership have come out criticizing the commentary of radio, television, and other mass media pundits. This is unbecoming, undignified, and completely unnecessary. We can hardly complain at Team Obama's attempts at censorship and media control, if we engage in similar behavior. The opinions expressed by conservative personalities often mirror the beliefs of millions of Americans. Running to condemn their opinions only further pushes conservative voters away from the Republican Party. The GOP is NOT responsible for the comments of pundits. It is not the job of any politician or GOP member to clarify, condemn, or comment.

Race Card Politics

Perhaps it is only natural that when the Presidency is held by a black man and the leader of the RNC is a black man, the issue of race in America would be a recurring theme. This unprecedented situation could provide a wonderful opportunity to showcase just how far this country has come in so short a time period. Certainly, there is no place else on this planet where racial relations have equalized so quickly or where people have worked so hard to ensure that they do. But you wouldn't know that to listen to politicians. How is the Party, or in fact the entire country, better served by comments such as Michael Steele's "I've been in the room and they've been scared of me.." when asked if white Republicans were afraid of "black folk?" Trying to earn credibility with one group by demonizing or marginalizing another is shameful. The continual engaging in race card politics is disingenuous and serves only to further divide.

Are there racists in the Republican electorate? Certainly. They are also a very small minority. Are there racists in the Democrat electorate? Certainly. They are also a very small minority. Continuing to elevate race as a factor in Republican politics unfairly portrays all Republicans as racists and insinuates that the Republican Party includes only whites as members. You will be hard pressed to find someone, no matter what their color or ethnic heritage (including Caucasians), who has not been the victim of racism or discrimination at some point in their lives. Continuing to point the finger in one direction is despicable.

Reactionary Responses

My inbox is full. Emails, newsletters, Twitter, Facebook, and a dozen networking sites all keeping me up to date on Republican politics. Disappointingly, almost all of them say some variation of the same thing, "Can you believe what Obama and Pelosi are trying to do this time?" Yes, yes I can believe it. They are doing exactly what they set out to do, exactly what they said that they were going to do from day one, destroy this country. What I don't see are emails, newsletters, Twitter, and Facebook posts detailing what the GOP is doing about it. I don't get posts explaining the Republican solutions to problems. I don't get daily messages giving me hope that this battle is under control.

The GOP seems to be reacting. Not leading. This is a huge mistake. By failing to tell Republican voters what is being done about the problems and focusing only on being the barer of bad news, people don't feel inspired or confident that the GOP can make a change, get back on track, and pull this jet out of its nose dive. Inspire us, the major media is frightening us just fine.

- Chapter 5 -

Renovating the GOP
From the Middle

While national politics gets the attention, a tremendous amount of untapped power rests in the hands of the state level GOP. Politicians who emerge onto the national scene have all come from the state level political arena. It is therefore essential that those who are "superstars" at the state and local level are supported, and groomed for conservative national leadership roles, while those who are RINOs are neutralized before they can inflict more harm.

The state level GOP has the opportunity to be the most influential force in Republican politics. They can engage the electorate, educate the voters, and more closely monitor politicians for hints of unethical behavior and RINO voting patterns. Some states do an excellent job of keeping the electorate informed and engaged. Others could do a much better job. At the national level, most of the focus is on the RNC, campaign finance, and the convention. It is therefore up to the state level GOP to make citizens aware of the politicians, the platforms, and the issues that are most important to their state.

States Rights & the 10th Amendment

While Team Obama is busy using Congress to grab unprecedented power for the federal government, as of last month (October 2009) 37 states have introduced or are proposing to introduce bills affirming State sovereignty under the 10th

Amendment to the Constitution. These states seek to demand that the federal government stop usurping State powers or handing down mandates that violate the Constitution.

Under the 10th Amendment to the Constitution, federal powers are limited to those delegated to it by the Constitution. Other than those specifically prohibited, all other powers, jurisdictions, and rights are held by the State and the people. Under the 10th Amendment, each State retains its sovereignty, freedom, and independence from the federal government. By affirming sovereignty, States are attempting to send a message that they will no longer be forced to financially support bankrupting social programs. A huge increase in unfunded mandates starting with the Clinton administration, increased by the Bush administration, and topped off by the Obama's $1 trillion "stimulus" plan impales with a double edged sword. These mandates require states to implement sweeping social programs, though the federal government provides no money for their funding. If states do not comply, they risk being cut off from federal tax dollars for other programs.

The state sovereignty issue is extremely important. Not only does it re-establish a line that must not be crossed by the federal government (the last cross created the Civil War), it brings state issues back under state control. Social national controversies, such as abortion, gay marriage, and capital punishment would arguably be better served were they returned to state or even local domain. In the same way that some counties are "dry" as in that they allow no liquor sales, the population of counties should make decisions about social issues inline with their population's mores and values.

Republicans must be on the front lines in state sovereignty issues. If your state has passed the State Sovereignty Resolution, this should be clearly detailed on the state GOP web site. If a proposal is pending or has yet to be proposed, this is an excellent opportunity to start organizing and informing the electorate.

Identifying Representatives and Their Positions

Before you can start a battle you need to be able to identify friends and enemies. In the world of politics, this is not always straight forward. Logic would dictate that those in your own party would be friends, while those on the other side of the fence would not. However, with a cast of characters that include RINOs and conservative Democrats, following party lines can be a big mistake. Perhaps even more upsetting is the fact that while politicians may say that they support an issue, kick backs, special interest groups, and favors may induce him or her to cast their ballot to the contrary.

An excellent source of information concerning your state and local representatives, their voting records, campaign finances, special interest group affiliations, and positions can be found at an exceptional site, www.VoteSmart.org which is provided by Project Vote Smart, a non-partisan, non-profit organization dedicated to protecting democracy through political transparency. The research organization provides an incredible service and should be the first port of call for all conservatives who want to make informed, educated decisions about politicians and issues.

Removing "Republicans in Name Only"

RINOs get their foot in the door at the local or state level. So logically, this is where to nip the practice in the bud. State leaders should be on the forefront of changing the practice of supporting those whose principles do not match that of the Republican Party. Politicians need to be put on notice that if they don't vote the will of their constituents, a more conservative candidate will be found, financed, and supported. Voters are tired of having "better of two evils" candidates from which to choose a representative. The only way to offer good, conservative candidates on a national level is to select and nurture good, conservative candidates at the ground level.

Clearly, some RINOs have been in power for a long time, making them more difficult to remove. But what is the option? Keeping them in place, year after year, has only served to undermine the economic and social fabric of this country. Even if it means losing the seat to the Democrats for the short term, removing RINOs is essential to the health of the Party and the security of the country.

Monitoring Ethics

One of the main complaints that voters have with politicians is the perceived lack of ethics. When tax cheats are promoted to higher levels of power, while a regular citizen who errors in tax calculations is fined and even jailed, it is easy to understand the frustration. Most people don't simply wake up and become unethical. There is often a pattern of unethical activities and behavior throughout their career. Continuing to financially and professionally support unethical behavior in politicians by overlooking their actions and continuing to promote them through the ranks into national level politics is immoral.

We can't be surprised at bad behavior when people are at the heights of power when they have exhibited bad behavior throughout their lives. State GOPs have an ethical obligation, to the Party, to the voters, and most importantly to the safety of our country, to remove unethical politicians. When GOPs are seen to be safe guarding the political process and protecting the public, regaining respect from the general population will become much easier.

Education

Arguably no other role can be as important for the state level GOP than that of political educator. If nothing else was obvious from the last election, vast segments of society possess a shocking ignorance both to the platforms and positions of the Republican Party and to the history of the Party itself. We can't afford to wait until the next election cycle and then try a "blitzkrieg" approach to educating the public. The state GOP must lead the way in educating the public about our values, our principles, and most importantly, our plans for the resurrection of the American Dream.

On the state level, the GOP can be very effective in creating and monitoring the effectiveness of educational programs that target specific demographics. While traditional education through commercials, pamphlets, doorstep chats, and speeches can be effective, States have so many more creative options available to them simply because they are better able to adapt their methods to local standards of acceptability. States are also better equipped than the national GOP to create a schedule of educational and public relations events to reach out to the voters.

State GOPs also have the added ability to micro-manage local educational efforts and the sponsorship of public events. Film contest, oratory contest, art contest, sponsorship for artist, the possibilities are endless. Create fun awareness campaigns. Educating the public is easier if it is done in a subtle, friendly way. The anger and threats and "how could you be so stupid" attitude will not win votes or awake up an uneducated electorate. It will only make them further entrenched in ignorance.

State level GOPs also have to face the fact that there will be anger. Conservatives feel rejected or deceived by the past decade of Republican core value deviation and may not be willing to listen to our platforms and pledges unless we can explain that we agree that things have gone off track. We must effectively explain that we have returned to core values and want the electorates help in getting things back on the right track. Humility will go a long way. But we also need to show that we are taking steps to fix the problem. Talk isn't enough.

The State GOP Web Site

One of the most effective tools that we have at our disposal is the internet. A great web site can be a 24 hours a day/ 7 days a week information and inspiration center. Ideally, the national GOP site would provide links to each state's GOP site. The state GOP site should provide an easy way for Republicans to navigate their way around state politics. Providing state political information, news, and activities help to create a cohesive, Republican team and unifies the many local organizations that have sprung up in support of specific issues.

State Party Platform

Some states have done an excellent job at showcasing their party platform. Others have failed to do so. But all should include the platform and the proposed solutions to the problems that face the state on their state GOP web site. Voters want to know exactly what they are supporting and more importantly, that party leaders have been thoughtful and consistent in reflecting on the issues. Simply passing down edicts without establishing ways in which Republicans can work towards achieving goals is ineffective. Many people feel duped by the past three administrations and while simple words are not enough to turn the tide, seeing the principles and values laid out in black and white, accompanied by proposed solutions will go a long way to re-engaging those who have wandered from the Party.

Understanding State Politics

State politics are largely a mystery to many Americans. Even those who actively participate in national elections may have little understanding of the mechanisms at the state level. However, it is at this level that the most effective and long lasting change can take place. For many Americans, the shocking greed, duplicity, and corruption at the national political level has created a renewed interest in state politics as a way to prevent the situation in the future. This is great for state politics. However, with limited information easily available, we run the risk of potential voters loosing interest or falling into apathy. The state GOP site should include, in easy to understand terms and diagrams, the roles of the various state and local representatives, how bills are created and passed, and a general guideline of what issues fall under the remit of the state government.

State Republican History

While the national heroes of the Republican Party are generally well known figures, on the state level, many amazing and inspiring people have slipped into the hazy of history. While it is not wise to focus too much energy on looking backwards, state level GOPs have a great educational tool in providing information about influential and inspiring Republicans who have made the state a better place to live. It is at the state level that the real diversity lay, which helps to create a bridge between the Republican Party and minority groups who have been preyed upon by Democrats for generations.

Transparency & Accountability

Americans are starting to understand the relationship between the problems with national level politicians and the people that are promoted up the ranks of power from a local and state level. This has inspired many to want more information about the people who are currently occupying state seats. People want to know how their state representatives are voting and what issues they support. Perhaps of equal importance, they want to know if the politicians are motivated to make real changes or if they are simply looking for a financially lucrative career.

The state GOP web site should provide a comprehensive list of all state and local politicians, their voting record, why they supported or rejected each bill, and the issues about which they are most passionate. The site should also include .pdf files of all of the bills proposed. Americans don't want to feel impotent, but without information, our hands are tied. With increasing frequency, voters want to be able to select candidates and nurture their careers, support them as our representatives and champions. This is far preferable to the current arrangement by where voters have to select from a group of largely unknown candidates. Again, people will become more politically active and aware if information is readily available. Knowing that their words and deeds are on-line for all to evaluate helps keep politicians doing the job that they were elected to perform.

News

While national politics affect us all, state level politics can have an immediate effect on the lives of citizens. The state level GOP should therefore be the internet home of politically aware citizens. News feeds should play an important part of the site, informing people about their representatives, how they are voting, what they are proposing, and what events are shaping the state.

Community

While a national Republican community is a wonderful step in the right direction, people are much more apt to organize, meet, and be active in community events on a state or regional level. For this reason, the state GOP site must have a community section that will allow people to engage and connect. Tips on creating a great web based community can be found under the national GOP site section in this book.

- Chapter 6 -

Renovating the GOP From the Bottom Up

It would be great if the mandates that we have given to the leaders of the Party inspired them to make quick, decisive, effective changes both to the way that they operate and the way that they lead. But, in a bureaucratic system, change can take time. Unfortunately, time is not a luxury that we have to enjoy. The real changes, the real force, the real power...comes from the ground. It comes from you and me.

Team Obama took over a socialist "grassroots" movement. Socialists, Alinksy-ites, radical racists, and other anti-Americans spent years planting seeds of discontent, hatred, and fear followed by decades of fertilizing it in the bull shit of indoctrination, misinformation, and manipulation, resulting in a harvest of pliable, angry, cult-like followers from Obama to lead at will. Some pundits have called for a Republican grassroots movement, a right-wing mirror of Obama's campaign. This is a mistake. Republicans don't want cult followers, we don't want to lead through lies and fear. We want an America that pays homage to the pioneer spirit upon which this country was founded.

Republicans, conservatives unaffiliated with the Republican Party, independents, and even conservative Democrats are rising up, joining groups, attending rallies and trying to stop the spread of this disease. We are witnessing a groundswell, a sudden, ferocious, eruption of angry Americans. These Americans won't be followers. They investigate the issues and want to hold people accountable, especially if those traitors happen to occupy seats within the Republican Party. But more than anything, they want to put this country back on the right track, close the loop holes that have turned this country into nirvana for illegal immigrants, and return the Constitution to its rightful position of sanctity. The only problem is that many of these groups, born in frustration, confused by the rapid disintegration of the country, feel impotent to make change. Groups small and large need to be able to organize, combine to create a united front, and lift their voices in unison to create a deafening sound that lets Team Obama know that we will not accept socialization without a fight.

Groundswell Power

Obama may have a grassroots movement to thank for his election, but Republicans are part of a groundswell. A groundswell is an uprising, an unexpected, angry, rapid eruption from underground. Based on Pelosi, Reid, et al vitriolic reaction to regular Americans who oppose sweeping socialization, the hate from the White House at Republican pundits, and the liberal media's continued attempts to minimize the scope and breadth of conservative protests around the country, Team Obama certainly seems surprised by the conservative groundswell. Whether this is because Team Obama had convinced themselves that real Americans actually want to be socialized or that the egomaniac believed that all would simply lay down for whatever anti-American, "new world order" plan he may imagine is unclear.

But a groundswell on its own is not enough to turn the tide of socialism and return American to the right path. It takes awareness of the issues on a local, state, and national level. It takes organization. It takes a game plan. And it takes a battlefield. Whether you are part of a small organization that wants to combine forces with other organizations in order to build power or you want to join or create a local organization in order to make a difference, the steps are the same and they all start in your own county. Welcome to the fight.

Taking Control of Local Politics

National level politics gets the news coverage. State level politics should act as a big sieve, separating the good from the bad. But the real power is on the ground level. Local government. I know that you will roll your eyes at the thought that one of your neighbors has any effect on who sits in the White House. But not only do they have a direct effect on who is elected, Democrat participation on the local level is more than double that of Republicans and nationwide 200,000 local Republican seats are empty. So while you are at Tea Party meetings and writing letters to Congressmen, that liberal loony or radical racist down the street from you is deciding who gets on the ballot and there are no conservatives at the committee meeting to counter.

County Precincts

In the United States, there are a total of 3,141 counties or county equivalents (parishes in Louisiana, boroughs in Alaska, etc.). Each county is divided into legislative districts, which are further divided into neighborhood precincts. Some states divide neighborhood precincts by city blocks, others by contiguous population, but however it is divided, those in your immediate neighborhood make up the population represented by your neighborhood precinct in what is commonly called the "Precinct Committee."

The Constitution of your state will dictate the makeup of the committee. Some states allow one committee person from each party, per 500 registered voters. Other states allot one committee person for each party period, with additional committee members allowed per established group of registered voters. Still others have gender quotas and require each party to have a certain number of male and female committee members. But no matter how your state frames the precinct, the precinct committee has amazing political power. Essentially, a precinct committee person is a representative of a political party.

Precinct Committee Representatives

If you've never heard of a precinct committee, you are not alone. Over the past forty years, interest in local level politics had dwindled, perhaps in part because most schools no longer teach civics. However, participation at the local level increased dramatically just prior to the last Presidential primaries when a virtually unknown Barack Obama recruited people in each county (through ACORN and similar groups) to add his name to the ballot.

Precinct Committee Representatives:
- Elect delegates to the party's National Presidential Convention.
- Elect delegates to the State Central Committee (the governing body of the party)
- Elect State Central Committee officers.
- Nominate candidates for vacancies in the state legislature
- Nominate candidates for vacancies in the county commission
- Participate in county and state platform conventions (where platforms are established)
- Recruit lobbyist to target specific elected officials

It should also be noted that the Precinct Committee Reps are also given in the name, phone number, address, email address, and the frequency in which they voted in the past four elections of all registered voters in their precinct. Obama's grassroots numbers don't seem quite so impressive when you understand that neighborhood precinct committee members and volunteers knew exactly who was an established Democrat and personally visited them with Obama propaganda.

It is at this level that the RINO problem starts. With almost full Democrat participation, and 200,000 empty Republican seats, some, eager to get into politics list themselves as Republicans in order to get onto the ballot. Others who might be called "moderate Republicans" who are conservative on financial issues but liberal on social issues take seats uncontested. This results in the current situation, where conservative Americans only have RINOs and moderate Republicans from which to choose at the state and national level elections.

The only way to counter this problem is participation. Conservatives MUST fill these empty seats. This will allow conservatives to nominate conservative politicians into state legislature and senate seats, which result in a conservative pool of politicians from which to select national leadership. This is not a problem that we can fix during a presidential election campaign, it must start now. We must retake control of local politics so that we have the pedestal from which to control state and national politics.

Whether you are an individual eager to make a difference or you are part of a conservative organization, the most important thing that you can do to take control of the country away from Pelosi and Obama is to either become a Precinct Committee Representative yourself or sponsor others to fill every empty seat in your county and challenge every RINO or moderate Republican that currently holds a seat. Becoming a Precinct Committee Representative is relatively straightforward. Contact the State GOP for exact requirements, but generally you will be given a nomination form and a list of registered voters in your area. Depending on the state you will need between 5 and 10 signatures from registered voters to be allotted a seat or be put on the ballot for the next election, depending on the state. Most seats go unopposed and the seats are simply awarded to the only person who submitted a nomination form. We can't leave the safety of our country to apathy. FILL THESE SEATS!!!

Precinct Committee Power

I want to repeat two facts.

There are nearly **200,000** empty
Republican Precinct Committee seats nationwide.

&

**Precinct Committee Reps nominate candidates
and elect delegates.**

Can there be anything more shocking than the fact the we already have the power not only to nominate conservative politicians into positions of leadership on the state and ultimately national level but also to rid ourselves of RINOs currently in power simply by participating in our local government? Is there anything more upsetting than discovering that we had the power to minimize the Obama Cult, had we only known where the power sits? Being a part of a Precinct Committee takes the dedication of only a few hours a month. Filling every one of these Republican Precinct Committee seats MUST be the #1 priority of every conservative organization in the country. We can rally, we can blog, we can complain all we want, but until we fill those seats with conservatives and use those seats to start nominating conservative candidates, it's all a waste of time. It's not too late.

Organizing

Americans all around the country, horrified at the sweeping socialist changes being implemented without their consent, are desperately looking for a hero. Unimpressed by the half-hearted attempts by national level politicians to compel any real change, people are organizing. In living rooms, in town halls, in bars, and in churches, Americans from all walks of life are creating small, local organizations in an effort to combine power and launch an attack against the socialist agenda. However, without direction, many of these small groups will reduce to "complaining clubs" instead of forces. Even larger organizations run the risk of losing their power and their members if they don't have a clear concept of how to use their power to effect change.

Understanding Organization Power

An organization is powerful only as long as it is gaining attention and achieving goals. Think back to what we discovered about Alinsky. His goals weren't noble and his attention seeking ranged from pathetic manipulations to down right disgusting threats, BUT they achieved HIS goals and he created a huge power base. Right now, organizations across the country are coming together to picket and protest Obama socialization. These organizations are getting attention, they are gaining momentum, and gaining membership. Many however are failing to achieve anything more than increased numbers. Success for them can only come if politicians take their numbers and anger into account and reverse their support for ObamaCare, mass takeovers of industries, and half hearted attempts at securing Americas safety. These organizations, in addition to showing force in the streets should use their numbers to fill local government and precinct committees with conservatives. In this way they are still showing force on a national level, but effecting real lasting change as well.

An organization doesn't have to be a huge global enterprise in order to have power. Some of the most effective organizations dominate their neighborhoods and effect positive changes, gaining local media attention while achieving localized goals. Positive changes in neighborhoods also acts as an education force in an area that may have suffered the indoctrination of liberals or radical racists. While we can't expect power changes from the top down, we also can't wait around for those in national positions of power to help our neighborhoods.

Creating a Mission

No organization can succeed if it doesn't have a goal or mission. Many Americans, angry and frustrated with the politicians currently in power and terrified at the rapid descent into socialism are looking to regain control by joining or starting organizations. It is essential that the organization has a clearly defined mission or goal. What do you realistically want this organization to achieve? If you aren't certain what you want to achieve, look around your community and identify issues that you feel could benefit from your championship. Some organizations focus on specific national issues such as pro-life or flat tax amendments. Others concentrate on local improvement or issues such as saving religious historical statues and artwork from county land when liberal groups demand the removal of a cross or the Ten Commandments on court house lawns, ending liberal indoctrination of public school children, or even cleaning up a community.

No matter what your goal, you should create a mission statement or a plan that outlines those goals. This will help insure that you don't get distracted. It also gives your organization a clear purpose. The difference between a successful organization and one that falls apart due to apathy comes down to actions. If the goal of your organization is too large or too abstract, people will have difficulty staying excited and motivated. So a goal such as "get rid of Obama" sounds nice, an achievable set of goals might be: 1) To Promote Christmas as a Christian Holiday; 2) To support the historic nativity scenes; 3) To influence shops to use the term Christmas; 4) fill precinct seats with conservatives.

In this way there are clear cut goals that have immediate effect. Communities whose nativity scenes have come under fire from atheists groups and liberals could certainly use an active organization supporting their continued existence. Christmas is a Christian holiday, celebrating the birth of Christ. While other groups have co-opted it into non-denomination specific celebrations, the holiday is at its core a Christian holiday. We don't require other religious groups to change their sacred days to accommodate non-believers. We shouldn't be forced to do so either. By establishing this as a goal it will be easier for people to brainstorm ideas on how to achieve the goal. No matter what the mission however, ALL conservative organizations MUST include the goal of procuring or filling Precinct Committee seats. Not only do these seats control power at the state and national levels, they are the ones who deal with local issues such as removing the Nativity Scene from parks and court house lawns.

Creating A Structure

Organizations work well if there is a structure and individuals are responsible for tasks that they enjoy. You want your organization to provide some fun, but also be inspiring. If you try and do everything yourself or you assign roles to people who can't or don't want to do them, you are setting yourself up to fail. An organization at minimum needs a person who will handle press and update web sites, a person who will handle fund raising, a person who will organize activities and events, and a person who will contact members and volunteers. Some of these roles can double up, but as your organization grows, having separate people in charge of each area will make things much easier.

Don't assign people roles just because they want to do them. The guy who can't balance his checkbook or is always begging money from you is NOT the best person to assign as treasurer or to handle fund raising. The guy who can't spell or who tends to get angry easily is not a great choice for dealing with the press. Clearly, someone who is disorganized won't make a good event organizer. So think. You want your organization to be a success, so pick the best people for the jobs.

Gaining Momentum

An organization goes from an idea to a force by gaining momentum, membership, and publicity. How do you get momentum? Where do you find members? Think about your mission and potential members will be easy to find.

If your goal is to remove liberal doctrine from the public schools:

- join the PTA
- appeal to parents directly
- contact church groups who may put information about your group into a church bulletin or newsletter
- contact your local newspaper or television station

If your goal is to protect Christmas as a Christian holiday your first stop should be churches and religious organizations.

Once you have members, you need an activity to start your organization on the road to success. If your organization wants to halt liberal indoctrination of school children, you might sponsor a get together where parents bring their children's school work, books, and handouts to identify liberal propaganda. Not only will this solidify your organization, it will also give you information. It is much more effective to be able to say, "We object to Mrs. Smith's 3rd grade class being forced to sing Obama my Savior" than to simply say "We object to liberal indoctrination."

Your activity doesn't have to be obviously linked to your mission. Many organizations use interim events to promote their activities and raise money. Bakes sales, donation drives, even community clean-ups can all be used as positive promotional events that tie in with your organization. One of the most important points to remember in gaining momentum is to make the activities enjoyable for members. People won't want to be involved if the entire organization becomes negative or too preachy. Make sure that people are having fun and are being recognized for their efforts.

Promote Your Organization

Promotion is one of the most important aspects of an organization's success. Unless people know about your organization, they can't join. Create a web site, start a blog, create a Facebook Group and Meetup Group. Get word online so that people can find you 24 hours a day. Keep your sites updated and informative. Avoid negativity. The goal is to create a conservative, Republican groundswell, not attack Democrats. Remember there are many Democrats who believe in conservative values, they have simply been indoctrinated to believe that they "belong" to the Democrat Party. By avoiding negativity, your organization will also be much more appealing to local radio stations, news channels, newspapers, and magazines.

Create a press kit. A press kit is set of promotional materials used to provide the media with information about you and your cause.

A simple press kit will include:

- A paragraph or two about yourself and any other key members of the organization.
- A fact sheet providing bullet points that list goals, statistics, why people should join.

- High quality images of your logo, flyers, posters, and photos of your organization in action.
- A press release outlining current organization news, events, and recent successes.
- A contact point. How do you want the media to contact you if they want to run a story or get a comment on an activity.

It is a great idea to promote your organization with pamphlets that inform the public about your goals, but also about the role of the Republican Party. Many people, jaded by politics, indoctrinated by liberals, or disgusted by the diversions of Republicans over the past decade won't listen to you. But they will often take literature, read through it and if it is well written and provides information where they can verify facts about the conservatives and Republicans for themselves, may be swayed to at least investigate voting Republican in the future.

Connecting With Other Groups

Networking is the name of the game. People who are active in one area are more likely to be active in others. Reach out to other local organizations and invite them to your events. You can find other conservative organizations through churches, conservative political organizations, business organizations, and of course the local Republican Party offices. Reach out to conservative politicians in your area. Explain your goals and efforts and that your primary mission is to ensure that conservative politicians win elections.

In connecting with other groups, make certain that they understand that your membership is available to help them at their events as well. If a small town group organized to defend Christmas as a Christian holiday combines with another small group removing liberal indoctrination from public schools, the picket line numbers quickly increase. Local press, especially those of liberal leanings may not even cover your event if there are only a handful of people, but if you have many groups coming together to show solidarity, you can get a lot of attention.

Community Relationships

People often get so excited about their organization that they fail to consider their perception in the community. Of course those who don't agree with your position aren't going to appreciate your existence. However, you can run afoul of even those who do support your cause if you stop being a good neighbor. A single sign in your yard, announcing your cause is accepted in all but gated communities. Thirty signs detailing every issue that you have and every grip or concern is not acceptable. It brings down the property value, makes the community look trashy, and impedes on your neighbors enjoyment of their own property. Remember to clean up after yourself after an event or a protest as well. Assign members to be part of a clean up crew if need be, but nothing turns a community off of a cause faster than the perception that they have been disrespected. Leaving garbage, signs, general clutter after your event will be seen as a sign of disrespect.

Most communities are happy to support peaceful protests as it is one of the most fundamental rights of the Constitution. You must remember however, that even those who don't agree with us, even those socialists, those liberals, those anti-Americans have the legal right to peacefully assemble and protest. Don't ruin your own reputation or marginalize the positive work of your group by engaging in negative attacks or disrupting peaceful protests. The real power is in the work that you do and in getting those precinct committee seats filled with conservatives. Yelling at someone is not going to change their opinion, but it may change the community's opinion about you.

- Chapter 7 -

Rules For Republican Radicals

Part of the reason that I wrote this book was to provide conservatives who want to make a difference with information about the methods that Team Obama has used, and continues to use, against us as individuals and against the Republican Party. Without understanding the "game" that Team Obama is playing, without understanding their "Playbook," it is very difficult to launch an effective battle against them. On the following pages, I have addressed the Alinsky methods and how we, as Republicans, can raise both an effective defense against Obama, but more importantly, an offense that pushes back the socialist advances at every governmental level.

Many of the areas in which Team Obama has been effective in striking blows against us are corrected simply by having a written and cohesive party platform, true to conservative values. Many people consider themselves Republicans, because they agree with the classic Republican values of a strong military, small government, and capitalistic economic system. Others may feel that their beliefs fall more in line with the classic Republican views on welfare, immigration, and social programs. But, most of us often don't have the time or energy to investigate past the issues that affect us personally or are confused by actions of a Republican Party that has disconnected from our values. This puts us all at a disadvantage when we are questioned by people who may genuinely want to know more about the Republican Party or when we are attacked about issues outside of our sphere of knowledge. A written, cohesive state and national platform provides stability to the party, an easy to understand point of reference for anyone who wants to understand our goals and ideals, and an effective shield against lies and smear tactics.

Alinsky laid down tactical rules designed to help his "community organizers" build power through manipulating their own people and intimidating, harassing, and ridiculing their opponents. As we have seen, these rules have been most affective when Alinsky's most famous student used them on the American public. However Alinsky's rules are not infallible and can be countered. On the following pages, I have addressed Alinsky's principles in hopes to create a useful Republican playbook.

Learning Lessons from Previous Battles

Sometimes you have to lose a battle to win the war. This is clearly the case today. Had we not lost the last election, we would still be dangerously ignorant of so many things.

- We would have no idea that NO ONE vets a person's credentials in advance, to insure that they are eligible to become President of the United States.

- We would not have a clue that socialist groups like ACORN are given millions and millions of tax payer dollars, using it to fund attacks on American values, socialist takeover bids, anti-American hate campaigns, illegal immigrant and low income housing scams, and tax evasion lessons.

- We wouldn't be aware that much of the news that we hear is nothing more than liberal opinions and propaganda designed to make us think that a socialist system is the best way forward.

- We wouldn't believe that anyone would want to destroy our economy so that they would have an excuse and the ability to remake it into a borderless, socialist state.

- And perhaps most importantly, we wouldn't conceive that so many people right here in this country would want to destroy traditional American values and the American Dream.

But now we do know and must prepare for a war that we can't afford to lose. What would any good military leader do when he or she finds weaknesses in defense systems? Identify the weaknesses, shore them up, and look out for ways that the enemy may attempt to get around the new defenses. We can do no less.

Republican Ethics

Considering the history of politics, it may seem comical to include a segment on ethics in a book about political strategy. For some, like Alinsky and Team Obama, the ends justify almost any means and ethics are simply something with which the "losers" console themselves. But ethics are important. Not only do they provide the foundation upon which to build a conservative, yet thoughtfully progressive country, but ethics provide inspiration to other fledgling democracies which in turn help to keep us safe. Perhaps more importantly, operating an ethical and transparent government helps to insure full citizen participation, important in maintaining a strong, proud, and free democracy.

But let us not kid ourselves, if a person's spiritual or religious beliefs insured that they acted in an ethical and moral manner in all things, politics wouldn't be a hotbed of intrigue and scandal. But it is. The threat of fire and brimstone has rarely been enough of a deterrent to keep men (and women) from sexual indiscretions, financial double dealing, drugs, alcohol, gambling and every other form of vice. Perhaps it is simply a quirk of human nature. Fear of getting "caught" by a spouse or answering for your sins in the after life simply isn't enough motivation to keep most people on the straight and narrow.

The temptations that swirl around politics must be intoxicating and perhaps in the days before mobile phone cameras, Twitter, computer hacking and all the other forms of electrical surveillance available today, ethical violations could be swept more easily under the carpet. But today's politicians have to understand that they are watched, filmed, recorded, and monitored (as are we all) virtually 24 hours a day, 7 days a week. A person can no longer "get away with" acting in an unethical manner. Even if their own moral compass doesn't compel ethical behavior, today it is simply a matter of self preservation.

Politicians that choose to act in an unethical manner, whether it is in the political arena or in their private life, put all Americans at risk. Those who act in an unethical manner in their professional lives undermine the entire political system. How can the government expect Joe Public to pay his taxes, especially in a fragile economy, when our elected officials finagle the system to avoid paying their taxes? How can we be expected to trust in a democracy that looks away when those elected to the highest State and National positions, lie, cheat, steal, often from their own constituents?

Politicians who act in an unethical manner in their personal lives can be even more dangerous. Personally, I don't particularly care what consenting adults do behind closed doors and I certainly don't want "bedroom police." In a perfect world, the private lives and the public lives of politicians might be separate issues. But this isn't a perfect world. Politicians who have "dirty secrets" have greatly increased exposure to blackmail or pressure to act in a way counter to their constituent's wishes. Of course there is also the issue of time and money. Politicians who are off gallivanting around when they are supposed to be voting on bills, reading proposed bills, meeting with constituents, and generally doing their job, put us all at risk. They are being paid to protect our interests and act as our representatives in the government. If they don't bother to turn up, we don't have a voice and we don't have any control. Governors Eliot Spitzer and Jim Sanford have both allegedly used public money (tens of thousands of dollars) to fund their extra marital affairs. When you consider that the amount of money Spitzer allegedly spent on prostitutes could have provided grade schools with computers or supported school music and arts programs or that the money Sanford allegedly spent on private jets back and forth to Columbia to visit his mistress would have paid for the physical therapy for dozens of wounded soldiers it is easy to see that their unethical acts ARE our business.

Exposure of their misdeeds also robs from those who gave them their lofty positions. As voters, we select a candidate whom we feel best represents the needs of our state or country. We support these people with campaign contributions, time and energy, and help to propel them throughout their career. Scandal often results in the disgraced politician being forced to resign his or her spot, only to be replaced by someone who does not represent our values. The disgraced politician has robbed us, not only of the money and time that we have invested, but of the political power that we have won.

However, we have to be ethical in our dictates on ethics. We can't condemn unethical behavior from our opponents, while turning a blind eye to the misdeeds done in our own party. Our representatives have to understand that unethical behavior will not be tolerated, no matter how high up the ladder they climb. In today's electronic surveillance world, their misdeeds will be discovered. Without requiring that those who represent us do so in an ethical manner, we have no one to blame but ourselves when they lie, cheat, steal, and don't do the job for which they have been hired.

Identifying the Enemy

While it may seem like common sense, before you can engage in any battle, you must be able to identify the enemy. This is not always as straight forward as it may seem. In politics, the enemy has always seemed to be voters of the opposing party. It is easy to blame the "dumb" voters of the other side since their votes result in the election of opposition representatives. Republicans largely see all Democrats as ultra-liberal, "bleeding hearts" who want to save the world on Middle America's tax dime and forgive all crime committed by the poor or emotionally damaged because "it's society's fault." Democrats see all Republicans as ultra-conservative, rich, old, white, religious nuts who want to inject themselves into the personal lives of citizens by mandating religion, sexuality, and procreation. And so it seems that our enemies are easy to identify. As a Republican, Democrats MUST be my enemy. Right? Wrong.

For decades, we have been taught that the Democrats are our enemies. The fact is, the majority of Americans hold a rather centrist view of the role of government, but fall slightly to the right or left on social issues. It is the minority of people who are actually ultra-liberal or ultra-conservative. However, in the Democratic Party, it is that very minority of ultra-liberals who are in power. This is an important distinction.

✪   Democrats are NOT the enemy. Specific members of the Democratic Party leadership ARE the enemy.

214

One of the most effective ways in which the Democratic leaders have gained new voters and increased campaign contributions is through misinformation. While painting their party as "mainstream," despite their true agenda being dramatically socialist (just look at the voting records of the likes of Obama and Pelosi), they have effectively painted the Republican Party as far right, suggesting that those of the very fringe of conservatism are a representative sample of all Republicans. New voters, largely at odds with the extreme right, feel that they have no choice but to vote Democrat or risk supporting something that the Democrat Party leadership assures them is akin to Nazism. Since as a political party, we have not effectively countered the label of "right-wing extremist," we can hardly be surprised when naïve voters are sucked into the Democrat's "army" largely by default.

✪   **The lack of a clear Republican Party platform is the enemy.**

If I was hired by Company A to sell a particular brand of tires, but I spent all my time talking about how bad Company A's tires are and suggesting that customers instead go by tires from Company B (who is secretly paying me a commission on the side), as soon as my deception was discovered, I would be out of a job. PERIOD. Yet in the Republican Party, people who have been hired to manage and promote conservative policy and positions, but instead vote for ultra-liberal positions, detrimental to the Republican Party, are routinely kept on board, for years (sometimes decades), while they continue to receive millions of dollars in salaries, funding, and kickbacks. With the finite number of seats available, these traitors also prevent someone who would champion conservative positions from taking the seat and doing the job properly.

There is no way to motivate conservative voter participation if the GOP continues to reward RINOs (Republicans in Name Only) with job security. There is a difference between a Republican who can't support a particular bill because of it's wording and those who continually side against conservative values and pro-American policies. The current party position of keeping a RINO in power simply to insure that the seat is occupied by someone who calls themselves a Republican is completely ridiculous. If he or she isn't voting

✪　　**RINOs must be removed from the party. PERIOD They are the enemy.**

In Alinsky's thirteenth rule, he counseled "community organizers" to; "Pick the target, freeze it, personalize it, and polarize it." He suggested finding a person with some degree of power within an organization, who was most likely to be intimidated and attack him or her. Actual blame was largely irrelevant as long as the target could be somehow connected to the issue. But selecting a target based on their perceived weakness, despite responsibility for a problem is unethical and disingenuous. It can backfire, lending public sympathy to the "underdog." It also doesn't solve the problem. It is essential that as Republicans we understand the issues, address the actual problem (not the distractions and diversions that politicians often place in the way), and hold accountable the people responsible.

When Nancy Pelosi declares herself "the most powerful woman in America" SHE is the enemy. When Barack Obama bankrupts our country to payback his political supporters or bows down to foreign dictators, apologizing for America, HE is the enemy. When Barney Frank opposes the Respect For Fallen Heroes Act, He is the enemy. When Chris Mathews uses his news program to express his opinions and pretends that those opinions are facts, HE is the enemy. Assigning blame to the entire party,

State, or industry doesn't solve the problem and acts to further push potential voters away. I believe that there are many people, currently registered with the Democratic Party who, if they were made aware of the true Republican platform, would find that they actually have Republican values. Further, if more people were aware of the actual issues and knew the authors of many of our disasters, they would be able to better judge the anti-American activities of some of those in power in the Democrat Party for themselves.

But, we can't afford to be hypocritical. Those within our own party must be held accountable for their misdeeds as well. We will never have a government that is by the people and for the people if those in power don't feel accountable to the people.

✪ **The actual "author of the disaster" is the enemy, NOT the party as a whole.**

The last chapter of this book, "Know Thy Enemy" details people who have been "authors of disaster" and are clear enemies of both the conservative Republican Party and a free, proud, America.

Dissecting Democrat Power

Team Obama used Alinsky's first rule, "Power is not only what you have, but what the enemy thinks that you have" to excellent advantage. Their "army" looked huge thanks to continual release of astronomic "hit rates" on their web sites, campaign contributions, and increased voter registration numbers. This was demoralizing to both Republican voters and to the GOP. Many, strapped for cash in this economy simply felt that they could ill afford to donate money to a losing party, hindering Republican efforts. The mass show of strength also attracted many independent voters. Psychologically people want to be on the "winning" side and Obama's press machine insinuated that a landslide was eminent.

But, when the glitter and paint was washed away, it was easy to see that much of the Team Obama "army" consisted of manipulated "hit rates" and allegedly fraudulent voter registrations and illegal foreign investors. As Republicans, we allowed ourselves to be sucked in and demoralized by smoke and mirrors.

✪ **Ignore the distractions of huge shows of force, they are usually smoke and mirrors.**

On the subject of frauds, illegal activities, and legal maneuvering, arguably no previous candidate has used the power of the legal system and knowledge of Constitutional loopholes to greater advantage. Whether it was using the courts to block University transcripts and birth certificate demands or green-light on-the-spot, no-id-needed, voter registration, Team Obama has made preemptive strikes against the American public's right to know and be protected. As Republicans and as Americans we need to understand that this is a tactic that will not go away. Battles will be won and lost without the public ever knowing the truth unless these loops holes are plugged, and clear, concise rules concerning public disclosure, qualification, and identification requirements are established and mandated by law. We must be prepared to shut down any attempts at legal trickery as a means of denying the public access to essential information.

✪ **We must plug up loopholes and be prepared for legal shenanigans and manipulations.**

Much of the power of the DNC lies in fear mongering. By painting a picture of Republicans as gun toting, racists the DNC has successfully been able to consolidate a large number of minority voters and groups under the Democrat umbrella. Republican policies and values favor a diverse ethnic Middle Class and our policies are designed to insure that people can easily and quickly assimilate, becoming valuable, self sufficient, members of America. Democrat policies keep people on welfare for generations, segregated thanks to a ban on a national language, and unwilling to assimilate into society. Yet their branding of us has been very successful.

The DNC has also been very successful in scaring women into voting against Republican policies primarily due to reproductive rights and military issues. This vision of Republicans as old men who want all women to be married, barefoot, and pregnant while all young men should be out killing someone is ridiculous and insulting, yet core to the DNC fight against us. And sadly, they have been able to convince an entire generation of women to vote the Democrat ticket. No where was this more obvious than in the attacks against Sarah Palin. In Sarah we have a modern, working mother, who is successful and driven in her career, while maintaining a loving family and home. She should be the "poster child" to the modern American woman, yet she is annihilated by women because of her personal feelings about abortion. The completely erroneous concept that Sarah, as Vice President, would have the power (or desire) to ban abortion and sexual education across the country was created and disseminated by the DNC through the media. Obama's jaw dropping, support of partial birth abortions was completely ignored by the press. While Sarah's personal views on abortion were expanded, twisted, and pulled all out of proportion, until the DNC claimed that a vote for Sarah would equal a vote for forcing an impregnated, pre-teen victim of a pedophile in to have a baby.

Obviously, since the DNC has been so effective in smearing Republicans and lying about Republican positions, they will continue to use this as their major weapon. But understanding why they have been so successful in disseminating misinformation is an essential component to ending it's usefulness as a tactic against us. The DNC have been successful in their endeavor to villainize Republicans due to media collusion, adherence to predictable responses, and visual branding.

There is little that we can do to prevent the DNC from using the liberal media to their advantage, despite their efforts to terminate conservative media outlets. But, while it seems like an oxymoron at the moment, journalism is supposed to be a respected profession in which the impartial truth about an issue or situation is revealed. In many cases in print and televised media, impartial "journalism" has simply been replaced by vitriolic opinion. Opinion is an important part of democracy. Without my ability to write my opinions, you wouldn't be able to read this book. I believe that thoughtful opinions, even those with which I disagree, are an essential component to democracy, but people must easily be able to recognize the difference between opinion shows masquerading as news and actual news shows. Sadly, thanks to format changes and subtle manipulations, there is seemingly little to differentiate between the two. This of course means that opinions or manufactured opinions designed to startle, inflame, or titillate, are being spread as statements of fact. As long as this is allowed to continue unchecked, real newsworthy items, such an Obama's support of partial birth abortions will be ignored in favor of the sort of made-up, headline grabbing opinions that ultimately helped to derail the McCain/Palin ticket.

✪ **We must insure that news sources are impartial and factual and opinion shows are clearly marketed as such.**

As a child, I was taught that if you can't say something nice about someone, don't say anything at all. I was told that it is best to ignore rumors and lies, since addressing them only gives them credibility. I was schooled to use appropriate, courteous behavior in public, that no one likes a liar or braggart, and perhaps most importantly, that cheaters never prosper. It's clear that my parents were NOT involved in politics when I was a child. Like me, Republicans (and many Democrat voters) adhere to these old rules of decorum and behavior. On the political scene however, this has sometimes been to our detriment. Our predictable response to attacks, lies, smears, and unethical behavior has been, no response.

When Tim Wilson blurted out "you lie" as Obama claimed that illegal immigrants would not be given free medical care under his proposed health care bill, Republicans (and Wilson himself) were shocked at the breech of decorum. Nancy Pelosi, Jim Clyburn (D SC), and Steny Hoyer (D Md) swung into overdrive, attacking Wilson, branding him a racist, and lobbying to sanction him. Eternally attention seeking, Jimmy Carter denounced Wilson and the entire Republican party as racists. However, it was clear that Wilson simply blurted out the words in shock at what was being said. Now lets compare Wilson's shocked utterance to the unchallenged behavior of scores of Democrats who hooted, hissed, and booed at President George Bush during his State of the Union address in 2005. Or the cheers of Pelosi et al for the Iraqi who pelted Bush with a shoe. Or the praise of Democrats when Senator Jim Webb announced that he felt like "punching President Bush." Wilson clearly suffered a breech of etiquette, but because Republicans have been hesitant to challenge bad behavior in opponents, when party members complained at the opportunist, over-the-top, disingenuous attack against Wilson, they came off sounding like scolded school kids moaning "well Jimmy did it too."

Republicans have been lax in attacking lies and smears, pointing our inconsistencies or flip flops, laying blame where it belongs, addressing ethics and professional behavior breeches, and pointing out cheaters. A degree of this is self preservation, a

221

politician doesn't want to go on record pointing out the lies or inconsistencies in a fellow politician if they fear that someone will turn around and point a finger back. A lot of it comes down to fear of the "R" word. No one wants to be branded a racist. It is virtually impossible to challenge a black politician or a policy that would disproportionately benefit blacks or the poor without being called a racist. The rest comes down to professional etiquette. Wilson may have uttered "you lie" while Obama was lying, but where is the Democrat etiquette police when one of their own, Alan Greyson Rep from Florida, calls a colleague a "whore" on national television?

I don't advocate Republicans taking their etiquette cues from Pelosi, Rangel, or Greyson. But we do need to play offense when it comes to professional standards of behavior and ethics. Our Representatives can't effectively represent us if they can't play on an even playing field and simply reacting like scolded, school children is not enough. If that means that they need to set Ms. Manners aside for a moment to call out a colleague who is not acting in a professional manner, then that is what they must do. If they face being called a racist for standing up for what is right, so be it. If they need to point out that an opponent is lying or trying to hide their own complacency in a problem, then that is exactly what I want to see them doing.

✪ **Republicans must set aside the etiquette book from time to time and respond to lies, smears, unethical behavior, and attacks fiercely and immediately.**

Visual branding is an extremely effective way of relaying a message, without actually saying anything verbally. By creating hundreds of mini-commercials, both supporting DNC positions and candidates, as well as those designed to malign the GOP, the DNC was able to subtly show through actors, that they are a party that embraces immigrants, ethnic and religious minorities, gays and lesbians, students, poor people, working class people, and families while portraying Republicans as John McCain, old, rich, and white. People new to the voting process or undecided, who see commercials or videos that show other people who are similar in look or beliefs, are naturally drawn to that party. By the same token, showing the Republicans as ONLY rich, old, white, men naturally puts up a barrier between the potential voter and the party who they feel doesn't represent them.

The fact that Republicans can be found in every ethnic, religious, sexual, and socio-economic group in the country is not evident to the general public. We have not done an effective job of reaching voters, partly because we continue to produce 1980's style full length commercials that say little visually or verbally. We have also missed the very photo opportunities that we need to insure that our brand is always in the headlines in a positive way. While we decried Obama as a fame seeker, more interested in the posing for the camera than for actually meeting troops, or answering question in town hall meetings, Obama's "photo ops" provided the media with a constant stream of positive stories and photos that they could use to push his campaign.

✪ **We must embrace visual opportunities that celebrate and promote the diversity of our party.**

The Republican Base

Over the past ten years, the Republican Party has lost cohesion. Many, for whom fiscal responsibility is key component to the Republican Party, left during the spending free-for-alls under Gorge Bush. Others who felt that the government should take a strong and immediate stand against illegal immigration left due to wishy-washy immigration policies. Still others refused to back John McCain as a Presidential candidate because of his very liberal stand on many key conservative issues. Potentially, millions of conservative Americans feel that the Republican Party has abandoned them, and so they simply didn't vote at all or voted for "hope" and "change." They have wandered away from the Party, but not the values and beliefs.

But, these wandering Republicans are not lost. As the Republican Party sets itself right and returns to the conservative values and core beliefs that inspire millions of Americans, many of those disenfranchised will return. Creating and publicizing our conservative state, and national platforms will help pull these voters back on board.

✪ **"Wandering" Republicans will return when they see that the Party returned to its conservative roots and goals.**

Many Republicans are disheartened. We look around our community and wonder where the work ethic, values, manners, and common sense have gone. We see crime, low graduation levels in schools, closed businesses, jobless figures rising, houses in foreclosure, parks and roads falling into states of disrepair all the while Congress shoves their hands deeper into our pockets for even more tax dollars to fund their favorite pet projects (swine odor and manure management, grape genetics studies, a tattoo removal clinic, etc.[75]), unnecessarily bailouts, and personal salary increases. For many, the trials and tribulations of Washington seem very far removed from the problems faced daily and they see no way of connecting the two. Voters from both parties frequently bemoan the quality of candidates from which they can choose at the national elections. Most of us have forgotten that like charity, politics begins at home.

---

[75] Morris, Dick "Catastrophe"

As Republicans, we should be as familiar (if not more so) with our local representatives as we are with national figures. While it is true that our national representative vote on matters of national importance, our local politicians help to steer local projects, determine city planning issues, and deal with the problems that face our communities. Not only can we help to shape our local future through political involvement, we have access to the very people who will be the next wave of state and national politicians. Insuring that they are ethical and driven by Republican values on a local level helps to insure that we don't get nasty RINO surprises in the future. People who are involved feel empowered.

✪ **We must embrace politics on a local level, both as a means to improve our community and as a way to guide the future of the party.**

Politicians are known to be "big talkers" full of ideas and promises, but often short on results. This disheartens the electorate and gives the impression that politicians either are unable or disinterested in working for their constituents. Republicans must become better at "tooting their own horn." This is another aspect of politics that is often counter to the acceptable standards of behavior learned as a child or to conduct considered professional in other industries. Many of us were taught that being a braggart was incredibly distasteful and that people who engaged in such boorish behavior should be avoided at all costs.

But, it is time that Republicans embrace positive promotion. I want to know when my city council rep. proposes legislation that will benefit my school district. I want to hear about it when my Senator helps to reform the electoral process making voting more secure. I want to know when my Congressman is instrumental in landing a contract that will bring jobs to my state.

Above all, I want to know when Republicans make positive contributions to my community, state, and my life. But, these issues and successes are not adequately promoted. Without adequate promotion, many in the general public never hear the names of those Republicans who are hard at work attempting to make our lives better. Voters respond to politicians who have proven and public track records of adhering to and promoting Republican values and beliefs.

✪ **Our base is empowered when they know the names of Republican representative at all levels and are aware of the successes that these people achieve on their constituents behalf.**

While the liberal media would have you believe that Republicans are all "fire and brimstone" Puritans, the Republican Party is not represented only by religious zealots. In fact, many Republicans are conservative centrist in their beliefs but tend to lean farther right on issues key to their family, such as military support, immigration reform, and social issues. Others find themselves squarely conservative on financial and security issues but lean a bit left on some social issues. Perhaps no social issue has been more widely used and abused by the liberals to drive a wedge between independent voters and Republicans or indeed between centrist Republicans and their far-right brethren, than the abortion debate.

When John McCain was announced as the front runner in the Republican primaries, many conservatives denounced him as being too liberal to support, refusing to vote rather than vote for someone who didn't meet their criteria. The so called Republican "fringe," who fall to the far right on social issues, generally on religious grounds, is a powerful force. This power was recognized recently by liberal media pendants who suggested that Republicans (meaning the centrist) should break with "fringe"

Republicans and join the Democrats. Clearly when the liberals start trying to divide the Republican Party, there is concern over the power of a more united GOP.

While this is completely understandable in principle to abstain from supporting the party nominee, it is short sighted in practice, resulting in a President that is unacceptable in ALL areas rather than one that is unacceptable in one area. Much like the couple who fantasize about all the things that they will do once they retire, but never save a dime towards retirement, refusing to back the Republican nominee simply because he or she may not support a single issue guarantees a failure. Those who refused to support McCain for fear that he was "all talk" on abortion and would not support actual legislation banning abortion, instead got a President who not only supports abortions and sends large chunks of tax payer money to fund abortions worldwide, but favors partial birth abortions.

Republicans of all beliefs need to remember that before we can even discuss the contentious social issues, we have to win the elections. Putting aside the issues that divide us, until a time when we are in power and can address these issues legitimately and practically is essential to Republican success.

✪   **"Fringe" Republicans must unite under a conservative GOP umbrella to insure victory. Their issues can only be addressed IF Republicans are in power.**

By the same token, many moderate Republicans fell prey to the scare tactics of Team Obama who insinuated that supporting the GOP ticket would insure a "morality police" state. Republicans who support pro-choice, same sex partnerships, or other contentious social issues were targeted by Democrats who claimed that their liberal position on social issues made them out of step with ultra-conservatives Republicans. Pro-choice,

Republican women in particular were targeted in a fear campaign using Sarah Palin's personal views on abortion and extrapolating that into an imagined national policy. The vitriol against Palin, particularly from women, centered on the media reports that Palin would force her own daughter to carry a baby to term in the event of rape. But, Palin hadn't suggested that her own feelings on the issue would dictate policy or that even if elected, she would have any power to effect a national legal change. This didn't stop the media from whipping up an anti-Palin frenzy. It also didn't prevent some Republicans from taking the bait and voting for Obama out of fear.

✪   **Providing a clear voting record for all candidates will help combat scare tactic attacks on the GOP. It will also remind voters that a candidate's job is to vote the will of constituents, not necessarily their personal beliefs.**

Expanding The Republican Base

In order to maintain power, a political party needs to be able to both maintain their core voter base and attract new voters. Due largely to a lack of clear values and stated platforms and coupled with a very effective smear campaign on behalf of Team Obama, the Republicans have failed not only to keep core demographics, they have not reached out to potential new members in an effective way.

Some statistics suggest that the number of people who classify themselves as "independent" voters is growing. Disenfranchised with major party politics, unclear of the real differences between parties, and general apathy towards career politicians, many independent voters want to take part in the process, but aren't certain that their vote matters. Whether these voters are true "middle-of-the-road" voters who simply want to wait and see which candidate from either party is most appealing to them or they don't find that either party truly represents their values and beliefs; winning over independent voters is key. But we can't wait until a hotly contested campaign to reach out.

In the 2008 election, many independent voters ultimately went with team Obama. For some, it was a matter of Obama's pitch being delivered more effectively. For others, fear of the media created ultra-radical right future drove them to Obama. Others simply chose the glitz and glamour of superstar Obama. And can we really blame them? If, as a voter, you have no idea of either candidate's positions or platforms, it simply comes down to a popularity contest. Obama seemed cool, confident, young, vital, and loved by millions around the globe. McCain seemed old and tired.

Obama's platform of "transparent" government really hit home with voters across the board. That he abandoned that policy the second he was elected is another matter, but the fact remains that people want a transparent political system. People want to be able to easily understand the political platform of both the party and the individual politician. They want to be able to quickly see the voting record of a candidate so that they can evaluate if he or she truly votes the will of the constituents. People want to be able to find out if a candidate has been in trouble or has conducted him or herself in an honorable way. There are few things more disheartening to voters than to find out too late that the person for whom they cast their vote, lied.

✪ **We must demand clear and concise platforms, positions, voting records, and bios, including any rules or ethics violations, of all politicians.**

Waiting until a tight election race to court independent voters is akin to calling for a date at 11 o'clock at night. Everybody

229

knows that you only want one thing.… Independent voters must be made to feel welcome and informed all year long, not just used for their vote at the last minute. This can be achieved largely through internet information and marketing.

The GOP web site should be an easy to understand and navigate portal which connects easily to the sites of each state and local party site as well as to the sites of all Republican politicians. Sites should be informative and convey a friendly professional tone. Each party site should provide a clear party platform, list and links to all Republican politicians in their jurisdiction, and information about the unique issues facing the state or area. Each politician's site should provide the party platform as well as their voting record, personal project goals and biography.

Today, people feel that they "know" someone who they frequently see on television. Politicians, especially at a state or local level rarely have the opportunity to create a connection with the voting public in a meaningful way. Video clips, podcasts, and interviews, filmed and posted on the politician's personal site as well as the state or local party sites are great ways to help people become familiar with a politician, feel connected, and be informed. When they feel connected, they continue to support.

E-newsletters are also a great way to stay connected to voters. Friendly and casual in tone, e-newsletters let people know what issues are being considered and what matters are up for debate as well as the successes and failures of local politicians. This type of medium is non-intrusive, people sign up for the newsletter, but can choose whether or not to read the newsletter. Since few people know when city council meetings take place or in fact what issues are before the council, e-newsletters inspire people to become involved in the political process.

The current GOP web site is completely reactionary, attempting to respond the smear tactic, Democrat claims. This is not effective and is in fact counter productive. We can't win this battle playing defense, we have to get out in front of the curve, provide information in a friendly and professional way, and let people investigate claims and make decisions for themselves. In a technology driven world, the Republican Party can't be seen as conservatively progressive or in touch if they can't get the message out to voters, in familiar ways. Modern voters want to pick and choose access through the internet, but want informative, non- propaganda filled mediums.

✪ **Republicans must stop being reactionary with their internet sites and messages and must instead provide a positive, easy to understand, informative internet based experience.**

America was built on legal immigration. People from around the world passed through Ellis Island and hoped that they would be approved for entry. Desperate to start a new life in the new world, many arrived with little more than the clothes on their backs and the desire to be Americans. These legal immigrants worked night and day and slept in cramped, dirty slums until they could get on their feet and make a better life for themselves and their families. Today legal immigrants still come to this country eager to become a part of the American Dream. Over 1 million were naturalized as US citizens last year. They are hard working, ambitious, and desperate to assimilate into American society. Most come from oppressive countries, heavily taxed, and micro-managed. The want limited government intervention. They believe in a free market system. Many possess the conservative values of strong family, education, and spiritual devotion. They embody the very principles upon which the country was founded. Yet they are not embraced by the Republican Party. The

Democrats take full advantage of this painting Republicans as racists and white supremacist eager to oust all immigrants.

The illegal immigration debate doesn't help our cause with legal immigrants either, though it should. Establishing a clear platform on immigration, including both our opposition to illegal immigration and support of legal immigrant is a start. But we must go further, explaining how illegal immigration hurts all Americans including legal immigrants. Until the immigrant community can see that we differentiate between those here legally, who we embrace, and those here illegally, we will be unsuccessful in reaching these patriotic, new Americans.

Republicans are missing a valuable opportunity. Legal immigrants are excited about participating in the political process. They vote, they get involved, and they encourage conservative American values in their children. Failing to reach out to these new Americans is a huge mistake with long term consequences, not only for the party but for America as a whole.

✪ **We must reach out to legal immigrants, assuring them that the principles that they came to America to find are alive and well in the Republican Party.**

Despite Team Obama throwing millions of dollars at the "youth vote," only an estimated 52% of people under 25 actually cast a vote. This number is not historical at all, as it mirrors the percentage of youth who turned out of the 1992 election. The major difference however was that large numbers of young people who identified themselves as Republicans still voted for Obama, who carried roughly 67% of all votes for those under 25. There is speculation that McCain's age was a factor. Obama's "coolness" was also sited. But two trends emerged as significant. In exit polls, only 4% of the respondents said that McCain's campaign reached out to them in any way, where 16% of Obama supporters stated that they had been contacted by Team Obama. And more telling, 69% of all voters under 25 felt that Obama was "in touch" with people like themselves.[76]

Clearly it is impossible to be all things to all people. But Team Obama did a much better job of providing voters with a reason to cast their vote for him. His team connected with these voters, addressed their issues, and engaged them in the voting process better than any previous Presidential candidate. He rode to the White House largely on a tide of young voters, in some states, these voters made the difference between his success or failure.

While a huge percentage of young people claimed in the exit poll that race was a factor in their choice for Obama, the win can't be explained away on the race factor alone, considering that white and latino youth overwhelmingly supported Obama as well, even when they considered themselves Republican. Clearly the Republican Party has failed not only to engage potential young voters, they have failed to engage young Republicans.

It all comes down to issues and packaging. While most demographics share common issues, the way that they are engaged and motivated may differ. Everyone may be concerned about the economy, but young college students will be particular concerned about student loans, loan defaults, entry level jobs, and economic factors particular to those just starting out in a professional or white collar career. They may be moderately interested in the challenges facing the over 65's but they won't be motivated by those issues alone. By the same token, the young, non-college educated voter will have different issues than their college student/graduate voting block. Minimum wages, apprenticeships and skills based training, shrinking domestic

---

[76] www.civicyouth.org

factory and farming output, child care, and other issues facing young people just starting out in blue collar professions will be of import to them.

Simply lumping all those under 30 into a single demographic and then largely ignoring them on the basis that they probably won't show up to vote is a tried and failed method. Not only do Republican candidates need their votes now, Republicans have a valuable opportunity to insure that the conservative values and beliefs that many already hold are nurtured and encouraged by the political process. So many young people have had years of ultra-liberal indoctrination thanks to extremist, anti-American "educators" such as Ward Churchill (who equated the victims of the World Trade Center disaster to Holocaust organizer Adolf Eichmann) and Cornel West (who blames problems in black society on white supremacist), the likes of which can be found in many Universities. Reaching out and giving young people a rational option is essential to prevent the continual socialization and moral decline of our country.

✪ **Republicans must actively and effectively engage young voters, both for votes today and for their lifelong political commitment.**

Team Obama very effectively branded the Republican Party as the party of rich, old, white, men. The GOP did little to challenge that image. In a time when, according to the census bureau, just over 50% of voters are female, roughly 34% are minorities, and a full 84% of people are considered middle class, or poor, allowing that brand to stick was and is political suicide. It is impossible to engage people, connect with people, or get them onside if they don't believe that you respect them or have their interests at heart.

Despite Republican superstars like Sarah Palin, Michael Steele, and Bobby Jindhal being well known in their own areas, prior to the election campaign, they were largely unknown by a national general public, even among Republicans. It was therefore tough for their eruption onto the national stage to seem like anything other than reactionary, half-hearted attempts to appeal to female and minority voters. Attempting to explain their decades of political service, after the national media and Team Obama had branded them as little more than tokens of appeasement put the GOP once again on the defensive and alienated independents and conservative democrats alike.

The Republican Party must do a better job of promoting not only the diversity of the voters whom they represent, but the diversity of the local and state level politicians who work hard supporting conservative policy. Increasing the public profiles of all Republican politicians must be a year round exercise, not simply a campaign after thought. By refusing to challenge the notion that we as a party are the party of only the "rich, old, white, man" we devalue the tremendous contributions of the majority of our members who are middle class and working class Americans. It devalues the young, the female, and the minority members and politicians who are dedicated to preserving conservative principles.

It should not be forgotten that this characteristic of Republicans as being "rich, old, white, men" was used as an insult. Are successful Americans and their families to be penalized simply because they have been able to achieve the American Dream? Only in the eyes of a socialist would a person's hard work and achievement be viewed as a negative. And the elderly? Well we already know what Team Obama thinks of the elderly from his completely unconstitutional health care proposal. Perhaps I am naïve, but I don't see why we can't celebrate the contributions of minorities without degrading the contributions of whites and in particular white men. The Democrat leadership, media, and many liberals seem completely unable to do so.

All of this of course is a Team Obama attempt to hide the fact that the Republican Party was instrumental in the creation and success and of the Civil Rights Movement, counting both Abraham Lincoln and Martin Luther King Jr among it's members. By welcoming those who assimilate into American society, work hard, support themselves, their families, and communities, the Republican Party has always been a guiding force in protecting America's melting pot. Republicans strongly support LEGAL immigration. But for the past decade the Democrat leadership has chosen to omit the word "legal" from its attacks on the GOP, claiming that we are against ALL immigration. This lie has been extrapolated into an anti-minority smear campaign. The Democratic Party as a whole has spent the past 40 plus years creating programs that propagate the cycle of poverty and keep people on welfare and in prison.

✪ **The Republican Party must refuse to accept inaccurate, slanderous labels. Challenging any such branding attempts with quick statistics will end the practice and help to embrace our diverse base.**

Show Me, Don't Just Tell Me

Before you can have effective strategies, you must have clear goals. Once Republicans have adopted clear and concise platforms, have created a brand that accurately represents the party, and have built an internet infrastructure that provides transparent, easy to understand information about the party at all levels and the politicians, it is time to wage war against Team Obama and the other ultra-liberals attempting to destroy our country. But we can't just tell people what we want to do or promise them that things will change under a Republican. People want proof, they want actions not words.

For Republicans to gain any credibility we must do the following:

1) Show the public
2) Inform the public
3) Empower the public.

Show the Public

In this technology driven world, simply telling people what you want them to know is no longer effective. Perhaps this a bi-product of years of being lied to by politicians (from all parties) and manipulated by the media or it may simply be a response to an instant gratification, visual world. Whatever the reason, people want to see what you have done and what you are doing, not just hear promises of what you may do in the future.

But, we can NOT rely on the liberal media to honestly cover our activities. Much like when a tornado hits a community and the media seems to hone in on the least intelligent person in the entire community, "journalists" have a bad habit of selecting a few extreme examples of Republican supporters and attempt to paint us all with the same brush. A brief flip through most mainstream news stations during a Republican protest showcases the point. Minimizing our numbers, maligning our message, and disregarding us, the same people who fabricated a European Obama Love Fest out of rock concert footage can hardly be trusted to give us honest coverage. So we must do it ourselves.

We must record every event, every protest. We must show people that the Republican Party and those who support our message are a diverse group of Americans who simply want to return the country to a responsible path. We must show our numbers. The liberal media suggests that Tea Parties are attended by a handful of disgruntled racists, not the hundreds of thousands of regular Americans frightened of spiraling debt to China, bottomless pits of kick backs and payoffs, the mass socialization of industries, and a foreign policy that sees our men and women vulnerable to the very same dictators to whom Obama is bowing and groveling.

We need to develop creative events, alternative activism, and flash mobs to engage younger Republicans and make visual statements that are easy to record and hard to ignore. Protests are most effective when they make tremendous visual impacts. Think of some of the most successful and memorable protests of the past few decades. Whether it is the sight of hundreds of big rig truck drivers slowly circling Washington to protest the price of gas or a single man standing in front of Chinese tanks in Tiananmen Square, visuals move people to think and to act.

Inform The Public

The days of people sitting patiently while a speaker peppers them with facts are long over. Short attention spans and unprecedented competition with entertainment for people's limited time has created an environment where information must be presented in a brief, fast paced, highly stylized way in order to reach any audience. During the campaign, Republicans lost out on many chances to engage the audience by using overly long monologues and responding to questions with lengthy answers. Today, if you can't master the "sound bite" (brief single sentence statements that fit easily into newscasts) you won't be successful in the public eye.

Republicans have to jump into the 21st century when it comes to information dissemination. Team Obama flooded the internet with commercials, videos, parodies, infomercials, mini-documentaries, and footage of speeches. He benefited from liberal indoctrination documentaries and films by far-left filmmakers such as Michael Moore. His supporters leased time on cable access shows and created "talk shows" to spread his message to the masses. Team Obama embraced visual media, making his message fast to view, easy to pass around, and available world wide 24 hours a day, 7 days a week.

Despite what the liberal media would like us to believe Hollywood is NOT exclusively the land of liberals. There are a lot of conservatives in entertainment and engaging film makers, documentarians, and media makers to create video clips, commercials, documentaries, etc is not difficult. While making a Michael Moore style documentary isn't free, millions of Americans have their own video equipment and editing software (both of which are relatively inexpensive). National, state, and local GOP and conservative groups should be sponsoring commercials and videos with Republican themes. Get people out there making the very thing that we need to spread our message.

As a messenger, the video is king. Think about the ACORN undercover videos. These undercover videos, shot by 20 year old Hannah Giles, a journalism student and journalist James O'Keefe for $1,300 resulted in the agency losing all federal funding, and relationships with the IRS, Planned Parenthood, the US Census, and Bank of America all being terminated. These two people and a video camera saved the American tax payer millions of dollars, and ended Obama's horrific ACORN as census taker plan. People who knew nothing about ACORN were able to understand in the few minutes of video that within the agency employees were advising people how to defraud the government and establish housing for prostitution and child trafficking. Obama, whose ties to ACORN are strong and decades long had to toss them under the bus to avoid the splash back. Those who had been rallying against ACORN for years, largely unsuccessfully, were able to marginalize the socialist front organization thanks to a few minutes of footage.

Empower the People

People are frustrated and angry. They don't want to wait for a savior or a hero. They want to do something. They want to make a difference. But they don't know how. It is the responsibility of every conservative in this country to:

1. Register to vote. If you aren't registered to vote and don't exercise the right that people have fought and died for, you have no right to complain when socialist, anti-Americans take over.

2. Find out if the Republicans seats in your precinct are filled if so, are the people conservatives? If not, step up and fill that seat. It takes only a few hours a month and makes all the difference in the world.

3. Join. There are organizations in your state and maybe in your community that support conservative causes. It is a great way to let your voice be heard and to connect with other like minded people.

4. Get involved in a way that is enjoyable for you. Whether it is making signs, lending your voice at protest rallies, making videos, blogging, reading and summarizing bills, or launching legal challenges, using your skills to help the conservative cause is an essential component to getting America back on track.

5. Challenge and attack (respectfully). The liberal media is full of misinformation, especially in the newspapers. Journalists don't bother to check facts and sources. Write letters to the editors challenging facts and supplying real information about the party platform, membership, and history.

Positive Protesting

Whether you are a member of an organization, an individual seeking to organize, a political candidate, or a GOP, you need to be familiar with organizational battle plans. Alinsky, to his credit, was great at distilling the elements that motivate and influence people. He counseled organizers to "Never Go Outside the Experience of Your People." Republicans and conservative organizations should heed this advice. People should play to their strengths. If you are a lawyer, use your legal skills to protest or to launch attacks, work with others who are filing Constitutional crisis suits, creating amendments to reaffirm states rights, or working to close legal loop holes. That doesn't mean that lawyers shouldn't grab picket signs or attend Tea Party rallies. They should. But it does mean that those who have specialist skills should use them.

People organize, protest, and launch attacks (legal please) because they are angry and frustrated. But in order to keep momentum going, events need to be fun, inspiring, and give participants the feeling that they are achieving their goals. Taking people out of their own comfort zone doesn't make events fun or inspiring. If you want to plan an event or protest, think about the things that you enjoy. Look at the people around you who will want to be involved. What do they enjoy? What are their skills? What do you hope to achieve from your event? By identifying the strengths and goals of those around you, devising events should be easy.

Many motorcycle enthusiasts are veterans. Veterans have MANY issues to protest at the moment. If you are part of a motorcycle club or have many members in your organization who are motorcyclists, what issues are most pressing to you? Poor care in veterans hospitals? Inconsistent policies in Iraq & Afghanistan? Cuts in military spending? Than focus on someone who you feel is responsible. Is it a Congressman or Senator who has continually voted against veterans issues? Or is this something that you need to take to Washington? Make a plan and reach out to others. Over a half a million people attend Sturgis each year. Can you imagine the effect of even a fraction of that many motorcyclists converging on Washington or your state capital to protest the treatment of vets? Talk about press coverage!

✪ **Look to the talents, skills, and lifestyles of your organization to devise effective and enjoyable protests and events.**

Of course this leads nicely into another truism from Alinsky, "Whenever Possible Go Outside of the Experience of the Enemy." Tea Party protests are wonderful ways to show our anger and our numbers. But they are getting to be expected. Do something different. Do something unexpected! What could be more outside the experience of most people than to have 100,000 motorcycle riders converge on the capital protesting the treatment of vets? Organizers should make themselves familiar with flash mob techniques, which create wonderful visuals (essential for publicity) or costumed protests. A few years ago when the Sierra Club participated in a protest against World Trade Organization policies, hundreds of people dressed as bright green sea turtles to protest fishing methods that killed the endangered creatures. Human chains encircling court houses and government buildings have been effective, as have art instillations that highlight issues dear to protestors.

Protests can be a great way to educate people. Hand out fliers, create placards and posters, use sheer numbers of people to send a message. Have a message. But remember the sound bite rule. Your message and the facts that support it must be brief, easy to understand, and simple. But above all, your events and protests should not be easy to ignore. Do the unexpected. Operate outside of the expected and FILM IT so that you can use your event to publicize your organization and keep your message firmly in the minds of viewers.

✪ **Effective protests and events are those that don't follow normal protocol. Do the unexpected, make a spectacle, and create an event that people can't ignore.**

Avoid never ending protests. Hunger strikes, sit-ins, chaining yourself to things, or any other form of protest that doesn't have a definite (relatively quick) end time will fail. People get bored. They lose interest. They lose focus. And those are just your members. The general public will be annoyed if they are inconvenienced for long periods of time and most people simply don't care if you starve yourself to death or not. Select a definite time period to protest, a few hours at most, and keep the goals reasonable and firmly in place.

✪ **Events and protests should be relatively short. People get bored easily.**

When protests start to look like bullying efforts, enemies gain sympathy. It is essential that organizers understand that their job is to protest, to create camaraderie, to raise awareness, and hopefully to make people consider conservative points of view. If a protest become violent or looks like a shouting match, the enemy wins. Organizers have to keep good control over an event in order to insure that opposition or the liberal media don't have the ability to label them as bullies. Conservatives should remember in all of their political dealings that opponents will do their best to turn any statement or activity into "proof" of racism, bigotry, hatred or intolerance. Organizers must think carefully about the timing and tone of events or protests to avoid giving the opposition the ability to appear victimized.

✪   **Conservatives need to be careful of their actions and messages to avoid creating "underdog" heroes of their opponents.**

Solutions

Protesting, complaining, and objecting won't amount to anything if you can't offer realistic solutions to the problem. This is why having a platform that includes Republican solutions and alternatives is an essential component of success in future political battles. It isn't enough to simply be opposed to something, we have to create responses that include real solutions to problems. It is especially important for people who put themselves on the "front lines" to be informed and sound bite ready. While protesting or interacting with the public or the press, you must be ready with short, simple sincere answers. People will ask you "well if you're so smart, what would YOU do?" and you must be ready with prepared responses. The only way to get people thinking, to engage voters, to change minds is to be able to give them solutions that are in fact better than what is currently on offer.

When you are part of an event or protest, either as a sponsor or a participant, prepare yourself. What issue in particular is the event or protest designed to address? Do you know the issues? Do you have solutions? If so, are they easy to convey? Simply showing up is not enough.

✪   **Protesting is not enough, you need to have solutions and be able to easily convey them in sound bite format.**

244

While having well thought out, succinct solutions helps you to quickly and confidently answer queries from the public and from the press in protests and events, it also offers you a great weapon to keep pressure on opponents. Conservatives have many opponents. Not only are the liberal, anti-American politicians and their supporters enemies, we have to contend with RINOs in our own party. When you have the ability to ask pointed questions such as, "Why did you support this bill when it is clearly in direct opposition to the Republican values and principles that you were elected to uphold?" some politicians will answer back that the bill was the "best" option available, as a way to attempt to deflect the criticism or will challenge you. Armed with solutions, you have the ability to stay on the offensive and keep the pressure on the target.

✪ **Having a solution puts pressure on those who have none to at least listen and contemplate.**

Ridicule as a Political Strategy

Alinsky believed that ridicule was the most potent weapon in his arsenal. It is almost impossible to combat ridicule and puts the target on the defensive. During the last election cycle, both the Republicans and Hillary Clinton faced unrelenting ridicule from the media and Team Obama. Republicans typically face ridicule from liberals on two fronts, past policies ("illegal war," economic policies, George Bush in general, etc.) and social issues. Past policies are an easy point of attack, simply because the attackers are attempting to judge a past event with "today's eyes." It is a way in which people who have limited information about current issues can continue to try and bludgeon the Republican Party with past issues.

Most social issue related ridicule comes from misunderstanding the actual position of the Republican Party. A lot of this is probably innocent. Thanks to decades of socialist and liberal indoctrination at schools and through the media, there are a lot of people who genuinely believe that Republicans are "old, rich, white, men" trying to keep the poor in the inner city and women barefoot and pregnant (after marriage of course).

As we have all witnessed in the 2008 Presidential elections, ridicule is a powerful weapon. Team Obama ridiculed the financial success of Senator McCain's wife, attempting to incite an atmosphere of class warfare. However, perhaps no candidate in history has been more ridiculed and maligned than Sarah Palin. Not only did Team Obama attack her experience, political success, and beliefs (all acceptable in political battles), they attacked her family, her children, her marriage, and her ability to be a mother. While other candidates have been quizzed about their personal lives, no other candidate has been so vilified, dissected, and degraded by the liberal media or an opposing candidate's campaign machine.

Exposing a candidate's family to ridicule is unacceptable. As a society, we depend on the best and brightest putting themselves forward to represent us in government. We can hardly expect the best and brightest to step forward, if they know that their children and spouses are going to be abused, harassed, and defamed. As Republicans, we must refuse to attack a fellow politician's family or speculate on their personal life, no matter what party they represent. But simply refusing to participate in ridiculing the family of a politician is not enough, we must denounce any and all who do engage in such ridicule.

✪ **You may attack a politician's actions, voting record, and his or her character, but it is never acceptable to ridicule a person's family or personal life.**

246

Fear of Ridicule as a Motivator

Everyone makes mistakes. But there is a significant difference between an honest mistake and a calculated ethical breach. Politicians from all parties have acted in unethical and inappropriate ways and have largely gotten away with it because their own party covers up the misdeed. Fearful of losing a seat or being painted with the same brush, political parties have been forced to become co-conspirators in illegal and unethical acts in order to "save the party." This can not continue.

Republicans must make it clear to the political hierarchy that illegal and unethical behavior will not be covered up or swept under the rug. Failure to address and confront those in our party who engage in illegal or unethical acts, simply render us all complicit in their crimes. It damages the reputation of the party as a whole and gives the impression that all politicians are untrustworthy or unethical. Further more, by being our own, best policing unit, we deny opposition forces one of the best weapons that they have to derail Republican candidacies and policies, the "surprise scandal."

✪ **Fear of public ridicule should be used to ensure that politicians, from all parties act in an ethical fashion.**

In the 2008 elections, Team Obama successfully campaigned for "transparency in government." This touched a cord with American voters (from all parties) who were frankly tired of constant lies and manipulations perpetrated by politicians and by the media. Of course, Obama's transparency pledge hardly survived election night. The disappointment from both supporters and detractors was/is palpable. From an ideological standpoint, this is a wonderful opportunity for Republicans to acknowledge and embrace the American people's

247

desire to be informed in an accurate way, without the spin, without the "moral garments."

From a practical standpoint, transparency has become a political necessity. We live in a time when almost everything that we do, say, or write can be recorded without our knowledge and posted online for the world to view. The reality of this fact must not be lost on conservative politicians and Republican Radicals.

✪ **If you wouldn't be proud to say it, write it, or do it in the light of day, DON'T. Republicans must be transparent in their dealings and moral, legal, and ethical in their words and deeds.**

Demanding Accuracy

Politics have always resided in a nasty arena. Slander, mud slinging, personal attacks, and double dealing have been standard fare throughout political history. However, recently, we Republicans have allowed our ideas, plans, and policies to be branded as "illegal," "unethical," and/or "anti-American" by the opposition and by the liberal media, without challenge. Republicans have been accused of backing an "illegal war" or proposing "anti-American immigration policies." We must not allow this branding to continue unchecked. It is essential that Republicans are ready to meet any opposition, with accuracy and information, and require that any opposition who tries to tar us with words such as "unethical" or "anti-American" be made to identify what aspects of the plan, policy or activity are actually met the definition of the word or phrase.

✪ **We must demand accuracy from our opponents. Those who would use shock or slander words to** attempt to discredit Republicans must be required to provide proof that a plan or activity is actually unethical, illegal, or anti-American.

By the same token, Republicans and Democrats alike have been guilty of labeling nearly every idea or concept put forward by an opposing party as unethical, illegal, or anti-American. This branding is taking place with such frequency that the terms have lost all meaning in political context.

Instead of branding every success or every idea put forward by the opposition as "unethical" or "anti-American" we must remember that the opposition is simply a group that has some differing opinions. Yes, there are those who behave in an unethical manner or who do wish the destruction of the United States, but they are the exception and not the rule. By rendering words such as "unethical" or "anti-American" impotent, the American people are robbed of the ability to differentiate truly bad behavior or destructive practices from those that simply come from the opposition. Truly anti-American policies and practices are swept away from public conscious along with all of the trivial or mundane that is similarly branded. "Unethical" or "anti-American" should be words that cause shock and disgust, today they are simply words used to describe almost every opposing view.

✪ We must stop branding every point upon which we disagree as "unethical" or "anti-American" and reserve those words for activities that genuinely meet the definition.

- Chapter 8 –

The Revolution Commences

Many a war is lost through lack of planning and direction. This war, the war to right our country and save its citizens from the socialist tide, is far too important to simply rush in and hope for the best. We have to have a step-by-step plan, implement it well, and gain both supporters and momentum along the way. We must address not only the overall goal of this war, but also identify the smaller battles that help insure and inspire victory.

-The Victory-

A thoughtfully and responsibly progressive, conservative America.

-The Battles-

To insure that conservative politicians occupy all Republican seats.

To insure that elected officials do the job for which they were hired.

To halt liberal advances against the Constitution, economy, and American society.

The information that follows lays out battle plans. But there are a few basic principles that will help the battle run more smoothly and in an organized fashion.

Work Smart.

Whether you want to develop a party platform, create a map of unmanned Republican precinct seats, or launch an education initiative, the essential first step is finding out if someone else is working on the project or has already completed your goal. Work smart. Redoing work that others have already completed or avoiding working with others who have a similar goal is not smart, it is a huge waste of time.

Focus on the battle at hand.

Your personal goal may be to end abortion, oust illegals, or finish the job in Afghanistan and Iraq, but without winning the war at hand, no ability exists to achieve those goals. It is essential that all conservatives fight the battles that award us the power to address societal issues at a later stage.

Integrate don't alienate.

Even in conservative circles, not everyone is going to agree on every issue. It is essential that people put their differences and personal agendas aside in order to win the war. We will need every conservative organization and conservative voter. It is also essential that we can reach out, educate, and integrate those who have been indoctrinated and scared away from the Republican Party.

Don't get dragged into diversions.

It is completely counterproductive to wage battles that won't win the war. Team Obama has been extremely effective at keeping the GOP and Republicans chasing diversions. This keeps the Republican Party a reactionary force. Focus on the battle plan and the battle, ignore Dem diversions.

Preparing for Battle

There are some organizational elements that should be addressed prior to entering the battle field.

Contact:

It is essential that you create a means for people to contact you. Create an email address that is JUST for politics.

This email address should be professional (not rude or derogatory).

GOOD: WinRepublicans2010@example.com
GOOD: SpringfieldConservatives@example.com

BAD: DieLiberalScum@example.com
BAD: ObamaSux@example.com

Your email address for political activities should NOT reveal anything about YOU. Remember there are a LOT of bad people out there, you want to avoid making yourself or your family a target.

BAD: BillSherman@example.com
BAD: ZacsMom@example.com

Inform:

Create a blog, Facebook page, etc. to keep people informed and up-to-date about your organization or political activities. Again, keep the name and content professional.

GOOD: KansasConservatives
GOOD: DetriotRepublicans

BAD: MiamiHatesDems

253

Remember that people who don't consider themselves Republicans or conservatives may also find your site. Do you want to inform and educate with grace and civility? Or do you want to defame and insult and insure that they don't engage? Make certain that you update frequently and add events far enough in advance so that people can add your event

Insure that your blog or web page has "comment moderation" enabled. This will allow you to read and approve comments from others before they appear on your blog or web page. Politics can get heated and unfortunately you may attract liberals who want to spread hate by attacking you or conservatives on your blog or web site. Comment moderation means that you have the ability to erase inappropriate comments before they appear on your site. But, it is really important that you remember the one simple rule of comment moderation: **Erase, don't engage!** People who post negative comments or personal attacks on other people's blogs do so in order to get a reaction. They crave your attention. They want nothing more than for you to try to insult them back or even try to inform them. They just want your reaction. It is a battle that you can't win. If you simply erase their comments and do NOT respond to them in any way, they will get tired and move on in search of someone who will engage them.

Connect

Don't be an army of one. Connect with other conservative and Republican organizations. They will offer assistance and the connection will insure that you aren't duplicating work which they may have already completed. You should also create a mechanism so that people can connect with you. Use your political email address and your blog, Facebook, web page, etc to provide a way for people to interact and participate.

254

-Battle-

To insure that conservative politicians occupy all Republican seats

-Battle Grounds-
Local Precincts
State Level Conservatives
Electing Conservatives

In order to win this battle, we need to win in three key areas. First, we need to fill ALL empty Precinct Committee Person seats with conservative people, as well as challenge any Republican seats currently held by RINOs. This will require recruiting conservatives in each precinct to dedicate themselves to several hours a month in committee meetings, as well as canvassing their neighborhood several times prior to election. Second, we need to identify conservative candidates to the Senate and Congress to support and champion. Perhaps most importantly, we need to educate and encourage voters to select conservative politicians at election time. This is done through a combination of informing people about the conservative platform and providing name recognition for conservative candidates.

Local Precincts:

Contact your state GOP office to find all Republican Precinct Committee seats in the state.

- Do they have a list of all Republican precinct seats?

- If so, does the list differentiate empty and occupied seats?

- If they do not have a list, how would they advise you going about compiling a list?

- Are there other groups or individuals who are compiling a similar list or want a similar list? Will they connect with you?

Determine which seats are empty, which are occupied by acceptable, conservative Precinct Committee Persons and which are occupied by RINOs.

- Create a list of empty seats and their boundaries.

- Create a list of seats occupied by acceptable conservatives so that you can lend support to those Precinct Committee Persons at election time.

- Create a list of seats occupied by RINOs so that an opposition candidate can be nurtured and supported.

What are the requirements to fill a precinct seat in your area? Generally there will be a combination of forms, identification, and a set number of signatures in support of the candidacy.

- Can you collect forms for each empty seat or will each individual candidate be required to collect their own forms?

- If your state allows you to collect the forms for all empty seats, make sure that you have extra. Remember, some states require ORIGINAL forms, not copies. Don't lose seats because of simple mistakes.

- If your state allows you to collect forms for each seat, make sure that you also collect the voters list for each precinct.

This will show the registered Republican voters in each precinct. These people will be more likely to lend their signature.

- How many signatures does your state require?

- What identification does your state require?

Use your connections (with other organizations and with people in your own group) to inform people about the Precinct Committee seats that are empty or occupied by RINOs.

- Start recruiting Precinct Committee Persons for each empty or challenge seat in your city or community (remember backup people are a GREAT idea!).

- Work with other conservative and Republicans organizations to help them start recruiting Precinct Committee Persons for their cities or communities. Make sure that they understand the requirements.

- Create a Precinct Committee Person "kit" that includes forms and instructions that you can provide to people in your state who don't live in your area.

Create an event to complete the requirements for each empty precinct seat and to challenge seats held by inappropriate people.

- Set up a group meeting for all people who want to be Precinct Committee Persons. Friday evening or Saturday morning meetings give candidates the ability to spend the weekend collecting the required signatures.

- Assist in insuring that forms are completed correctly.

- Make certain that candidates are equipped with voter lists for their appropriate precinct and send them out to get the required signatures.

Create a follow up meeting to turn in the candidate's forms based on the requirements of your area.

- If you are allowed to turn in forms on behalf of candidates, collect the forms.

- If not, schedule a convenient time for everyone to drop their forms.

- Identify and assist people who have been unable to generate required signatures.

Be prepared for unexpected problems or setbacks.

- People do drop out. They may have family commitments or personal problems that prevent them from either completing the forms/signatures or ultimately being a Committee Person. Think ahead and have back up people in place, ready to complete forms, get signatures and take those empty seats. Be gracious with those who back out, we still need their votes!

- Always get extra signatures. Make sure that each form has more signatures than required. Some signatures may be ultimately disqualified, so make sure that you have more than required for security.

- Don't lie or falsify. Only REAL people who REALLY sign their REAL name need sign a candidate's form.

Check Up!

- Some states award uncontested seats to the person who puts their name forward and only place seats with more than one candidate on the ballot. Others will put all names on the ballot, even if only one person is running.

- Make sure that all candidates have met the requirements and if your state requires it, has their name on the ballot.

- Pinpoint any contested seats. Any contested seat that is occupied by a RINO should be identified for intense precinct campaigning. We must ensure that the conservative candidate can oust the RINO and this is only achieved by campaigning.

You should now have a solid foundation of conservatives who want to fill empty seats or run against RINOs for Precinct Committee seats. You also have neatly packaged, small areas divided by precinct for effective canvassing. Each Precinct candidate should become very familiar with the voters in their area. Not only does this assure their own success as a Precinct Committee person and a positive conservative voice in their community, but also facilitates the creation of groundswell support for conservative politicians across the state. It is at this very small, local level where real differences can be made, both in educating voters about the conservative platform and engaging people to back positive, conservative changes on a local, state, and national level.

It is essential that in addition to having a strong Precinct team, we also take the time to discover the truly conservative candidates on a local and state level, reach out to them, and promote them along with the promotion of Precinct members.

State Candidates:

Connect with conservative Senators and Congress people in your state, especially those who are up for election.

- Connect with the GOP state office. Are there truly conservative Senators and Congress Persons on the ballot? If so, reach out to them.

- The GOP and in particular the conservative politicians with whom you have connected should have campaign materials. Offer to send out their campaign materials with the Precinct Committee candidates as they canvas their neighborhood.

Where RINOs are running for re-election or for a higher office, find out if there are conservatives running against them that could use your help.

- Connect with conservative politicians in hotly contested areas. Offer to promote them on a "groundswell" level by distributing their campaign materials with the Precinct Committee candidates.

- If the conservative politicians are campaigning in your area, coordinate a meet and greet so that the Precinct candidates can take part in any campaign activities.

- Remember, people learn by repetition. The more frequently they hear the names of conservative candidates in positive ways, the more likely they will vote for them.

- Use meet and greets as photo opportunities. These are GREAT for your web site, blog or Facebook and should be used as a promotional vehicle in your press kit.

You should now have Precinct Committee persons, connections with conservative state politicians, and promotional materials. This puts you in the perfect position to start preparing for the election. You can NOT wait until the last minute. Start thinking about ways that you can generate positive attention for conservative candidates and generate votes.

Election:

Rule One – **Positive Repetition** - People vote the names that they remember. So make sure, in the weeks up to the election, that voters know the names of conservative candidates.

Rule Two – **Connect Connect Connect** – People vote for people who they feel will really represent them, people that understand them, and have connected with them on some level. This makes the Precinct Committee person a very important position. A good Committee person will engage with their neighborhood throughout the year, not just the day before the election.

Connect with pro-conservative or unbiased journalists on a local level. Creating a network of supportive journalists will give your candidates a voice and a presence.

- Connect with journalists who will be interested in profiling conservative candidates and conservative awareness events.

- Make yourself familiar with press releases, their function, and their uses. Send press releases when appropriate.

- Let journalists know that you are available to provide a conservative reaction to political local, state, and national news.

Organize local events. Local events can be a great way to inform people about the conservative position or as a way to protest ultra-liberal travesties.

- Don't organize events for your home or business. This is unsafe. Remember, those who don't have conservative values sometimes act in uncivilized and even violent ways.

- Information events should be about educating people in a friendly and most importantly non-patronizing manner. Provide information about the Republican Party's history and about the current conservative platform.

- Protesting events should be tasteful and BRIEF! Remember, there are many, MANY people, Republicans, Independents, and Democrats, that are sick of the problems in Washington and in their state and community. Protesting should ALWAYS be both a "we are mad as hell" and a "here is the conservative solution."

- Don't try to hide the Party's recent deviation. There will always be those who say, "well Bush started it" or something of the sort. Don't rise to that level. Instead acknowledge that politicians have deviated from the conservative platform to disastrous result and that that very deviation is why you are here today, rallying to get the country back on track.

- All events should include campaign materials so that people can take information away with them. This is a great way to educate and create memorable repetition for conservative candidates.

Precinct candidates should organize canvassing days to meet the voters in their precinct.

- Remember, canvassing is about friendly conversation NOT combat. The candidate's job is to provide information about themselves and conservative candidates in a confident and professional way not to try and force their opinions onto people.

- Precinct Committee candidates should make notes about the supportive people that they meet. Keep addresses and contact details of these voters so that they can be issued voting reminders prior to election day.

- Canvassing should include dispensing campaign materials provided by conservative candidates and the GOP.

- You can also prepare flyers that include the party platform, election date, time, and place, and the name of conservative candidates. Remember, people vote the names they remember.

Organize a voter registration drive.

- Contact your county's board of registrars. They will provide you with information and materials such as registration forms.

- You can register people door-to-door or at busy places such as shopping centers, Universities, libraries, etc. If you are registering people at a location, book your space well in advance.

- Organize volunteers to man the registration tables or go door-to-door.

- Voting drives BY LAW must be non-partisan. You CAN NOT endorse a party or candidate. The goal is to get more people voting.

- The Federal Election Commission requires that a sign be placed near the registration table or a notice be given (if registering people door-to-door) that states: "Our voter registration services are available without regard to voters' political preference."

- Make certain that you have enough clip boards, pens, forms, etc. BUT some states prohibit any freebees (no candy, treats, balloons, etc.).

- Make certain that people know what you are doing. Make big "register to vote here" signs.

- Make certain that completed forms are stored and delivered to the board of registrars in the manner that they authorize. Any deviation could be a fraud. It goes without saying, but be honorable.

- Make certain that you know the registration requirements. There are residency, age, identification, and qualification requirements, some of which vary between states. Make certain that you are informed and create an "information page" so that others are informed as well.

- Some states require those registering to vote to declare a party affiliation, others do not. Make certain that you know your state's rules.

- In many states, people can register to vote online. Make sure that you can provide that info. so that those who are too busy to register during the drive can do so at home.

In the run up to the election, final canvassing and information drives should be organized. Remember, people vote based on personal connections and name recognition. Make certain that precinct candidates and conservative politicians are at the forefront of people's minds.

- Precinct Committee candidates should be out, door-to-door in their neighborhood insuring that people are aware of the election date and are familiar with the names of conservative candidates on a precinct, local, and a state level.

- Provide last minute materials including poll location and hours.

- Final information events should push the conservative agenda and conservative candidates.

- Precinct candidates should evaluate any issues that prevent voting. Do conservative voters in your precinct need help getting to and from the polls? If so, organize transportation.

Election Day is extremely important. Precinct candidates and conservative volunteers should be on hand (based on election rules in your community) to meet and greet voters and remind voters of the names of conservative candidates.

- Remember, voters gravitate towards winners. Conservatives MUST present a friendly, professional, and united group and provide name recognition at the polls. This is the time for confident approachability, not angry urgency.

Get people to the polls.

- If you or precinct candidates have committed to getting home bound people to the polls, make certain that you follow through. People will wonder how conservatives can correct national problems if they can't meet local transportation commitments.

- Make sure that you get people home again too, but don't grill people. They know that you want a conservative win.

Winning conservative seats is all about organization. If you can help recruit conservatives at the precinct level who are excited about creating a conservative groundswell, we can win this battle. It isn't about creating one champion who leads the country. Not at this point. It is about creating an army of voters who are educated as to the conservative platform. It is about creating an army of conservative politicians that are dedicated to resurrecting the American Dream and moving the country back to the right track. From this group of strong, dedicated, state level conservative politicians, future Presidential elections should have a larger number of appropriate candidates from which to choose.

Maintain the groundswell. You have helped to create a political machine. By recruiting conservative Precinct Committee members and organizing canvassing, information events, and protests, you have created a means to reach out to every voter in your community, even long after the election. Encourage Precinct Committee members to continue to reach out to their community by keeping people informed of important political events. This helps voters to be better educated and feel in control. Keep using your blog, Facebook, and newsletters, etc to maintain connection with voters and Precinct Committee members. This will be important as we move on to the next battle of ousting RINOs.

-Battle-

To insure that elected officials do the job for which they were hired.

-Battle Grounds-
Identify Conservatives, Moderate Republicans, & RINOs
Put Wayward Republicans On Notice
Expel RINOs and Replace with Conservative Republicans
Term Limits

Once elected, politicians reveal their true colors. Unfortunately, this sometimes means that those whom we have supported and nurtured turn out to be disappointing. It is therefore essential that politicians are monitored. This helps to keep them on the right track if they are distracted and helps to identify those who will require expulsion. There is no excuse for supporting RINOs for years, let alone decades (Arlan Specter). Identify true conservative politicians. These people must be supported financially and with our voices and votes. Moderate Republicans may be acceptable depending upon what areas they diverge. RINOs are NEVER acceptable. They must be identified and removed. PERIOD.

But we should not stop there. While RINOs are robbing our Party of power, there are politicians of all varieties who are using their position to amass personal fortunes through kick backs and side deals at voter's expense. Others use their power to create legacy seats for their children. The founding fathers saw political service as a way for successful people to lend their expertise to the operation of the country, for a short period of time. It was never intended to be a lifetime career. It was certainly never intended to establish a hereditary ruling class. However, with politicians "holding" seats open for their children and friends, this is exactly what is happening. Not only are some politicians creating family political dynasties, they are robbing voters of the right to choose representatives for themselves. While politicians such as Biden are holding seats open for months (even years) so that their children can occupy the seat in the future, when seats are granted without the benefit of campaigns and elections, we get politicians like Nancy Pelosi who was gifted her first seat and has been protected from any real challenger for the entirety of her career.

It is essential that politicians do the job for which they were hired, which is to vote the dictates of their constituents. I feel that by forbidding any sort of "seat holding" and establishing term limits, we help to insure that voters maintain control over politicians and ultimately over the direction of the country.

Identify Conservatives, Moderate Republicans, & RINOs:

The only way to take control of the political process is to make certain that voters have control over the politicians who represent them. Unfortunately, much of what politicians do is behind closed doors. This makes it difficult to monitor their votes, proposed legislation, and behavior.

Get familiar with www.VoteSmart.org which is an excellent source of information about state representatives, their voting records, campaign finances, special interest group affiliations, and positions.

- Make a spread sheet of all Republican politicians on the state level, for your state.

- Next to each politicians name identify them as conservatives, moderate Republican, and RINOs.

- Those who are squarely conservative should be championed for continued state level support or potential national level political promotion. Check ethics!

- Next to the names of moderate Republicans and RINOs, identify which issues they support or reject that fall without conservative platform parameters.

It isn't enough that YOU know who the real conservatives are and who should be put on notice or expelled. You need to share your information and gain information from others.

- Share your list with the conservative organizations with which you connected.

- Ask these connections to supply additional information about the people on the list if they have information. This is a great way to weed out people for ethical violations or to clarify moderate positions, if there was a legitimate reason for a non-conservative vote on an issue. In this way, a clear picture of politicians who are worthy of support and those who need expelled develops.

- Post the list of Republicans on your blog, Facebook page, or newsletter to insure that Precinct Committee members and members of the general public who have connected with you, are aware of the status of politicians.

- Encourage people to keep an eye out on the news or in the papers about the positive and negative activities of Republicans on a state and local level. Use the connections that you have created to stay informed.

Put Wayward Republicans On Notice:

Republicans who have fallen afoul of conservative platform positions must be identified and either nudged back in line or expelled.

- Politicians must be given the benefit of the doubt. If they have strayed off course, it may simply be because they have buckled to pressure from other politicians or it may be because they have lost touch with their constituents. However, they may have deviated because they do not agree with the conservative platform and have voted based on their true agenda.

- Republican politicians must be alerted in a friendly but firm way that they are expected to vote and propose legislation in support of conservative positions. They should be made aware that they are being given the benefit of the doubt in past voting, but any deviations from this day forward will result in a loss of support and active engagement to find a conservative challenger.

- Unfortunately, many politicians do not respond to the concerns of single voters. It is therefore important that edicts are sent from organizations or precinct committee persons. This alerts politicians to the fact that you have "weight" behind your words.

- Sometimes petitions can be effective, especially if they contain a LOT of signatures. Circulate a petition among your contacts, to compel a politician to vote appropriately.

- RINOs who refuse to perform the job for which they were hired must be identified and removed.

Expel RINOs and Replace with Conservative Republicans:

Removing RINOs is only an option when an acceptable conservative replacement can be found, nurtured, and propelled. This must be a top priority.

- Compile an "offense" flyer showing the voting record and legislation proposal record of the RINO. This will be very useful when campaigning against the RINO. Voters want to know how specifically the politician has failed.

- Will the GOP support a conservative challenger over the RINO incumbent? If they will, the process is much easier. However, often GOP organizations are hesitant to change direction and continue to support RINOs once they are in.

- Work with conservative organizations to identify a potential conservative local politician who would be best to challenge the RINO for the Republican seat.

Once a conservative challenger is identified and is onboard to run against the RINO, the election machine must kick in again.

- Use the same precinct canvassing techniques to inform voters about the conservative challenger and educate them to not simply choose the "Republican" candidate whose name they recognize.

- Precinct Committee members must be kept informed about RINOs and the conservative challengers that should be supported so that they can vote appropriately for delegates and promotions.

- A delicate balance must be maintained when attacking RINOs. You need to marginalize the RINO without damaging the Republican brand. This is achieved by promoting the conservative challenger as a modern conservative republican while exposing the RINO as a traitor without linking his or her name to the Republican brand.

Example:
Jack Jackson is a thoughtfully progressive, conservative Republican.

Jo Joseph is a traitor to his state who supported Obama's "stimulus" scam.

By using the name of the challenger with the terms, conservative and Republican, people will associate Jackson as THE Republican. Where avoiding using the Republican brand with Joseph and instead focusing on negative specifics, we can start to disassociate the RINO with the Republican Party.

- It is essential that you remember that repetition equals recognition and often, people vote for the name they recognize, not the best candidate. Don't push the RINO's name inadvertently by continual reference. Once it has been established that the RINO is a traitor, only reference the conservative challenger's name.

In commercials, video, and electronic media, we should avoid saying the name of the RINO as much as possible so as to avoid establishing recognition. Photos, especially those that are less than flattering, coupled with the issues upon which the RINO has let us down are sufficient.

Term Limits:

From the infancy of the American Revolution, the issue of limiting terms of office as a means of pressuring democracy has been important. While early versions of government in the United States established term limits, when the Constitution was ultimately ratified, the issue of term limits was not specifically addressed. While even Thomas Jefferson pointed that the omission of specific terms limits was a potential disaster, since culture dictated that political service was temporary and members of Congress rotated frequently, mandatory limits were not deemed necessary.

After the Civil War, a new breed of career politicians developed who saw their financial success lay in a lifetime of power. By the end of the last century, turn over in Congress was almost nonexistent. Once elected, today's Congressmen maintain their positions, virtually unchallenged, for their entire working life. Essentially, today's politicians embody the very "perpetuity of office" and "ruling class" establishment that created the necessity of the American Revolution.

At various points over the past sixty years Republicans have attempted to pass legislation requiring term limits. In 1952, Republican sponsored term limit legislation passed with a bare majority in the House, but failed to reach the 2/3rd majority required in Congress. Throughout the 1990's various pushes to establish term limits have passed on a state level, but failed on a national level. Of course, asking a group of people who are amassing fortunes by staying in power to vote against their self interests and vote themselves out of power is unrealistic. However, the success of term limits on a state level and Washington's complete disregard for the wishes of the American people clearly illustrate that term limits need to be addressed and established on a national level.

Conservative candidates at the state level who identify themselves as proponents of national term limits are especially champion worthy. Not only does this establish that they believe in the true spirit of the Constitution and the intent of the Founding Fathers, but also shows that they are committed to the betterment of the country and not the establishment of a family political dynasty. Across the political spectrum, Americans are uncomfortable with the idea of a "ruling class" of politicians. Conservatives who include term limits as part of their campaign platform will appeal to independent voters as well as conservatives.

-Battle-

To halt liberal advances against the Constitution, economy, and American society.

-Battle Grounds-
Identify Areas Where Liberals Are Attacking Our Country
Identify Organizations and Politicians Who Are Challenging
Liberal Advances
Create Groundswell Campaigns Against Liberal Attacks

Liberals have spent decades creating mechanisms to destroy the American Dream. It is only in this past election that many of us had even heard of ACORN, yet the organization had been quietly dealing hate and discord while scamming the government out of millions of tax payer dollars annually for forty years. Unfortunately, ACORN is not alone. There are hundreds of organizations, with thousands of braches, quietly chipping away at the foundation of this great country. Like termites, unless we can find their nests and rid ourselves of these pests, the structure, security, and stability of this country will crumble.

Identify Areas Where Liberals Are Attacking Our Country:

Everywhere you look, the liberal agenda is evident. Amoral people are portrayed as "heroes" on television. America is portrayed as an evil place in schools. Social programs hemorrhage tax payer money supporting generation after generation on welfare. Illegals rush across the border to have anchor babies in the US to guarantee them a lifetime welfare check. But disabled military families need to depend on private charity to insure that they have Christmas dinner or can meet their rent payments. Something is seriously wrong. But for many people, so many things are "so wrong" that it can be difficult to focus on a single battle field. Frankly, that is the point. Liberals attack on so many fronts simultaneously that it can seem almost impossible to counter. However, if conservatives can address the individual issues and break up the attack into small, manageable battles, we can turn the tide on the liberal advancement and take back the country.

No one can tackle ALL issues. It is much more effective to select a single issue or a small number of issues upon which you can really focus.

- Select an issue about which you are passionate.

- If you can't settle on an issue, the next chapter of this book addresses many issues facing conservative America. You may find it easier to select an issue to champion after reading that chapter.

Once you have selected an issue or a small group of issues, think about where the battle field for these issues reside.

- While you should select issues upon which you can be passionate, it is also important to look at where and how you might be able to be most effective.

- Often people have local issues, as well as state or national issues. This can help keep you motivated by winning small local battles, especially since larger battles tend to move along at a slower pace.

- Local issues often go virtually unchallenged because people are unaware of the activities of national liberal organizations in their communities.

- Become as familiar as possible with the enemy's activities on a local, state, and national level.

Identify Organizations and Politicians Who Are Challenging Liberal Advances:

There are national organizations as well as state and national conservative politicians who are already dedicated to stopping liberal attacks in their tracks.

- Connect with organizations and politicians who are battling liberals over your issue(s).

- Do these national organizations have local chapters that might be more pro-active on a local level? If not, perhaps you could start a local chapter.

- Conservative politicians who are battling liberal onslaughts should be championed, even if they are not in your local area or state.

- Be proactive in alerting national organizations to local problems. Parents didn't know that their own children were being forced to sing pro-Obama chants in school. It was only when a YouTube clip was posted that parents became aware of the indoctrination. If you can help alert those with power to local travesties, you can get a great deal accomplished.

Create Groundswell Campaigns Against Liberal Attacks:

You have created the mechanism to get things done on a local level. The connections that you made through Precinct Committee campaigns, canvassing, informational events, and protesting have given you the ability to educate conservatives in your area about the anti-American activities that take place locally. While parents across the country were mad at the Obama indoctrination songs, think how much angrier they would be if it was happening in THEIR children's school!

Use your connection network to keep people informed about local anti-American activities.

- Keep people up-to-date with blog posts, Facebook posts, and any newsletters that you produce.

- Keep Precinct Committee members up-to-date so that they can inform their community about potential threats.

Make certain that the general public is aware of the liberal activities in your community.

- Organize information and protest events to highlight the liberal attacks locally.

- Remember these events can be a great way to garner votes, inform people about the conservative agenda and Republican Party. Make certain that you are prepared.

- Make certain that you stay connected with supportive members of the media.

Some issues are simply a matter of saying "no you can't do that" such as the Obama songs in grade schools. Other issues require specific solutions. These issues often involve a liberal group attempting to force new legislation. Immigration, health care, abortion, etc. these issues all rely on conservatives having a better solution.

- Write down your agenda or your goal so that you will be less likely to get distracted by liberals who often use a rapid fire attack methods of shouting you down so that you can't answer questions or point out their lies.

- For "you can't do that" issues, be prepared with analogies. Why did Wilson get attacked for saying "You Lie" at the President when Democrats haven't been admonished for reading the paper during State of the Union addresses or wishing Bush dead in news clips?

- For solution based issues, make certain that you have the conservative platform, including proposed solutions at hand.

The enemy of my enemy is my friend.

- When organizing events and protests against liberal activities, make sure you reach out to other organizations who share your target, even if they don't share your core cause.

- Your goal is numbers and attention. Don't worry about cohesive beliefs among protesters.

- Think outside the box. If you want to protest the treatment of military personnel at a poorly run local hospital, reaching out to veterans groups is a great idea. But many police, fire, and rescue people are vets too, as are motorcycle riders, pilots, and chaplains. Reach out to high school and college ROTC members. Looking for patriots? Try the local 4H and FFA clubs, church groups, and historical recreation clubs. The point is, by thinking about ALL of the people affected by a single issue you can reach out to many people who you might otherwise fail to consider.

Liberals have done an exceptional job of shoring up their positions and fighting battles often before the rest of us have any idea that an issue exists. Obama's college transcripts and birth certificate issues are perfect examples. Long before the voting public was aware of the existence of Barack Obama, his people were already filing law suits to seal records. We have to learn to use the power of the law as well.

As Liberal loons attempt to force feed a 2,000 page health care bill through Washington, despite the fact that no one seems to have read it, the need for "Bill Reading Groups" is pretty clear.

- Bill Reading Groups divide up weighty bills, read the bills, and provide summaries to politicians, media, and the general public.

- Some Bill Reading Groups have started online. If you enjoy reading, this may be a great way to get involved.

- If you want to start your own Bill Reading Group, posting your findings on line is a great way to inform and educate thousands, maybe millions of people without leaving your desk.

While I certainly wouldn't advise people to file frivolous law suits, many of the dodgy tricks played on voters in the last election campaign revolved around using the legal system to block pertinent information from voters.

- A great way to counter legal maneuverings is by monitoring the filings of lawyers frequently used by liberal groups. By staying abreast of suits that they are filing, we can avoid the shock and ultimate paralysis caused by surprise legal wranglings.

- Conservative lawyers should use their expertise to devise creative solutions to pressing problems. This can be through challenging liberal lawyer's efforts to weaken the Constitution, strengthening state sovereignty, or by using local laws and ordnances to address social issues.

- There are a lot of lawsuits out there against liberal attacks that are flying under the radar, largely thanks to liberal media bias. Many of these worthy suits are filed by small firms or individual lawyers who are finding themselves fighting battalions of lawyers backed by liberal money. Those in legal fields should certainly consider lending their time and expertise to help even up the fight.

Liberal media bias is damaging the country in ways that last generations. When far left positions are stated as "unbiased" and factual, millions of Americans are getting a dramatically askew view of the country, its citizens, and the leadership. Rather than listen to or read liberal indoctrination media, many conservatives simply turn the channel or avoid particular newspapers. However, by ignoring the indoctrination, we are simply avoiding the fact that millions of people are being mislead.

- Media listens to money. The best way to counter liberal indoctrination media is to organize boycotts against sponsors and advertisers. The goal is NOT to stop them advertising on a particular show, channel, or newspaper, but rather that they demand accuracy and unbiased coverage AND that opinion pieces are clearly identified as opinion pieces.

- Circulation in papers and viewer numbers for mainstream news shows are down thanks to the internet. That means that editors and producers fight for every consumer. Organizing a signature campaign can be a great way to get attention, simply because editors and producers don't have the luxury of ignoring people. Petition against biased news. Rally against opinion as fact shows. Get a lot of signatures and you can actually create a change in programming.

- File complaints. Broadcasters and print media are regulated on a state and national level. File complaints detailing the exact compliance issue. Generally you must list the date and time, segment name, and exact issue with a piece. How exactly did the show deceive the public? Which statement was a lie? Broadcasters and media producers can be fined if they are found to be behaving contrary to licensing requirements.

- Make certain that you can counter misstatements with facts. It isn't enough to write a letter to the editor stating that a news piece was wrong. You should be able to state the facts and why their assertions should be retracted. Unfortunately, many "journalists" don't bother to do much research. Provide the facts and many editors and producers will retract.

- Chapter 9 -

American Issues
Conservative Values

When I was much younger, I attended a lot of rock concerts. There was always a point in any concert when the tempo changed. After blistering guitar solos and blinding light shows the stage would grow dark, the crowd would quiet, and the band would launch into a power ballad. As the song started, a single tiny speck of light could be seen in the darkness as some fan held their lighter above their head. But it didn't take long before the entire audience was bathed in the golden glow of thousands of lighters held high. I understand that now kids hold their opened cell phones over their head instead of lighters, but the effect is the same. While a single tiny flame or the back light of a single cell phone hardly pierces the darkness, the combined effect of a thousand such lights can be blinding. As conservatives, we need only to hold our little lighter or open cell phone high above our heads for the combined light to expose the darkness in politics and to send the cockroaches in all parties scurrying for darkness.

With so many things wrong in Washington and in the country (thanks to Washington), people can become overwhelmed with the problems and inactive in their shock and depression. Conservatives should be well versed in all issues that affect this country, however, it is natural for some issues to be more important to you than others. The issue about which you are passionate becomes that tiny light in the darkness. This is especially true if you seek to actively change the system. Whether you are a politician seeking to reconnect with the electorate, someone contemplating taking a precinct seat, a conservative organizer, or simply a conservative who wants to be effective in turning the tide against Obama's socialist agenda, choosing a single cause about which you are passionate, is an important step in creating that blinding conservative light.

On the pages that follow, I have addressed my opinions on some of the issues which I feel are most pressing. Clearly, my opinions do not mirror those of every other conservative. But, hopefully this will give you food for thought as you select an issue to champion. While I hope to shed light on the truly dangerous associations, influences, and motivations of Barack Obama, this book is also designed to be a useable, useful playbook to battle against the well organized and funded socialist tide. Without the decades of organization and indoctrination, and lacking the hundreds of millions of dollars conned out of the government and provided by foreign supporters of a weak America, we have to use creativity and dedication to wage this battle and win.

Proof of Eligibility

I don't know if Barack Obama was born in the US or not, but the issues surrounding the controversy highlight two important issues that must be addressed. First, while the Constitution establishes requirements that must be met in order to be the President, apparently there is no consensus as to who is supposed to verify the credentials for eligibility. The Federal Elections Committee claimed that it is not within their jurisdiction to make such checks, claiming that it was the job of each state's Secretary of State. The Secretary of State for several states have suggested that they simply stamped the paperwork that was presented from the FEC, believing that all relevant checks had been made. This is unacceptable. Not only does it put the country in danger of being lead by a person who has divided loyalties, it opens the door to lengthy and distracting "prove you're a citizen" lawsuits with each future Presidential campaign.

Establishing a clear cut chain of responsibility is essential, as is establishing eligibility prior to any name going to the primaries. The American public should not be vested financially or emotionally into a candidate before the eligibility issue is resolved. All Americans deserve certainty in their candidates.

Second, there has been much debate over the definition of the term "Natural Born" as it exists in the Constitution. It is essential that we return to the words and intent of the framers of the Constitution for determination of a definition. Arguably, "natural born" in the context of the times would have been a person born of two married American citizens. Further, even in the 18th century, the legitimate child of two citizens born outside of the confines of their home country was considered a "natural born" citizen, provided that the father was in service of the government. While times have changed, and a child's legitimacy or illegitimacy by virtue of married parents no longer holds the same weight, a clear cut definition of what constitutes a "natural born" citizen must be established to prevent a return of this issue in the future.

H.R. 1503 – Presidential Eligibility Act

This Act would amend the 1971 Federal Election Campaign Act to require a copy of the candidate's birth certificate and any other documentation that would be required to establish that a candidate meets the Constitutional requirements to be the President.

Transparency in Candidates

When a candidate runs for office, he or she is embarking on a job interview on a massive scale. The candidate uses skills of persuasion to convince to us, the employers, that he or she is the best person to fill that particular role. They may rely on charm and personality, but much of what we as employers base our decision upon is background and experience. Entire industries have sprung up to verify that employees are who they say that they are and have the credentials to back up their assertions. The higher up the employment ladder you go, the more thorough the checks become. You want to know if the person handling your open heart surgery came in top in the class or failed that course because he or she didn't bother to attend.

All of us have to submit records that prove that we meet the criteria for a particular job. If we don't meet those requirements, we don't get the job. Simple. It is this system of checks that protects the public from someone deciding that they want to be an architect or a doctor or a lawyer or a police officer or a pilot or any other occupation without having the proper training and education. Can you imagine going to a job interview and telling the potential employer, "I refuse to show you my background or provide you any proof at all that I am qualified for this job?" In Barack Obama we have just such a refusal. While every other candidate was trying to put a positive spin on a bad grade here and a tardy for partying there, Obama was filing law suits across the country to bar us, his potential employers, from accessing and evaluating his background.

I am not suggesting that a bad grade in political science would make you a bad politician, anymore than I would suggest that good grade in endocrinology guarantees that you will be a great doctor. I am also not suggesting that a "misspent youth" whether it is in ultra-liberal activism or the Hells Angels prevents you from being a perfect candidate later in life. In fact some of those extreme life experiences make for the best employees. I am suggesting however that as a potential employer, I have the right to evaluate your background and make a determination for myself as to whether or not you would be the best fit for a particular position. Most of us have blips in our background. Whether it is a bad grade, a period of unemployment, or a stint in prison, we have to explain our actions and our experiences and have our lives evaluated in order to get a job. Should a person applying for the job of leader of the free world be required to provide less information than the guy applying to be a fry maker at McDonalds?

As an American voter, I have the right and responsibility to evaluate any political candidate to determine their fitness for the job. This includes their education, their employment experience, and any criminal or financial records. If they have bad patches in their past, I have the right to be informed and determine for myself if I think that it is germane to the job. PERIOD.

A bill to end politicians using legal wranglings to hide their education, background, financial associations, criminal convictions, or other ethical violations must be passed in order to assure the American voter has all relevant information with which to make an informed and educated decision as to the suitability of the candidate.

Military

Can there be a greater calling than that of the selfless defense of our country and the freedoms upon which she was founded? Yet those who accept the challenges are routinely denied the respect and protection that they were promised and deserve. As a country we do not do nearly enough to repay the debt that every American owes to these men and women.

There should be no question as to our military being the best equipped and best trained in the world. Reports from the field suggesting that our solders do not have the equipment that they require are unconscionable. The level of medical care afforded some of those returning wounded warriors is shocking and shameful. Protecting those who protect us must be a top priority for conservatives and indeed for the entire country.

- Our military should be the best equipped, most modern military in the world.

- Safe voting procedures for military personnel overseas must be developed and protected. It is unbelievable that those who are protecting our democracy are denied the ability to participate.

- Protection from predatory lenders, and alternatives to foreclosure and bankruptcy should be available to all military personnel.

- Clearly defined housing, education, and career options and programs should be available for every military person leaving the service.

- Military hospitals should be the finest hospitals in the world, offering the most advanced treatments and rehabilitation therapies for wounded soldiers.

- All military personnel should have access to the best mental health treatments and therapies available.

- Homeless and veteran should never be words that could be used in the same sentence.

Some areas have excellent care. Others have limited access to services or the services are of poor quality. The fact is, many services provided to military personnel and their families are provided by volunteers. Our military families deserve better than to have to depend on volunteers to meet their needs. Many military families also find that once their service ends, the support ends as well. Military people have put their lives on the line for this country, they should receive some support throughout their lives. Freedom is not free, and it is high time that we as a country started paying the debt that we owe these men and women.

News & Media

The First Amendment protects the right to free speech. It doesn't protect the right of the media to dress up opinions as facts. I greatly enjoy the commentary of many of those who are opinion purveyors, some with whom I agree on many issues. But it is getting increasingly difficult, in many mediums, to distinguish the news, which is supposed to be unbiased, fact based reporting and opinions. Many television news shows splice factual news with opinion to such a degree as to blur the line between the two completely. In my opinion, this accounts for a great deal of vitriol shown by voters on both sides of political debates.

It is irresponsible for news programs to masquerade opinions as news. Opinion shows and opinion purveyors have an important place in the lives of viewers. They often open people's minds to other points of view or act as a polemic synthesizing people's own beliefs. But in an environment where the ultra-liberals threaten to force conservative news and opinion mediums out of business through the poorly named "Fairness Doctrine," it is even more important that the difference between what is opinion and what is unbiased news reporting is clear.

Economy

Barack Obama is NOT an economist. Nancy Pelosi is NOT an economist. John McCain, Harry Reid, Joe Bidden…..not an economist among them. So why are these people making sweeping economic changes to the way that our country operates?

Our free market system serves us well. It is only when the government steps in to try and take control and scrape a little more off the top for themselves that the entire structure collapses, which of course gives them additional room to take more money and control. In our history, every time the government has tried to step in and grant new powers for themselves the country has been devastated. It created the catalyst for the Civil War, the Wall Street Crash, the Great Depression, the debilitating welfare reforms of the 1960's, the oil and agricultural disasters of the 1970's and of course the current financial debacle.

The job of the President may include that of chief guardian of the economy. But as a guardian, that role doesn't have the Constitutional authority to control the economy. The guard at the local shopping mall is there to guard the peaceful and lawful ebb and flow of trade, he isn't supposed to go about determining prices, choosing who buys what, or forcing shoppers to pay for the trinkets of other shoppers who can't afford them.

There is a significant difference between government regulation and free market regulation. As we have seen, government regulation operates through the use of kick backs, side deals, political favors, and special interests. Free market regulation comes primarily from competition and when evenly applied, civil law. Consumers determine what they will and will not pay for items. They determine where they will spend their money based on a whole host of factors. Companies that want to stay in business respond accordingly. As long as the laws that are in place to protect consumers are actually applied, the free market system chugs along nicely.

However, over the past decade, a system of government regulation coupled with a practice of turning a blind eye to the legal shenanigans of big business has created a complete disaster. To make matters worse, instead of simply enforcing the laws that already exist to protect consumers and ensure that the market moves along consistently, Washington seeks further regulation in an effort to mimic the free market controls.

While a system completely free of regulation is certainly not the answer, enforcing the laws that currently exist, ending the government preferential treatment of big business to the determent of small businesses, and using regulatory powers to protect the consumer surely would be a step in the right direction. The first thing that springs to mind when I hear the name Obama or Pelosi and the word economy used in the same sentence is that famous Ronald Reagan quote "The nine most terrifying words in the English language are: 'I'm from the government and I'm here to help.'"

Foreign Policy

Foreign policy that begins and ends with apologizing for America is not a foreign policy that is effective or honorable. Groveling to foreign leaders, especially in terror sponsoring countries and those with appalling human rights records doesn't ingratiate us to others or make them want to change their ways. It simply marks us as weak and duplicitous. Further, Obama continues to play candidate for ruler of an, as of yet, only imagined "new world order," a role that doesn't sit well with any other democratic nation in the world.

Energy Dependency

The "global warming" debate aside, one of the greatest threats to our security as a sovereign nation can be found in our baffling dependency on terror supporting countries and enemies for our energy. We teach children not to take candy from the creepy guy on the corner, but then turn around and base our entire economic survival on the creepy guys overseas. It makes no sense. Of course if we had no way of producing our own energy, we would be compelled to deal with countries, no matter what their politics. But this clearly isn't the case.

Different sources provide varying statistics as to when Saudi oil is expected to run out. But, no matter whether the wells dry up in 5 years or 50 years, the problem remains. As a country we must become energy self-sufficient, sooner rather than later. Of course developing cleaner more efficient sources of energy is important for the progress and future stability of this country. But, developing new technologies takes time. Team Obama's plan is to kowtow to both the Arab oil producers and to environmental groups by refusing to utilize the energy that we have right here at home is baffling. In a country where jobs, especially in certain sectors, are scarce and energy prices are high, continuing to prevent oil producers in the US from tapping into our own energy sources is madness.

Energy producers must be allowed to provide the energy that this country needs, while investing in the development of cleaner, renewable sources of energy. Our dependency on foreign oil must end.

Welfare

Republicans are often unfairly categorized as being anti-welfare or anti-poor as a way of painting us as uncaring, corporate types unconcerned with the trials and tribulations of the less fortunate. The fact that middle-class Republicans outstrip Democrats in charitable donations of course paints a different picture. Conservatives are aware that there are times in some people's lives when they need a helping hand. Welfare is supposed to address those times and provide temporary financial help to Americans who are truly in desperate need, enabling them to get back on their feet and able to return quickly to being productive members of society.

Welfare programs have virtually bankrupted some states. Welfare generations, welfare scams, and of course illegal immigrants sponging off the system has robbed tax payers and those who are generally needy alike. There is no reason, with dirty streets, unkempt parks, graffiti targeted buildings, and failing infrastructures why anyone who is receipt of welfare is not working to improve their community. Several years ago, I conducted an online experiment where I outlined the following basic welfare plan for my state and asked for comments.

This was the plan:

On the 1st day of January, everyone who is currently in receipt of welfare, social security, or medical benefits from the State of New York will be issued a letter detailing the time and place of their review meeting. Meetings are mandatory and will take place within 30 days from the date of letter issue.

- You must bring proof of your identity and you will be finger printed.

- If you have a disability, bring your medical records, you will be assessed by a state medical board.

- If you are not working, but are able bodied, you will be give a mandatory job. These jobs will be dependant on your skill level. If you are unskilled you will be given menial labor positions (cleaning streets, landscaping parks, renovating neighborhoods, etc.)

- If you are pregnant or have children under school age, you will be required to bring your child to daily parenting classes.

- Only those who are truly unable to work will be in receipt of welfare monies after February 1st.

- From February 1st, in order to receive money you will be required to work. If you refuse to do the assigned job, fail to come to work, or behave inappropriately on the job, you will not receive any money from the State.

- If you wish to advance out of manual labor positions or to increase your pay you may attend free evening and weekend courses or you may join the armed services.

In my opinion the above scenario would:

- Help eliminate the illegal immigration problem. Since Americans would be forced to work, there would be no job incentives for illegals to come into the US.

- Do away with welfare fraud since people would be finger printed and must work to earn.

- Renovate the community.

- Give people who may have never had a job the self esteem and living skills needed so that they would be inspired to move off the welfare system.

The reaction to the above posted plan was very interesting. Conservatives and independents largely approved of the plan with some tweaks, such as establishing time limits and drug testing. However, I received emails from liberals who claimed that the plan was unfair to the poor. This really illustrates the difference in basic beliefs between conservatives and liberals when it comes to welfare. Conservatives believe in equal opportunities. No matter where you come from, with your own hard work and initiative you can succeed. Liberals believe in equal results, that no matter where you come from you should be made equal to middle America, at tax payer expense.

Welfare must be reformed. Rife with fraud, financially crippling, tempting to illegals, and ineffective in combating poverty, the current welfare system is a colossal failure. Some of the suggestions that I have listed in my example are in place in some states thanks to the Welfare Reform Act of 1996. However, as with most government action, they are half heartedly applied, burdened by bureaucracy, and poorly executed.

Affirmative Action

The time for Affirmative Action is long gone. The idea that minorities and women can't achieve on their own merits is debasing. It reeks of what George W Bush called the "soft bigotry of low expectations." Preferential hiring practices, greatly lowered University admission requirements, and quotas do little to support the notion of equality for all. William Bradford Reynolds, Assistant Attorney General for Civil Rights under Ronald Reagan once said that Affirmative Action is "demeaning because it says people are going to get ahead not because of what they can do but because of race."[77]

---

[77] Stein, *Harry City Journal* Now the GOP is For Affirmative Action? August 2006

Affirmative Action has created a new racism. Politicians and in fact most white Americans are so afraid of being branded as racists that we publicly bend over backwards to avoid any chance of being so labeled. However, instead of ending racism, those who are now denied employment, college placement, and advancement because they are white can hardly be expected to see the reverse discrimination as a positive thing. Perhaps more importantly, Affirmative Action does nothing to help integrate America. Penalizing people for being one race is just as insidious now as it was 70 years ago. However, instead of correcting the problem, we have swung wildly in the other direction, simply changing the racial group targeted.

In order to truly be equal, Affirmative Action and other preferential practices must be abolished. To do otherwise suggests that blacks, other minorities, and women are inferior and can't succeed without a hand out. This is not the message that we want to teach another generation.

Illegal Immigration

Immigration is a hot button issue, not only between Republicans and Democrats, but between conservative and moderates within the Republican Party. Conservatives generally favor a strict enforcement of the law which would result in potentially hundreds of thousands if not millions of illegals being rounded up throughout the country and expelled. Moderates tend to favor a quasi-amnesty program where those here illegally could apply for guest worker status, provided that they register and pass background checks. Both conservative and moderate Republicans support tighter border enforcement and stiffer penalties for employers who hire illegal immigrants.

Personally, I think that happy medium between to two Republican positions could be found. While strictly speaking, enforcing current legislation would be the "letter of the law" thing to do, it is impractical for several reasons, none the least of which is that creating millions of refuges would irreparably damage our position worldwide and at home. Families being forcibly evicted from their homes on international television, screaming mothers, crying babies and all that goes with that action falls afoul of the very Judeo-Christian beliefs that many of us share. By the same token, amnesty is no incentive to prevent new illegal immigrants from entering the country.

I have seen several proposals that would incorporate the two positions.

- Tighten border security to stop or at least greatly slow the tide of illegal immigrants.

- Establish an amnesty date by which all employers must register any illegal workers. After that date any employer with unregistered illegal workers would face criminal prosecution.

- Those illegally in this country would have a period of one year to either voluntarily leave or register and submit to the usual immigration checks (health, background, etc).

- If they pass the checks and are employed, they would be allowed to stay, though they would have three years to complete full citizenship requirements, be expected to pay taxes, and learn English.

- If they are not employed, don't meet immigration eligibility (background checks etc) they would be deported.

- There would be no anchor babies. At least one parent must be a legal US citizen in order to give a child citizenship.

- Anyone charged with a felony during the amnesty period or prior to being granted citizenship and subsequently found guilty of committing a felony, would be deported after serving the sentence.

- No form of public assistance (welfare) would be available to any non-citizen.

This type of plan would do several things. Let us say, for ease of argument that the immigration initiative started on January 1, 2010. From that date no (or few) illegal immigrants would be able to enter due to tighter controls. This leaves only those currently in the country to address. All parties would be aware that they had an entire year from that date to meet compliance. Those who could meet immigration requirements would have a year to register and begin the citizenship procedures. Those who could not meet the requirements (criminal background, unemployed, etc) would have a year to make their arrangements and return home. Anyone either employing an unregistered illegal immigrant after January 1, 2011, or being in the country unregistered after that point would be prosecuted.

For American citizens, this type of plan would help protect them from illegal immigrants with criminal records and end the incredible tax burden of supporting illegals on welfare. For those here illegally, the plan would give them a set time period within which to apply for citizenship or return to their own county. Those who qualify for citizenship would be able to set out of the shadows and take their place in American society, welcomed as positive contributors to the country.

No matter what the plan, the goal of the Republican Party in regards to illegal immigration is to first, make it very clear that LEGAL immigration and ILLEGAL immigration are two completely different things. Legal immigrants typically share our core conservative values, they work hard to contribute to society, care for their family, and assimilate into America. They should be welcomed into the Republican Party with open arms. Second, we need to establish a plan that is both just to American citizens and humane to those who are here illegally.

Language

Conservatives typically believe that English should be legally established as the official language of the United States. A single language helps people to assimilate, gives those new to the country the incentive to learn the language in order to fully participate in society, and saves the tax payer. By nurturing partnerships between educational facilities, community centers, libraries, and churches, community based programs to improve literacy for all adults, including English as a second language for legal citizens could be developed. This of course leads to a better integration between foreign born citizens and the American born public. A termination of multi-lingual forms and services also helps combat illegal immigration.

Voting

Voting is a cherished right in this country. But it seems as if the last several election cycles have seen a dramatic increase in voter registration and polling station shenanigans and fraud. Whether it is ACORN registering Disney characters and the dead, recounts where only one party's votes are considered "valid," or the Black Panthers "guarding" polling places, it is disingenuous for America to decry the voting fraud in emerging democracies while our own system is so askew.

Better safe guards need to be put into place to protect voters and the electoral process. A February 2008 Congressional Cooperative Election Study revealed that 62% of people believed that vote fraud was a common occurrence. Even if voter fraud is not as rife as many believe, the impression that the system is unfair or slanted towards a certain party or candidate undermines the entire process.

- The voter registration system must be clarified and strictly enforced to prevent the "nursing home trawling" and illegal immigrant voting that has transpired.

- Transparency needs to be established to protect absentee voters and in particular those in the military whose experienced considerable election challenges in the last election cycle.

- Anti-intimidation laws need to be passed or enforced to prevent groups from blocking or "patrolling" polling places.

- A transparent chain of custody needs to be established so that all people believe that their vote is being counted correctly.

The mere idea that in the greatest democracy in the world, voter fraud exists is appalling. The fact that it has become almost an accepted as a fact of life is shocking. When men and women join the military and go to foreign lands to protect our country, help spread democracy, and make this world a safer place, the fact that right here at home democracy is being tampered with to the benefit of politicians is disgusting. Conservatives (and in fact ALL

Americans) must make a stand to stop the erosion of one of our most cherished rights.

Education

Education provides a veritable smorgasbord of issues upon which to focus.

- Socialist indoctrination

- Savior Obama spirituals

- Anti-white and anti-American versions of history, current events, world events, and politics

- Inappropriate sexual references and pro-homosexuality lessons

And that's just in grade school. Our children are being robbed of music and arts programs. Schools can't afford uniforms or equipment for sports or band. Yet states spend hundreds of millions of dollars educating illegals and school districts are compelled, by strong teachers unions to continue to pay teachers removed for incompetence, sexual improprieties, and behavior problems. Some teachers are clearly stars. But a quick review of YouTube shows that there are a shocking number of teachers who seem unable to grasp basic English. Ebonics, slang, and improper use of language permeate in some areas, yet these teachers are protected thanks to a union whose usefulness has passed. Of course there is also the controversial school voucher system.

Whether it's tighter control over a curriculum, supporting a school voucher system, ending educational spending on illegals, or removing the power of the teachers unions so that those teachers who are incompetent, inappropriate, or simply ignorant can be culled from the pack, safeguarding our children and the educational system is paramount to the future of this country.

Grade school isn't the only area of education where there are considerable problems. Falling graduation rates, kids graduating without basic skills, and almost non-existent vocational courses or apprenticeships in many areas leave kids completely unprepared for life in a competitive adult world. Those who do seek to attend college or university are met with lowered entrance requirements for some and racial quota systems that keep some of the best and the brightest from attending. The societal knock on effect of having a sizeable percentage of mediocre students occupying higher education seats is obvious.

Feminism

The feminist movement was supposed to free women from the shadows and shackles of fathers and husbands, giving them the ability to follow their own paths, achieve their own goals, and nurture their own opinions and beliefs. Unfortunately, the domineering men of the past have been largely replaced by the domineering women of modern media, who deem ultra-liberal positions the only ones viable for women. Unless a woman agrees with the opinions of the likes of Nancy Pelosi, Joy Behar, or Whoopi Goldberg, they are attacked for being "ignorant," "racist," or "white terrorists." Conservative female voters are maligned and called "backward" while conservative female politicians are called "stupid" and "dangerous." While women in politics have always had a tough row to hoe, the past presidential campaign has certainly revealed that women are unfortunately their own worst enemy.

I have no idea who envisioned the concept that ALL women should think alike, believe in the same things, and vote the same way. Clearly women have a wide variety of experiences, backgrounds, religious and spiritual foundations, social and financial spheres, goals, expectations, beliefs, and opinions. It is therefore incomprehensible that millions of people with such varied backgrounds would all be expected to believe the exact same thing and vote accordingly simply because of their gender. Until women in positions of power and in particular those in the media accept that women are not all carbon copies of each other sharing sex organs and an opinion, women will never occupy a position of equality in the United States.

Women make up half of the electorate power in the United States. However, as long as there are women in the public eye who continue to demand fealty and require all that women agree with their very liberal opinions, the oppression of women will continue and women will be marginalized in politics and in government. It is only when women are so vicious and condescending to other women that men feel comfortable to do the same. The feminist movement fails when we replace one group who demand that all women act a certain way and believe a certain thing, with another group who demand that all women act a certain way and believe a certain thing.

Tackling Controversial Issues

Clearly there are many others areas that are important to conservatives. The issues that I focused on have a wide base of appeal and are best dealt with on a national level. However there are many issues that I believe, are better handled on a local or state level.

Abortion

In many counties across the country local residents have made determinations as to what types of behavior and services they find acceptable in their community. So called Sunday "blue laws" restrict commercial activity, prohibit or restrict the sale of alcohol, prohibit the sale of cars, and restrict sporting and hunting activities on Sundays. Many communities also ban or restrict gambling on certain days or in its entirety. These laws rely on the voting public in local communities to make decisions about what behaviors and services are acceptable within their county.

The abortion issue is one of the most divisive in politics. While the lines are often drawn down religious boundaries as to whether you approve or disapprove of the availability of abortions, even within the pro-life community there are varying positions on such issues as the "morning after" pill or in regards to what should be done with a pregnancy that resulted from rape or incest. One thing is certain however, given the current liberal climate of "abortion-as-birth-control" and Obama's support of partial birth abortions, a national referendum on abortion is unlikely. However, were abortions or even facilities that offer abortions banned or restricted on a county level, people would have a greater chance of achieving their goals, at least within their own community. Abortion is a prefect example of an issue that could potentially be addressed on a county or state level, which would avoid the will of the people being usurped by the liberal media and liberal population centers.

Judicial Reform

In many areas across the country, prosecutors receive increased salaries and promotions based on the number of people charged with a crime and the percentage of people convicted. However with tremendous pressure to avoid costly trials and fierce competition for federal prison money, an unethical, competing agenda has emerged in which prosecutors are encouraged to avoid trial but incarcerate more people. Despite a drop in the crime rate, the conviction and incarceration rates have almost tripled. The vast majority of these people are middle class and working class people charged with drug possession and insufficient funds checks. Perhaps most shocking, less than 5% of these people ever go to trial.

Wait a minute! Hold the phone!! How can people in America be tossed into prison for a joint or a bounced check without even a trial? That is completely impossible!! Yet, people are essentially fast tracked from arrest to incarceration, often for crimes that were previously considered misdemeanors, emotionally and financially devastating families, sending children into the foster care system, and destroying lives. The knock on effect to families and communities is almost immeasurable.

Middle and working class poor people are most at risk of being fast tracked to prison. Often people in these economic groups earn too much to qualify for the public defender program. Yet are unable to afford to hire attorneys on their own. This leaves this group extremely vulnerable. In an effort to increase conviction rates while discouraging trials, prosecutors in many communities have developed "deferment" programs. These programs offer people charged with a crime an incredible deal. If they will simply sign a piece of paper agreeing to accept responsibility for the crime and pay a monthly "deferment fee," all will be forgiven; they can go home, they won't have to hire an attorney to defend them in trial, and as long as they follow some simple rules, all charges will be dropped at a certain point in the future. The only problem, in some communities, less than10% can live up to those "simple rules" resulting in tens of thousands of people sentenced and sent to prison, without a trial.

So just what types of rules violations result in a one way ticket to prison? The violation must be pretty severe in order to warrant a person being sent to prison right? How about job loss. A parking ticket. A late deferment fee payment. These have all resulted in middle class Americans being robbed their due process and sent to prison without a trial, all so that prosecutors can earn bonuses and pay raises and states can get more federal money. Not that it should matter, but this situation doesn't affect a handful of "unlucky" people, it effects tens of thousands of people across the country, not to mention the families and in particular the children that are dumped into an already strained and flawed foster care system.

Of course a system that provides middle class Americans a one way ticket to the state penitentiary is not the only problem facing the judicial system. Prosecutors, like Mike Nifong of Duke Lacrosse Rape Case fame, who are aware that the person that they are prosecuting is innocent, but continue to do so in order to cultivate press relations and launch political careers, are becoming increasingly common. Without financial resources to defend themselves and state bar associations that protect lawyers (and even those who pretend to be lawyers) with the full force of their power, once targeted, it is almost impossible for those who are not extremely wealthy to defend their innocence. Legal experts suggest that as many as 14% of all people convicted are in fact innocent of any crime. In communities where district attorneys and judges are elected positions, high conviction rates and a tough stance on crime, coupled with lots of television "face time" are essential for success, leading to ever increasing instances of "conviction at all costs."

We live in a country that is supposed to be the shinning star of democracy and justice in the world. Yet in many communities, citizens are prayed upon and incarcerated for the financial gain of attorneys and state coffers. People who want to champion justice reform should investigate their own county system. Are deferment agreements pushed? What percentage of those who accept deferment agreements are ultimately incarcerated? Are cases in your county being retried due to "prosecutorial misconduct?" Does the state bar association publish the names of attorneys who have been sanctioned or disciplined? If you live in a community with a less than stellar reputation when it comes to justice, everyone is at risk. Justice reform can happen on a local level and should be a top priority of anyone who values the sanctity of the Constitution and the principles upon which this country was founded.

Sanctuary Cities

The establishment of so called "sanctuary cities" where officials are commanded to turn a blind eye to illegal immigration is unconscionable. However, decisions to create a "sanctuary" are made largely at the precinct committee level. With seats allotted to Republicans largely unfilled, these measures are often passed on the liberal vote alone. By simply filling the seats allotted to us with conservatives and voting against "sanctuary" status we can gain a powerful weapon in the fight against illegal immigration.

Community Specific Issues

Many communities face liberal onslaughts. Whether this is in the form of attacks against historical and religious icons, denying ROTC groups the ability to operate, assaults against Christmas, Thanksgiving, and Easter holidays, or other community specific issues, looking around your neighborhood and singling out areas that could use the power of conservative organization is a great way to start taking back our country.

- Chapter 10 –

You & I

As I run through a final edit of this book, which has been a labor of love and of loathing for me, I feel compelled to share with readers a few final thoughts before this book is released and is no longer in my control.

I came to research Saul Alinsky and Barrack Obama in a backwards sort of way. In 2008, I was busy researching disbarred former District Attorney Mike Nifong (of the Duke Lacrosse Rape Case fame) for a piece about the prosecutorial misconduct. I discovered that many prominent politicians were former prosecutors who were propelled into fame and prominence due to either a single high-profile legal case or an almost unblemished record of convictions. When you start compiling statistics about the misconduct, abuse of power, and dishonesty that is shockingly common in a profession that not only gives almost unequalled power to prosecutors but rewards them for convictions at all costs, a frightening picture of not only our justice system but of our political landscape, emerges.

It was during this time that I became very interested in the backgrounds of those politicians who had navigated their way into the combat zone for the highest office in the land. Gone was the "everyman" who had to be prodded into public service and did so only to lend his expertise for the betterment of the country, replaced by career politicians who had little background outside of an early legal career and a lifetime of campaigning. And then, there emerged Barrack Obama, a candidate whose background was opaque at best, whose own writings and associations suggested someone who should be on a terrorist watch list instead of running for the Presidency. Obama had carefully eliminated almost every verifiable aspect of his past, requiring people to read his books and believe his versions, as nothing else was available. Ultimately, Obama's own reliance on Alinsky doctrine and both he and his wife's references to Alinsky inspired me to research the man and ultimately to write this book.

I say that this book has been a labor of love and loathing. Despite my travels and youthful indiscretions or perhaps because of them, I love America. Having lived and worked abroad a great deal, I know that while there are those who "hate" America, far more people still cling to the ideals of the American Dream and hope that someday, they can save up enough money to come and be a part of the American experience as a citizen. I have heard the heavily accented voices of people who may never see this land break out into choruses of "God Bless America." I have seen the tears in people's eyes as they sit on the Staten Island Ferry and glimpse the Statue of Liberty for the first time. After two decades of international travel, I have never been in a cab in a foreign country when the driver didn't tell me that he had been to the US or was saving to go on vacation. I have rarely met a person who didn't love America.

I have met a great number of people around the world however, who hate our politicians. I have experienced the crippling taxes of foreign countries, the year long wait lists for medical services, the substandard health care, factory-like education system, and woefully inadequate public services. Not in third world countries, but in European capitals. In countries that Obama wants to emulate. This is where the loathing part of this book comes in. Having experienced what Obama wants for our future and having identified how he intends on taking us all there, I felt that there had to be something that I could do to try and stem the tide. This book is my effort.

Ronald Reagan once said, "Freedom is never more than one generation away from extinction." We are the parents of that generation.

Conservative America, YOU and I are now all that stands in the way of American extinction.

YOU and I are all that prevents a humbled and hobbled America being offered up as the sacrificial lamb of a man whose aspirations are that of leader of the New World Order.

YOU and I are all that stands between socialist ruin and the Resurrection of the American Dream.

So many have lived and died to give Americans unequalled rights and freedoms.

Now defending America depends upon YOU and I.

Alexandrea Merrell

About Alexandrea Merrell

Alexandrea Merrell grew up in the Midwest, the oldest child of a military aviator and his wife, a University professor and author. At 18, she moved to Boston to pursue a career in journalism as a foreign correspondent, but faced with a years long waiting list for the program, at 19 Merrell relocated to New York City. After attending Hofstra University and New York University, where she studied political science and economics, she spent her early career pursuing acting while writing business articles, corporate portfolios, and customer service manuals for the financial and property industries.

Through her twenties and thirties, despite having three children and working in several different industries, Merrell continued to write. In addition to penning multiple drama screen plays, she researched and wrote several documentaries focusing on social issues. One such documentary, which focused on the failure of antiquated anti-stalking laws to protect people from modern day electronic and internet stalking, lead to Merrell being offered a place at film school.

During her tenure as a "mature student," Merrell focused on writing and producing projects about criminal justice reform, civil rights, First Amendment limitations, and politics, culminating in her Dissertation: "Televised For the Court of Public Opinion: Disintegrating Civil Rights in Expose Television" which focused on the media's usurpation of people's right to be presumed innocent until proven guilty in a court of law. Almost two decades after originally leaving school, Merrell graduated with a Masters Degree in Television and Film Project Development. Merrell then attended law school before returning to writing full time.

In 2008, Merrell began to blog about the ethical and legal irregularities in the Presidential campaign. Continued reference by Obama and his wife to Saul Alinsky lead Merrell to research the corporate terrorist and the links between his organization and Obama. Her findings lead her to write "Rules For Republican Radicals" which dissects the tactics and techniques used by Team Obama to manipulate the media and voters.

Alexandrea Merrell continues to write about politics and social issues from a conservative perspective; both contributing daily commentary and opinions on events that affect Americans and providing guidance to those who wish to become involved in politics or organize political organizations. She also continues to write both fiction and factual pieces for print media and producing projects for film and television.

You can read more of her work at AlexandreaMerrell.com

Breinigsville, PA USA
12 August 2010
243515BV00001B/11/P